BIOLOGICALLY INSPIRED COOPERATIVE COMPUTING

T0189403

IFIP – The International Federation for Information Processing

IFIP was founded in 1960 under the auspices of UNESCO, following the First World Computer Congress held in Paris the previous year. An umbrella organization for societies working in information processing, IFIP's aim is two-fold: to support information processing within its member countries and to encourage technology transfer to developing nations. As its mission statement clearly states,

> *IFIP's mission is to be the leading, truly international, apolitical organization which encourages and assists in the development, exploitation and application of information technology for the benefit of all people.*

IFIP is a non-profitmaking organization, run almost solely by 2500 volunteers. It operates through a number of technical committees, which organize events and publications. IFIP's events range from an international congress to local seminars, but the most important are:

• The IFIP World Computer Congress, held every second year;
• Open conferences;
• Working conferences.

The flagship event is the IFIP World Computer Congress, at which both invited and contributed papers are presented. Contributed papers are rigorously refereed and the rejection rate is high.

As with the Congress, participation in the open conferences is open to all and papers may be invited or submitted. Again, submitted papers are stringently refereed.

The working conferences are structured differently. They are usually run by a working group and attendance is small and by invitation only. Their purpose is to create an atmosphere conducive to innovation and development. Refereeing is less rigorous and papers are subjected to extensive group discussion.

Publications arising from IFIP events vary. The papers presented at the IFIP World Computer Congress and at open conferences are published as conference proceedings, while the results of the working conferences are often published as collections of selected and edited papers.

Any national society whose primary activity is in information may apply to become a full member of IFIP, although full membership is restricted to one society per country. Full members are entitled to vote at the annual General Assembly, National societies preferring a less committed involvement may apply for associate or corresponding membership. Associate members enjoy the same benefits as full members, but without voting rights. Corresponding members are not represented in IFIP bodies. Affiliated membership is open to non-national societies, and individual and honorary membership schemes are also offered.

BIOLOGICALLY INSPIRED COOPERATIVE COMPUTING

*IFIP 19th World Computer Congress,
TC 10: 1st IFIP International Conference on
Biologically Inspired Computing, August 21-24, 2006,
Santiago, Chile*

Edited by

Yi Pan
Georgia State University, USA

Franz J. Rammig
Universität Paderborn, Germany

Hartmut Schmeck
Universität Karlsruhe (TH), Germany

Mauricio Solar
Universidad de Santiago de Chile, Chile

 Springer

Biologically Inspired Cooperative Computing

Edited by Y. Pan, F. Rammig, H. Schmeck, and M. Solar

p. cm. (IFIP International Federation for Information Processing, a Springer Series in Computer Science)

ISSN: 1571-5736 / 1861-2288 (Internet)

ISBN: 13: 978-1-4419-4184-8   eISBN: 10: 0-387-34733-X
Printed on acid-free paper   eISBN: 13: 978-0-387-34733-2

9 8 7 6 5 4 3 2 1
springer.com

Preface

In the world of information technology, it is no longer the computer in the classical sense where the majority of IT applications is executed; computing is everywhere. More than 20 billion processors have already been fabricated and the majority of them can be assumed to still be operational. At the same time, virtually every PC worldwide is connected via the Internet. This combination of traditional and embedded computing creates an artifact of a complexity, heterogeneity, and volatility unmanageable by classical means.

Each of our technical artifacts with a built-in processor can be seen as a *"Thing that Thinks"*, a term introduced by MIT's Thinglab. It can be expected that in the near future these billions of *Things that Think* will become an *"Internet of Things"*, a term originating from ETH Zurich. This means that we will be constantly surrounded by a virtual "organism" of *Things that Think*. This organism needs novel, adequate design, evolution, and management means which is also one of the core challenges addressed by the recent German priority research program on *Organic Computing*.

A new paradigm in computing is to take many simple autonomous objects or agents and let them jointly perform a complex task, without having the need for centralized control. In this paradigm, these simple objects interact locally with their environment using simple rules. An important inspiration for this model is nature itself, where many such systems can be found. Applications include optimization algorithms, communications networks, scheduling and decision making, supply-chain management, and robotics.

There are many disciplines involved in making such systems work: from artificial intelligence to energy aware systems. Often these disciplines have their own field of focus, have their own conferences, or only deal with specialized sub-problems (e.g. swarm intelligence, biologically inspired computation, sensor networks). The IFIP Conference on Biologically Inspired Cooperative Computing is a first attempt to bridge this separation of the scientific community.

At the same time it is the dignified forum to celebrate the 30th anniversary of TC10, IFIP's Technical Committee on Computer Systems Technology. This unique conference brings together the various fields covered by the individual working groups of TC10 and opens the perspective to explore boundaries.

Combining the areas of expertise of TC10's working groups, a highly attractive program could be compiled. The Working Group 10.1 (*Computer-aided Systems Theory*, Chair: Charles Rattray, UK) brought in the point of view of *Modeling and Reasoning* about Collaborative Self-Organizing Systems. Aspects of *Collaborative Sensing and Processing Systems* have been contributed with support of Working Group 10.3 (*Concurrent Systems*, Chair: Kemal Ebcioglu, USA). The important topic of *Dependability* of Collaborative Self-Organizing Systems is been looked at under the auspices of Working Group 10.4 (*Dependable Computing and Fault Tolerance*, Post-chair: Jean Arlat, France). Finally, *Design and Technology* of Collaborative Self-Organizing Systems are studied by contributions of this conference. For these aspects Tiziana Margaria, Germany was responsible, acting for Working Group 10.5 (*Design and Engineering of Electronic Systems*).

There are three remarkable keynote contributions to this conference. They provide a deep insight into major challenges of Biologically Inspired Cooperative Computing:

- *An Immune System Paradigm for the Assurance of Dependability of Collaborative Self-Organizing Systems* (by Algirdas Avizienis, Vytautas Magnus University, Kaunas, Lithuania and University of California, Los Angeles, USA),
- *99% (Biological) Inspiration ...*
  (by Michael G. Hinchey and Roy Sterritt, NASA Goddard Space Flight Center, Greenbelt, USA, and University of Ulster, Jordanstown, Northern Ireland, rsp.)
- *Biologically-Inspired Design: Getting It Wrong and Getting It Right*
  (by Steve R. White, IBM Thomas J. Watson Research Center).

The contributions to the program of this conference have been selected from submissions originating from North and South America, Asia and Europe. We would like to thank the members of the program committee for the careful reviewing of all submissions, which formed the basis for selecting this attractive program.

We welcome all participants of this 1st IFIP Conference on Biologically Inspired Cooperative Computing – BICC 2006 and look forward to an inspiring series of talks and discussions, embedded into a range of conferences of the IFIP World Computer Conference 2006.

Franz J.Rammig (Germany)   *Yi Pan* (USA)
Mauricio Solar (Chile)   *Hartmut Schmeck* (Germany)
(Conference Co-Chairs)   (Program Co-Chairs)

Program Committee

Content

An Immune System Paradigm for the Assurance of Dependability of Collaborative Self-organizing Systems

Algirdas Avižienis

Vytautas Magnus University, Kaunas, Lithuania
and
University of California, Los Angeles, USA

Abstract. In collaborative self-organizing computing systems a complex task is performed by relatively simple autonomous agents that act without centralized control. Disruption of a task can be caused by agents that produce harmful outputs due to internal failures or due to maliciously introduced alterations of their functions. The probability of such harmful outputs is minimized by the application of a design principle called "the immune system paradigm" that provides individual agents with an all-hardware fault tolerance infrastructure. The paradigm and its application are described in this paper.

1 Dependability Issues of Collaborative Self-Organizing Systems

Self-organizing computing systems can be considered to be a class of distributed computing systems. To assure the dependability of conventional distributed systems, fault tolerance techniques are employed [1]. Individual elements of the distributed system are grouped into clusters, and consensus algorithms are implemented by members of the cluster [2], or mutual diagnosis is carried out within the cluster.

Self-organizing systems differ from conventional distributed systems in that their structure is dynamic [3]. Relatively simple autonomous agents act without central control in jointly carrying out a complex task. The dynamic nature of such systems makes the implementation of consensus or mutual diagnosis impractical, since constant membership of the clusters of agents cannot be assured as the system evolves. An agent that suffers an internal fault or external interference may fail and produce harmful outputs that disrupt the task being carried out by the collaborative system. Even more harmful can be maliciously introduced (by intrusion or by malicious software) alterations of the agent's function that lead to deliberately harmful outputs.

Please use the following format when citing this chapter:

Avižienis, A., 2006, in IFIP International Federation for Information Processing, Volume 216, Biologically Inspired Cooperative Computing, eds. Pan, Y., Rammig, F., Schmeck, H., Solar, M., (Boston: Springer), pp. 1–6.

The biological analogy of the fault or interference that affects an agent is an infection that can lead to loss of the agent's functions and also to transmission of the infection to other agents that receive the harmful outputs, possibly causing an epidemic. The biologically inspired solution that I have proposed is the introduction within the agent of a fault tolerance mechanism, called the fault tolerance infrastructure (FTI), that is analogous to the immune system of a human being [4,5]. Every agent has its own FTI and therefore consensus algorithms are no longer necessary to protect the system.

2   A Design Principle: the Immune System Paradigm

My objective is to design the FTI for an autonomous agent that is part of a self-organizing system. I assume that the agent is composed of both hardware and software subsystems and communicates to other agents via wireless links. Then I will employ the following three analogies to derive a design principle called "the immune system paradigm":

    (1) the human body is analogous to hardware,
    (2) consciousness is analogous to software,
    (3) the immune system of the body is analogous to the fault tolerance infrastructure FTI.

In the determination of the properties that the FTI must possess four fundamental attributes of the immune system are especially relevant [6]:

    (1) It is a part of the body that functions (i.e. detects and reacts to threats) continuously and autonomously, independently of consciousness.
    (2) Its elements (lymph nodes, other lymphoid organs, lymphocytes) are distributed throughout the body, serving all its organs.
    (3) It has its own communication links – the network of lymphatic vessels.
    (4) Its elements (cells, organs, and vessels) themselves are self-defended, redundant and in several cases diverse.

Now we can identify the properties that the FTI must have in order to justify the immune system analogy. They are as follows:

    (1a) The FTI consists of hardware and firmware elements only.
    (1b) The FTI is independent of (that is, it requires no support from) any software of the agent, but can communicate with it.
    (1c) The FTI supports (provides protected decision algorithms for) multichannel computing by the agent, including diverse hardware and software channels that provide design fault tolerance for the agent's hardware and software.
    (2) The FTI is compatible with (i.e., protects) a wide range of the agent's hardware components, including processors, memories, supporting chipsets, discs, power supplies, fans and various peripherals.
    (3) Elements of the FTI are distributed throughout the agent's hardware and are interconnected by their own autonomous communication links.
    (4) The FTI is fully fault-tolerant itself and requires no external support. It is not susceptible to attacks by intrusion or malicious software and is not affected by natural or design faults of the agent's hardware and software.

(5) An additional essential requirement is that the FTI provides status outputs to those other agents with which it can communicate. The outputs indicate the state of the agent's health: perfect or undergoing recovery action. Upon failure of the agent's function the FTI shuts down all its outputs and issues a permanent status output indicating failure.

The above listed set of design requirements is called the immune system paradigm. It defines an FTI that can be considered to be the agent's immune system that defends its "body" (i.e., hardware) against "infections" caused by internal faults, external interference, intrusions, and attacks by malicious software. The FTI also informs the other agents in its environment of its state of health. Such an FTI is generic, that is, it can serve a variety of agents. Furthermore it is transparent to the agent's software, compatible with other defenses used by the agent, and fully self-protected by fault tolerance.

A different and independently devised analogy of the immune system is the "Artificial Immune System" (AIS) of S. Forrest and S. A. Hofmeyr [7]. Its origins are in computer security research, where the motivating objective was protection against illegal intrusions. The analogy of the body is a local-area broadcast network, and the AIS protects it by detecting connections that are not normally observed on the LAN. Immune responses are not included in the model of the AIS, while they are the essence of the FTI.

3   Architecture of the Fault Tolerance Infrastructure

The preceding sections have presented a general discussion of an FTI that serves as the analog of an immune system for the hardware of an agent of a self-organizing system. Such an FTI can be placed on a single hardware component, or it can be used to protect a board with several components, or an entire chassis [5]. To demonstrate that the FTI is a practically implementable and rather simple hardware structure, this and the next section describe an FTI design that was intended to protect a system composed of Intel P6 processors and associated chip sets and was first presented in [5].

The FTI is a system composed of four types of special-purpose controllers called "nodes". The nodes are ASICs (Application-Specific Integrated Circuits) that are controlled by hard-wired sequencers or by read-only microcode. The basic structure of the FTI is shown in Figure 1. The figure does not show the redundant nodes needed for fault tolerance of the FTI itself. The C (Computing) node is a COTS processor or other hardware component of the agent being protected by the FTI. One A (Adapter) node is provided for each C node. All error signal outputs and recovery command inputs of the C node are connected to its A node. Within the FTI, all A nodes are connected to one M (Monitor) node via the M (Monitor) bus. Each A node also has a direct input (the A line) to the M node. The A nodes convey the C node error messages to the M node. They also receive recovery commands from the M node and issue them to C node inputs.

The A line serves to request M node attention for an incoming error message. The M node stores in ROM the responses to error signals from every type of C node and the sequences for its own recovery. It also stores system configuration and system time data and its own activity records. The M node is connected to the S3 (Startup, Shutdown, Survival) node. The functions of the S3 node are to control power-on and power-off sequences for the entire agent, to generate fault-tolerant clock signals and to provide non-volatile, radiation-hardened storage for system time and configuration. The S3 node has a backup power supply (e.g. a battery) and remains on at all times during the life of the FTI.

The D (Decision) node provides fault-tolerant comparison and voting services for the C nodes, including decision algorithms for N-version software executing on diverse processors (C-nodes). Fast response of the D node is assured by hardware implementation of the decision algorithms. The D node also keeps a log of disagreements in the decisions. The second function of the D node is to serve as a communication link between the software of the C nodes and the M node. C nodes may request configuration and M node activity data or send power control commands. The D node has a built-in A node (the A port) that links it to the M node.Another function of the FTI is to provide fault tolerant power management for the entire agent system, including individual power switches for every C node, as shown in Figure 1. Every node except the S3 has a power switch. The FTI has its own fault-tolerant power supply (IP).

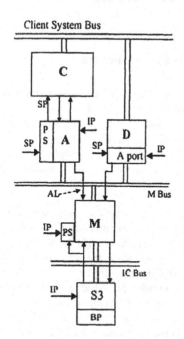

SP: System Power

IP: Infrastructure Power

BP: Backup Power

PS: Power Switch

C: Computing Node

A: Adapter Node

D: Decision Node

M: Monitor Node

S3:Startup,Shutdown, Survival Node

AL: A-Line

Note: Redundant nodes are not shown

Fig. 1. Basic Structure of the FTI

4   Fault Tolerance of the FTI

The partitioning of the FTI is motivated by the need to make it fault-tolerant. The A and D nodes are self-checking pairs, since high error detection coverage is essential, while spare C and D nodes can be provided for recovery under M node control. The M node must be continuously available, therefore triplication and voting (TMR) is needed, with spare M nodes added for longer life.

The S3 nodes manage M node replacement and also shut the agent down in the case of failure or global catastrophic events (temporary power loss, heavy radiation, etc.). They are protected by the use of two or more self-checking pairs with backup power. S3 nodes were separated from M nodes to make the node that must survive catastrophic events as small as possible. The S3 nodes also provide outputs to the agent's environment that indicate the health status of the agent: perfect, undergoing protective action or failed.

The all-hardware implementation of the FTI makes it safe from software bugs and external attacks. The one exception is the power management command from C to M nodes (via the D node) which could be used to shut the system down. Special protection is needed here. Hardware design faults in the FTI nodes could be handled by design diversity of self-checking pairs and of M nodes, although the logic of the nodes is very simple and their complete verification should be possible.

When interconnected, the FTI and the original autonomous agent form a computing system that is protected against most causes of system failure. An example system of this type is called DiSTARS: Diversifiable Self Testing And Repairing System and is discussed in detail in [1]. DiSTARS is the first example of an implementation of the immune system paradigm. Much detail of implementation of the FTI is presented in the U.S. patent application disclosure "Self-Testing and – Repairing Fault Tolerance Infrastructure for Computer Systems" by A. Avižienis, filed June 19, 2001.

5. In Conclusion: Some Challenges

The use of the FTI is likely to be affordable for most agents, since the A, M, D, and S3 nodes have a simple internal structure, as shown in [5] and the above mentioned disclosure. It is more interesting to consider that there are some truly challenging missions that can only be justified if their computing systems with the FTI have very high coverage with respect to design faults and to catastrophic transients due to radiation. Furthermore, extensive sparing and efficient power management can also be provided by the FTI. Given that the MTBF of contemporary processor and memory chips is approaching 1000 years, missions that can be contemplated include the 1000-day manned mission to Mars [8] with the dependability of a 10-hour flight of a commercial airliner. Another fascinating possibility is an unmanned very long life interstellar mission using a fault-tolerant relay chain of modest-cost DiSTARS type spacecraft [9]. Both missions are discussed in [5].

References

1. A.Avižienis, J.-C. Laprie, B. Randell, C. Landwehr. Basic concepts and taxonomy of dependable and secure computing. *IEEE Trans. On Dependable and Secure Computing,* 1(1):11-33, January-March 2004.
2. N.A. Lynch. Distributed algorithms. Morgan Kaufmann, 1996.
3. F. Heylighen, C. Gershenson, The meaning of self-organization in computers. *IEEE Intelligent Systems,* July/August 2003, pp. 72-75.
4. A. Avižienis. Toward systematic design of fault-tolerant systems. *Computer,* 30(4):51-58, April 1997.
5. A.Avižienis, A fault tolerance infrastructure for dependable computing with high performance COTS components. *Proc. of the Int. Conference on Dependable Systems and Networks (DSN 2000),* New York, June 2000, pages 492-500.
6. G.J.V. Nossal. Life, death and the immune system. *Scientific American,* 269(33)52-62, September 1993.
7. S.A. Hofmeyr, S. Forrest. Immunity by design: An artificial immune system. *Proc. 1999 Genetic and Evolutionary Computation Conference,* pages 1289-1296. Morgan-Kaufmann, 1999.
8. Special report: sending astronauts to Mars. *Scientific American,* 282(3):40-63, March 2000.
9. A. Avižienis. The hundred year spacecraft. *Proceedings of the 1st NASA/DoD Workshop on Evolvable Hardware,* Pasadena, CA, July 1999, pp. 233-239.

99% (Biological) Inspiration ...

Michael G. Hinchey[1] and Roy Sterritt[2]

[1] NASA Goddard Space Flight Center, Greenbelt, MD 20771, USA
[2] University of Ulster, School of Computing and Mathematics,
Northern Ireland

Abstract.   Greater understanding of biology in modern times has enabled significant breakthroughs in improving healthcare, quality of life, and eliminating many diseases and congenital illnesses. Simultaneously there is a move towards emulating nature and copying many of the wonders uncovered in biology, resulting in "biologically inspired" systems. Significant results have been reported in a wide range of areas, with systems inspired by nature enabling exploration, communication, and advances that were never dreamed possible just a few years ago. We warn, that as in many other fields of endeavor, we should be *inspired* by nature and biology, not engage in mimicry. We describe some results of biological inspiration that augur promise in terms of improving the safety and security of systems, and in developing self-managing systems, that we hope will ultimately lead to self-governing systems.

1   Introduction

Thomas Alva Edison described invention as 1% inspiration and 99% perspiration. This quotation is attributed to him with multiple variations, some describing invention, others describing genius.[*]

We cannot possibly hope to match the inventiveness and genius of nature. We can be *inspired* by nature and influenced by it, but to attempt to mimic nature is likely to have very limited success, as early pioneers of flight discovered.

---

[*] The earliest recorded quotation is from a press conference, quoted by James D. Newton in *Uncommon Friends* (1929): "None of my inventions came by accident. I see a worthwhile need to be met and I make trial after trial until it comes. What it boils down to is one per cent inspiration and ninety-nine per cent perspiration."

Please use the following format when citing this chapter:

Hinchey, M.G., Sterritt, R., 2006, in IFIP International Federation for Information Processing, Volume 216, Biologically Inspired Cooperative Computing, eds. Pan, Y., Rammig, F., Schmeck, H., Solar, M., (Boston: Springer), pp. 7–20.

Icarus attempted to escape the Labyrinth in which he was imprisoned with his father, Daedalus, by building wings from feathers and wax. Despite Deadalus's warning not to fly so low as to get the feathers wet, nor so near the sun as to melt the wax, Icarus flew too high, the wax did indeed melt, and he fell to his death.

In 1809, a Viennese watchmaker named Degen claimed to have flown with similar apparatus. In reality, he only hopped a short distance, and was supported by a balloon. Early attempts at mechanical flight involved the use of aircraft with wings that flapped like a bird's. But clearly, trying to copy birds was not going to work:

> Since the days of Bishop Wilkins the scheme of flying by artificial wings has been much ridiculed; and indeed the idea of attaching wings to the arms of a man is ridiculous enough, as the pectoral muscles of a bird occupy more than two-thirds of its whole muscular strength, whereas in man the muscles, that could operate upon wings thus attached, would probably not exceed one-tenth of his whole mass. There is no proof that, weight for weight, a man is comparatively weaker than a bird ... [1].

It was only when inventors such as Otto Lilienthal, building on the work of Cayley, moved away from directly mimicking nature, and adopted fixed wings, originally as gliders and later as monoplanes, and eventually as aircraft with wings and a tail, as Cayley had identified was needed for flight [2], that success was achieved [1]. Even then, early aircraft had very limited success (the Wright brothers' historic first powered flight at Kitty Hawk, North Carolina, in 1903 only lasted 12 seconds and 120 feet [3]), and required the addition of gas-powered engine for thrust and the Wright brothers' identification of an effective means of lateral control, for a feasible heavier-than-air craft to be possible.

Aircraft as we know them now bear very little resemblance to birds. Flight was *inspired* by nature, but hundreds of years were spent trying to copy nature, with little success. Inspiration was vital—otherwise man would never have attempted to fly. But direct mimicry was the wrong direction. Similarly we believe that computing systems may benefit much by being *inspired* by biology, but should not attempt to copy biology slavishly.

> To invent an airplane is nothing.
> To build one is something.
> But to fly is everything.
> *Otto Lilienthal (1848-1896)*

2   Biologically-Inspired Computing

> We've discovered the secret of life.
> *Francis Crick (1916-2004)*

The Nobel prize-winning discovery, in 1953, of the double helix structure of DNA and its encoding was revolutionary. It has opened a whole new world of understanding of biology and the way in which nature works. Simultaneously, it has resulted in several new fields of scientific research: genetics, genomics, computational biology, and bioinformatics, to name but a few.

The understanding of how nature encodes biological information and determines how living organisms will develop and evolve has enabled us to improve the quality of life, eliminate certain diseases, cure congenital defects in unborn children, and make significant advances in controlling and eventually eliminating life-threatening conditions.

This greater understanding of the biology of living organisms has also indicated a parallel with computing systems: molecules in living cells interact, grow, and transform according to the "program" dictated by DNA.   Indeed, the goal of bioinformatics is to develop "in silico" models of in vitro and in vivo biological experiments [4].

Paradigms of Computing are emerging based on modeling and developing computer-based systems exploiting ideas that are observed in nature.   This includes building self-management and self-governance mechanisms that are inspired by the human body's autonomic nervous system into computer systems, modeling evolutionary systems analogous to colonies of ants or other insects, and developing highly-efficient and highly-complex distributed systems from large numbers of (often quite simple) largely homogeneous components to reflect the behavior of flocks of birds, swarms of bees, herds of animals, or schools of fish.

This field of "Biologically-Inspired Computing", often known in other incarnations by other names, such as: Autonomic Computing, Organic Computing, Biomimetics, and Artificial Life, amongst others, is poised at the intersection of Computer Science, Engineering, Mathematics, and the Life Sciences [5].   Successes have been reported in the fields of drug discovery, data communications, computer animation, control and command, exploration systems for space, undersea, and harsh environments, to name but a few, and augur much promise for future progress [5, 6].

3   The Autonomic Nervous System

> The nervous system and the automatic machine are fundamentally alike in that they are devices, which make decisions on the basis of decisions they made in the past.
> *Norbert Weiner (1894-1964)*

Inspiration from human biology, in the form of the autonomic nervous system (ANS), is the focus of the Autonomic Computing initiative.   The idea is that mechanisms that are "autonomic", in-built, and requiring no conscious thought in the human body are used as inspiration for building mechanisms that will enable a computer system to become self-managing [7].

The human (and animal) body's *sympathetic nervous system (SyNS)* deals with defense and protection ("fight or flight") and the *parasympathetic nervous system (PaNS)* deals with long-term health of the body ("rest and digest"), performing the vegetative functions of the body such as circulation of the blood, intestinal activity, and secretion of chemicals (hormones) that circulate in the blood.   So too an autonomic system tries to ensure the continued health and well-being of a computer-based system by sending and monitoring various signals in the system.

The general properties of an autonomic (self-managing) system can be summarised by four objectives: being self-configuring, self-healing, self-optimizing and self-protecting, and four attributes: self-awareness, self-situated, self-monitoring and self-adjusting (Figure 1). Essentially, the objectives represent broad system requirements, while the attributes identify basic implementation mechanisms [8].

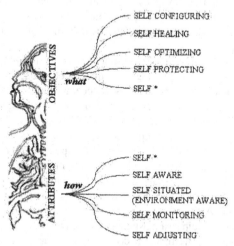

Fig. 1 Autonomic System Properties

In achieving such self-managing objectives, a system must be aware of its internal state (self-aware) and current external operating conditions (self-situated). Changing circumstances are detected through self-monitoring, and adaptations are made accordingly (self-adjusting). As such, a system must have knowledge of its available resources, its components, their desired performance characteristics, their current status, and the status of inter-connections with other systems, along with rules and policies of how these may be adjusted. Such ability to operate in a heterogeneous environment will require the use of open standards to enable global understanding and communication with other systems [5].

These mechanisms are not independent entities. For instance, if an attack is successful, this will necessitate self-healing actions, and a mix of self-configuration and self-optimization, in the first instance to ensure dependability and continued operation of the system, and later to increase self-protection against similar future attacks. Finally, these self-mechanisms should ensure that there is minimal disruption to users, avoiding significant delays in processing.

At the heart of the architecture of any autonomic system are sensors and effectors. A control loop is created by monitoring behavior through sensors, comparing this with expectations (knowledge, as in historical and current data, rules and beliefs), planning what action is necessary (if any), and then executing that action through effectors. The closed loop of feedback control provides the basic backbone structure for each system component [9].

The autonomic environment requires that autonomic elements and, in particular, autonomic managers for these elements communicate with one another concerning self-* activities, in order to ensure the robustness of the environment. Figure 2 depicts that the autonomic manager communications (AM⇔AM) also includes a reflex signal. This may be facilitated through the additional concept of a pulse monitor—PBM (an extension of the embedded system's heart-beat monitor, or HBM, which safeguards vital processes through the emission of a regular "I am alive" signal to another process) with the capability to encode health and urgency signals as a pulse [10]. Together with the standard event messages on the autonomic communications channel, this provides dynamics within autonomic responses and multiple loops of control, such as reflex reactions among the autonomic managers. This reflex component may be used to safeguard the autonomic element by communicating its health to another AE. The component may also be utilized to communicate environmental health information.

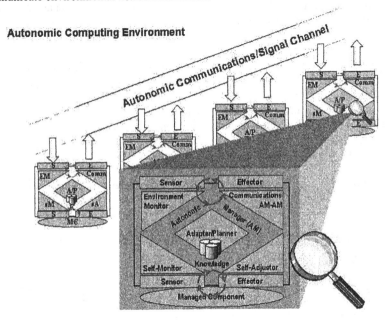

Fig. 2 Autonomic System Environment consisting of Autonomic Elements

An important aspect concerning the reflex reaction and the pulse monitor is the minimization of data sent—essentially only a "signal" is transmitted. Strictly speaking, this is not mandatory; more information may be sent, yet the additional information must not compromise the reflex reaction. For instance, in the absence of bandwidth concerns, information that can be acted upon quickly and not incur processing delays could be sent. The important aspect is that the information must be in a form that can be acted upon immediately and not involve processing delays (such as is the case of event correlation) [11].

Just as the beat of the heart has a double beat ("lub-dub", as it is referred to by the medical profession) the autonomic element's pulse monitor may have a double beat encoded—a *self* health/urgency measure and an *environment* health/urgency measure

[12]. These match directly with the two control loops within the AE, and the self-awareness and environment awareness properties.

4   Inspiration from Human Biology

> We still do not know one thousandth of one percent of what nature has revealed to us.
> *Albert Einstein (1879-1955)*

4.1 New Metaphors

In this emerging field of biologically-inspired computing, we are seeking inspiration for new approaches from (obviously, pre-existing) biological mechanisms, and in fact a whole plethora of further self-* properties are being proposed and developed, leading to the coining of the term *selfware*.

The biological cell cycle is often described as a circle of cell life and division. A cell divides into two "daughter cells" and both of these cells live, "eat", grow, copy their genetic material and divide again producing two more daughter cells. Since each daughter cell has a copy of the same genes in its nucleus, daughter cells are "clones" of each other. This "twinning" goes on and on with each cell cycle. This is a natural process.

Very fast cell cycles occur during development causing a single cell to make many copies of itself as it grows and differentiates into an embryo. Some very fast cell cycles also occur in adult animals. Hair, skin and gut cells have very fast cell cycles to replace cells that die naturally. Scientists now believe that some forms of cancer may be caused by cells not dying quickly enough, rather than cycling out of control.

But there is a kind of "parking spot" in the cell cycle, called "quiescence". A *quiescent* cell has left the cell cycle; it has stopped dividing (Figure 3). Quiescent cells may re-enter the cell cycle at some later time, or they may not; it depends on the type of cell. Most nerve cells stay quiescent forever. On the other hand, some quiescent cells may later re-enter the cell cycle in order to create more cells (for example, during pubescent development) [13].

We have been considering self-destruction as a means of providing an intrinsic safety mechanism against non-desirable emergent behavior from the selfware. It is believed that a cell knows when to commit suicide because cells are programmed to do so—self-destruction (sD) is an intrinsic property. This sD is delayed due to the continuous receipt of biochemical retrieves. This process is referred to as *apoptosis*, meaning "drop out", used by the Greeks to refer to the Autumn dropping of leaves from trees; i.e., loss of cells that ought to die in the midst of the living structure. The process has also been nicknamed "death by default" where cells are prevented from putting an end to themselves due to constant receipt of biochemical "stay alive" signals.

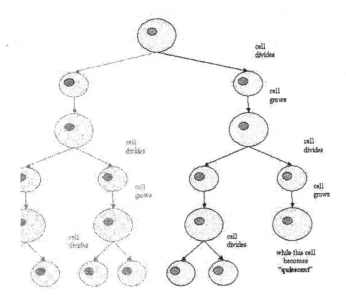

Fig. 3 Cycle of cell life - featuring a quiescent cell

Further investigations into the apoptosis process have discovered more details about the self-destruct program. Whenever a cell divides, it simultaneously receives orders to kill itself. Without a reprieve signal, the cell does indeed self-destruct. It is believed that the reason for this is self-protection, as the most dangerous time for the body is when a cell divides, since if just one of the billions of cells locks into division the result is a tumor, while simultaneously a cell must divide to build and maintain a body [14, 15, 16].

4.2 Inspiration

Of course, each of these techniques and mechanisms is useful in achieving autonomicity and in mimicking the autonomic nervous system (ANS). But while the inspiration comes substantially from that of the human (or animal) body, the techniques are not those that the ANS actually uses.

There *are* signals sent around the human body in the form of hormones and pulses, amongst others, in the blood. But in modern computer science and engineering, we have developed many efficient communication mechanisms that do not rely on signals flowing through miles of unnecessary channels (veins and arteries), but may be directly routed or broadcast using wireless communications.

We do not know precisely how apoptosis and quiescence works, nor specifically their roles. But they certainly offer interesting ideas for future security and safety mechanisms in computer-based systems [6].

These techniques are *inspired* by nature, but not necessarily implemented as they are by nature. In many cases, we can make some optimizations or improvements; in other cases we simply do not understand enough of how nature works to implement these directly, but they can certainly inspire interesting metaphors for self-management and self-governance.

5 Swarms

> What is not good for the swarm is not good for the bee.
> *Marcus Aurelius (A.D. 121-180)*

We are all familiar with swarms in nature. The mere mention of the word "swarm" conjures up images of large groupings of small insects, such as bees (apiidae) or locusts (acridiidae), each insect having a simple role, but with the swarm as a whole producing complex behavior.

Strictly speaking, such emergence of complex behavior is not limited to swarms, and we see similar complex social structures occurring with higher order animals and insects that don't swarm *per se*: colonies of ants, flocks of birds, packs of wolves, etc. These groupings behave like swarms[†] in many ways [17].

A *swarm* consists of a large number of simple entities that have local interactions (including interactions with the environment) [29]. The result of the combination of simple behaviors (the microscopic behavior) is the emergence of complex behavior (the macroscopic behavior) and the ability to achieve significant results as a "team" [18]. Basing collaborative computing systems on the concept of a swarm allows us to build complex systems, with often surprising behavior, from simple components.

Intelligent swarm technology is based on swarm technology where the individual members of the swarm also exhibit independent intelligence [19]. Intelligent swarms may be homogeneous or heterogeneous, or may start out as homogeneous and evolve as in different environments they "learn" different things, develop new (different) goals, and eventually become heterogeneous, reflecting different capabilities and a societal structure.

Agent swarms have been used as a computer modeling technique and have also been used as a tool to study complex systems [20]. Examples of simulations that have been undertaken include flocks of birds as well as business and economics and ecological systems.

In *swarm simulations*, each of the agents is given certain parameters that it tries to maximize. Swarm simulations have been developed that exhibit unlikely emergent behavior. These emergent behaviors are the sums of often simple individual behaviors, but, when aggregated, form complex and often unexpected behaviors.

Swarm intelligence techniques (note the slight difference in terminology from "intelligent swarms") are population-based stochastic methods used in combinatorial

---

[†] The term "swarm", as we use it here, refers to a (possibly large) grouping of simple components collaborating to achieve some goal and produce significant results. The term should not be taken to imply that these components fly (or are airborne); they may equally well be on the surface of the Earth, under the surface, under water, or indeed operating on other planets.

optimization problems, where the collective behavior of relatively simple individuals arises from their local interactions with their environment to give rise to the emergence of functional global patterns.

Swarm robotics refers to the application of swarm intelligence techniques to the analysis of swarms where the embodiment of the "agents" is as physical robotic devices.

5.1 Swarm Inspiration

The idea that swarms can be used to solve complex problems has been taken up in several areas of computer science.   These include the use of analogies to the pheromone trails used by ants (to leave trails for the colony to follow to stores of food) in software to solve the traveling salesman problem, allowing the software to "find" the shortest route by following the route with the most "digital pheromone", meaning it is the shortest (as on longer routes the concentration of pheromone would be lower due to being spread over a greater distance) [17, 21].   The approach is an example of *Ant Colony Optimization*, a very interesting approach that is inspired by the social behavior of ants, and uses their behavior patterns as models for solving difficult combinational optimization problems [22].

Swarm behavior is also being investigated for use in such applications as telephone switching, network routing, data categorizing, and shortest path optimizations.   Swarm radio and "swarmcasting" of television over the internet is an approach to file-sharing that is inspired substantially by swarms.   The approach exploits under-utilized uplinks to download part of the file to other users and then allow for the receipt of portions of the file from those users.   The result is that streaming video is possible even without a high-speed internet connection.

Research at Penn State University has focused on the use of particle swarms for the development of quantitative structure activity relationships (QSAR) models used in the area of drug design [23].   The research created models using artificial neural networks and k-nearest neighbor and kernel regression.   Binary and niching particle swarms were used to solve feature selection and feature weighting problems.

Particle swarms have influenced the field of computer animation also. Rather than scripting the path of each individual bird in a flock, the Boids project [24] elaborated a particle swarm with the simulated birds being the particles.   The aggregate motion of the simulated flock is much like that in nature: it is the result of the dense interaction of the relatively simple behaviors of each of the (simulated) birds, where each bird chooses its own path.

5.2 Swarms for Exploration

NASA is investigating the use of swarm technologies for the development of sustainable exploration missions that will be autonomous and exhibit autonomic properties [25].   The idea is that biologically-inspired swarms of smaller spacecraft offer greater redundancy (and, consequently, greater protection of assets), reduced costs and risks, and the ability to explore regions of space where a single large spacecraft would be impractical.

ANTS is a NASA concept mission, a collaboration between NASA Goddard Space Flight Center and NASA Langley Research Center, which aims at the development of revolutionary mission architectures and the exploitation of artificial intelligence techniques and the paradigm of biological inspiration in future space exploration. The mission concept includes the use of swarm technologies for both spacecraft and surface-based rovers, and consists of several submissions:

- *SARA: The Saturn Autonomous Ring Array* will launch 1000 pico-class spacecraft, organized as ten sub-swarms, each with specialized instruments, to perform *in situ* exploration of Saturn's rings, by which to understand their constitution and how they were formed. The concept mission will require self-configuring structures for nuclear propulsion and control, which lies beyond the scope of this paper. Additionally, autonomous operation is necessary for both maneuvering around Saturn's rings and collision avoidance.
- *PAM: Prospecting Asteroid Mission* will also launch 1000 pico-class spacecraft, but here with the aim of exploring the asteroid belt and collecting data on particular asteroids of interest for potential future mining operations.
- *LARA: ANTS Application Lunar Base Activities* will exploit new NASA-developed technologies in the field of miniaturized robotics, which may form the basis of remote landers to be launched to the moon from remote sites, and may exploit innovative techniques to allow rovers to move in an amoeboid-like fashion over the moon's uneven terrain.

5.3 Inspiration and Improvement

ANTS, although a nice acronym, is actually somewhat of a misnomer—other than the LARA submission, the concept mission is more inspired by swarms of bees or flocks of birds than by colonies of ants.

But even then, ANTS is merely *inspired* by birds and bees. As we discussed in Section 1, the pioneers of flight found that directly attempting to mimic avian flight was the wrong way forward. Similarly, ANTS spacecraft in the PAM and SARA submissions will not attempt to fly like birds (in any case it would not be practical to build them with wings, a short tail, a curved sternum and hollow bones, in the way birds have evolved from *Archaeopteryx,* a dromaeosaurid from the late Jurrasic and Cretaceous periods and the earliest known flying creature).

In PAM, illustrated in Figure 4, a swarm of autonomous pico-class (approximately 1kg) spacecraft will explore the asteroid belt for asteroids with certain characteristics. In this mission, a transport ship, launched from Earth, will travel to a point in space where gravitational forces on small objects (such as pico-class spacecraft) are all but negligible. From this point, termed a Lagrangian, 1000 spacecraft, which will have been assembled *en route* from Earth, will be launched into the asteroid belt.

Approximately 80 percent of the spacecraft will be workers that will carry the specialized instruments (e.g., a magnetometer or an x-ray, gamma-ray, visible/IR, or neutral mass spectrometer) and will obtain specific types of data. Some will be coordinators (called leaders) that have rules that decide the types of asteroids and data the mission is interested in and that will coordinate the efforts of the workers. The third type of spacecraft are messengers that will coordinate communication between the rulers and workers, and communications with the Earth ground station.

The swarm will form sub-swarms under the control of a ruler, which contains models of the types of science that it wants to perform. The ruler will coordinate workers, each of which uses its individual instrument to collect data on specific asteroids and feed this information back to the ruler, who will determine which asteroids are worth examining further. If the data matches the profile of a type of asteroid that is of interest, an imaging spacecraft will be sent to the asteroid to ascertain the exact location and to create a rough model to be used by other spacecraft for maneuvering around the asteroid. Other teams of spacecraft will then coordinate to finish mapping the asteroid to form a complete model.

This is *not* how birds flock nor bees swarm.[‡] Birds form flocks in response to a *flocking call* issued by one of the birds.   Birds in the flock continue in the flight pattern by "following" another bird. It is thought that collisions are avoided via *flight calls*, whereby birds let other birds know where they are via sound. In ANTS, the spacecraft do not "broadcast" in this way; spacecraft do not communicate with each other directly, but rather via a *messenger* that coordinates communications between the spacecraft and with Earth.   Collision-avoidance (both collisions with other spacecraft and with asteroids) in ANTS is achieved by keeping models of locations, which will be achieved via various means.   Since movement will be enabled only by simple thrusters, it is anticipated that many of the spacecraft will be lost due to collisions.

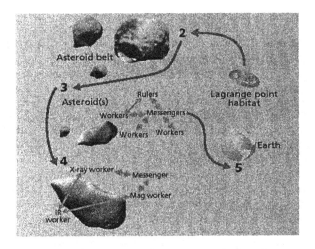

Fig. 4 ANTS PAM (Prospecting Asteroid Mission) scenario

In many senses, this is more efficient than the broadcast mechanism of the flocking calls and flight calls.   There is less communication overhead, and the spacecraft are not continually having to update the information on where other spacecraft are located relative to them.   Of course we can tolerate certain losses of spacecraft (one of the motivations for a swarm-based approach is to have redundancy and avoid mission loss due to a single incident), as long as the number of incidents is within certain boundaries, whereas a flock of birds could not tolerate continual losses due to collisions.

[‡] Not all species of bee swarm; there are several solitary species.

ANTS spacecraft will also need to have protection mechanisms built in, such as going into sleep mode to protect solar sails (used for power) during solar storms. This is analogous to a flock of birds taking shelter in severe weather, but the spacecraft do not have to land and find shelter, they merely have to alter their position and lower their sails to avoid damage from electrical charges, etc.

Similarly, flocks of birds and swarms of bees do not form sub-swarms as is envisioned in ANTS, nor do they take instructions directly from a leader. While flocks and swarms in nature do occasionally allow for an alternate to take over a particular role (e.g., the establishment of a new queen in a hive), this is not so efficient as in ANTS where a worker with a damaged instrument, instead of becoming useless, can take over the role of messenger, or even leader.

The ANTS swarm, collaborating to collect science data from the asteroid belt, is clearly inspired by nature and the biology of birds and bees, but exhibits enhancements over nature by virtue of techniques and approaches known to us from the fields of computing and engineering.

6   Conclusions

The human race has gained much from a greater understanding of biology. Understanding how the "program" of life works has made it possible to prevent many undesirable conditions, cure certain diseases and afflictions, devise new treatments and drugs and understand better when they can be used, etc.

Notwithstanding this greater understanding of biology, most of these advancements were due to the exploitation of modern computing technology and its application to biological problems, and in particular the ability to develop and explore (search) models of reality.   We begin with such models, and enhance them with concepts not seen in nature or the real world [26], but deriving from advancements in computing and engineering.

Such modeling of biological phenomena and nature has enabled us to better understand the behavior patterns of insects, birds, and mammals. Simultaneously, an understanding of biology and nature has enabled the creation of a whole field of biologically-inspired computing.   Ingenuity in nature has sparked imaginations and inspired ideas for means of developing complex computer systems that reduce complexity, enable the development of classes of system which we could never have achieved without this inspiration, and move towards self-governance of systems.

Biologically-inspired computing involves looking at biology and nature and models of it, and then adapting it and improving on it with advances made in computing technology and engineering.

Unlike Edison, at least in this context, we see the inspiration as being 99% of the effort, and believe that computing can benefit in many ways from biological inspiration.   We believe that biologically-inspired computing should be 99% (biological) inspiration, combined with 1% mimicry.

Look deep into nature, and you will understand everything better.
Albert Einstein (1879-1955)

Acknowledgements

We are grateful to the organizers of BICC 2006 for inviting this talk and associated paper.

Autonomic apoptosis was introduced in [14], and quiescence in [6]. More detailed expositions of the ANTS concept mission, and specifically the PAM submission, are given in [25,27, 28].

Part of this work has been supported by the NASA Office of Systems and Mission Assurance (OSMA) through its Software Assurance Research Program (SARP) project, *Formal Approaches to Swarm Technologies (FAST),* and by NASA Software Engineering Laboratory, Goddard Space Flight Center (Code 581).

This research is partly supported at University of Ulster by the Computer Science Research Institute (CSRI) and the Centre for Software Process Technologies (CSPT) which is funded by Invest NI through the Centres of Excellence Programme, under the EU Peace II initiative.

Some of the technologies described in this paper are patent-pending and assigned to the United States government.

References

1. O. Lilienthal, "Practical Experiments for the Development of Human Flight," *The Aeronautical Annual,* pp 7-20, 1896.
2. G. Cayley, "On Aeriel Naviation," *Nicholson's Journal,* November 1809.
3. B. Gates, "The Wright Brothers," *Time,* 29 March 1999.
4. J. Cohen, "Bioinformatics—an Introduction for Computer Scientists," *ACM Computing Surveys,* 36(2):122-158, June 2004.
5. M.G. Hinchey and R. Sterritt, "Self-managing Software," *IEEE Computer* 39(2):107-109, February 2006.
6. R. Sterritt and M.G. Hinchey, "Biologically-Inspired Concepts for Autonomic Self-Protection in Multiagent Systems," In *Proc. 3rd Int. Workshop Safety and Security in Multiagent Systems (SASEMAS 2006) at AAMAS,* Hakodate, Japan, 8-12 May 2006.
7. R. Sterritt, "Towards Autonomic Computing: Effective Event Management," In *Proc. 27th Ann. IEEE/NASA Software Engineering Workshop (SEW),* MD, USA, 3-5 Dec. 2002, IEEE Computer Society Press, pp. 40-47.
8. R. Sterritt and D.W. Bustard, "Autonomic Computing: a Means of Achieving Dependability?" In *Proc. IEEE Int. Conf. Engineering of Computer Based Systems (ECBS'03),* Huntsville, AL, USA, 7-11 April 2003, pp. 247-251.
9. R. Sterritt and D.W. Bustard, "Towards an Autonomic Computing Environment," In *Proc. IEEE DEXA 2003 Workshops - 1st Int. Workshop Autonomic Computing Systems,* Prague, Czech Republic, 1-5 September 2003, pp. 694-698.
10. R. Sterritt, "Pulse Monitoring: Extending the Health-check for the Autonomic GRID," In *Proc. IEEE Workshop Autonomic Computing Principles and Architectures (AUCOPA 2003) at INDIN 2003,* Banff, AB, Canada, 22-23 August 2003, pp. 433-440.
11. R. Sterritt and D.F. Bantz, "PAC-MEN: Personal Autonomic Computing Monitoring Environments," In *Proc IEEE DEXA 2004 Workshops - 2nd Int. Workshop Self-Adaptive and Autonomic Computing Systems (SAACS 04),* Zaragoza, Spain, 30 Aug–3 Sept. 2004.

12. R. Sterritt and M.G. Hinchey, "SPAACE:: Self- Properties for an Autonomous and Autonomic Computing Environment," *In Proc. Software Engineering Research and Practice (SERP '05)*, Las Vegas, NV, 27-29 June 2005, CREA Press.

13. J. Love, *Science Explained*, 1999.

14. R. Sterritt and M.G. Hinchey, "Apoptosis and Self-Destruct: A Contribution to Autonomic Agents?" In *Proc. FAABS-III, 3rd NASA/IEEE Workshop on Formal Approaches to Agent-Based Systems*, 26-27 April 2004, Greenbelt, MD, Springer Verlag LNCS 3228, 2005.

15. R. Sterritt and M.G. Hinchey, "Engineering Ultimate Self-Protection in Autonomic Agents for Space Exploration Missions," In *Proc. IEEE Workshop on the Engineering of Autonomic Systems (EASe 2005) at 12th Ann. IEEE Int. Conf. Engineering of Computer Based Systems (ECBS 2005)*, Greenbelt, MD, USA, 3-8 April 2005, IEEE Computer Society Press, pp. 506-511.

16. R. Sterritt and M.G. Hinchey, "Biologically-Inspired Concepts for Self-Managing Ubiquitous and Pervasive Computing Environments" In *Proc. WRAC-II, 2nd NASA/IEEE Workshop on Radical Agent Concepts*, Sept. 2005, Greenbelt, MD, Springer Verlag LNCS 3825, 2006.

17. M.G. Hinchey, J.L. Rash, W.F. Truszkowski, C.A. Rouff and R. Sterritt, "Autonomous and Autonomic Swarms," *In Proc. Autonomic & Autonomous Space Exploration Systems (A&A-SES-1) at 2005 Int. Conf. Software Engineering Research and Practice (SERP'05)*, Las Vegas, NV, 27-29 June 2005, CREA Press, pp 36-42,

18. E. Bonabeau, G. Théraulax, "Swarm Smarts," *Scientific American*, Mar 2000, pp 72-79.

19. G. Beni and J. Want, "Swarm Intelligence," In *Proc. Seventh Annual Meeting of the Robotics Society of Japan*, Tokyo, Japan, 1989, pp 425-428, RSJ Press.

20. D.E. Hiebler, "The Swarm Simulation System and Individual-Based Modeling," In *Proc. Decision Support 2001: Advanced Technology for Natural Resource Management*, Toronto, Canada, September 1994.

21. M. Dorigo and L.M. Gambardella, "Ant Colonies for the Traveling Salesman Problem," *BioSystems*, 43:73-81, 1997.

22. M. Dorigo and T. Stützle, *Ant Colony Optimization*, MIT Press, Cambridge, MA, 2004.

23. W. Cedeno and D.K. Agrafiotis. "Combining Particle Swarms and k-nearest Neighbors for the Development of Quantitative Structure-Activity Relationships," *Int. J. Comput. Res.*, 11(4):443-452, 2003.

24. C.W. Reynolds, "Flocks, Herds, and Schools: A Distributed Behavior Model," *Computer Graphics*, 21(4):25-34, 1987.

25. W.F. Truszkowski, M.G. Hinchey, J.L. Rash and C.A. Rouff, "Autonomous and Autonomic Systems: A Paradigm for Future Space Exploration Missions," *IEEE Trans. on Systems, Man, and Cybernetics—Part C*, 36(3):May 2006.

26. I. Peterson, "Calculating Swarms," *Science News*, 158(20):314, 11 November 2000.

27. C.A. Rouff, M.G. Hinchey, J.L. Rash and W.F. Truszkowski, "Experiences Applying Formal Approaches in the Development of Swarm-Based Exploration Missions," *Int. J. of Software Tools for Technology Transfer*, to appear, 2006.

28. W.F. Truszkowski, M.G. Hinchey, J.L. Rash and C.A. Rouff, "NASA's Swarm Missions: The Challenge of Building Autonomous Software," *IEEE IT Prof.* 6(5):47-52, 2004.

29. G. Beni, "The Concept of Cellular Robotics," In *Proc. 1988 IEEE International Symposium on Intelligent Control*, pp 57-62, IEEE Computer Society Press.

30. E. Bonabeau, M. Dorigo and G. Théraulax, "Inspiration for Optimization from Social Insect Behaviour," *Nature* 406:39-42, 6 July 2000.

Biologically-Inspired Design: Getting It Wrong and Getting It Right

Steve R. White

IBM Thomas J. Watson Research Center, P.O. Box 704,
Yorktown Heights, NY 10598 srwhite@watson.ibm.com

Abstract. Large, complex computing systems have many similarities to biological systems, at least at a high level. They consist of a very large number of components, the interactions between which are complex and dynamic, and the overall behavior of the system is not always predictable even if the components are well understood. These similarities have led the computing community to look to biology for design inspiration. But computing systems are not biological systems. Care must be taken when applying biological designs to computing systems, and we need to avoid applying them when they are not appropriate. We review three areas in which we have used biology as an inspiration to understand and construct computing systems. The first is the epidemiology of computer viruses, in which biological models are used to predict the speed and scope of global virus spread. The second is global defenses against computer viruses, in which the mammalian immune system is the starting point for design. The third is self-assembling autonomic systems, in which the components of a system connect locally, without global control, to provide a desired global function. In each area, we look at an approach that seems very biologically motivated, but that turns out to yield poor results. Then, we look at an approach that works well, and contrast it with the prior misstep. Perhaps unsurprisingly, attempting to reason by analogy is fraught with dangers. Rather, it is critical to have a detailed, rigorous understanding of the system being constructed and the technologies being used, and to understand the differences between the biological system and the computing system, as well as their similarities.

1 Introduction

There is no doubt that computing systems are complex. They are arguably the most complex artifacts ever produced by humans. As computing systems become ever more complex, we naturally look to other fields to understand what tools and techniques we might bring to bear on the problems that we encounter. Computer

Please use the following format when citing this chapter:

White, S.R., 2006, in IFIP International Federation for Information Processing, Volume 216, Biologically Inspired Cooperative Computing, eds. Pan, Y., Rammig, F., Schmeck, H., Solar, M., (Boston: Springer), pp. 21–32.

scientists have long looked to mathematics, and even physics, for algorithms and methodologies. We have also, though perhaps less often, looked to biology.

But biological systems are quite different from computing systems, often radically so. We would not want to build a computer that counts on its fingers, or types on a keyboard. Why, even the term "biologically-inspired design" should make us a little nervous. We do not refer to the "mathematically-inspired design" of computing systems, or even to "physics-inspired design." We refer to mathematical algorithms, or techniques borrowed from physics, that help us design better computing systems. What, then, is the role of biological inspiration?

In the remainder of this paper, we turn our attention to three problems in computing systems in which people have used biology as an inspiration to understand and construct computing systems. The first is the epidemiology of computer viruses, in which biological models are used to predict the speed and scope of global virus spread. The second is global defenses against computer viruses, in which the mammalian immune system is the starting point for design. The third is self-assembling autonomic systems, in which the components of a system connect locally, without global control, to provide a desired global function. In each problem area, we look at an approach that seems very biologically motivated, but that turns out to yield poor results. Then, we look at an approach that works well, and contrast it with the prior misstep. Finally, we summarize the reasons why one biologically-motivated approach fails, while another succeeds. We conclude that reasoning by analogy is dangerous, but that a deeper understanding of the differences, as well as the similarities, between biological and computing systems can help us avoid the pitfalls of biologically-inspired design.

This is a cautionary tale.

2 Computer Virus Epidemiology

Ever since Len Adleman coined the term "computer virus" to describe a self-replicating program [1], the temptation to use biological analogies for them has been overwhelming. Computer viruses authors have used techniques such a "polymorphism," in which a virus changes its form with each succeeding generation in an attempt to evade detection, in much the same way as certain biological viruses mutate rapidly to evade the body's defenses. Anti-virus programmers developed techniques such as looking in files for bit strings that were found in known viruses but not in normal programs, much like the mammalian immune system produces cells that bind to viruses but not to cells in the body.

There has also been an overwhelming temptation to use models of biological virus spread to model computer virus spread. This temptation is understandable. Both kinds of viruses infect individuals, whether they are mammals or computers. Both spread from one individual to another via infection vectors, whether it is sneezing or sending files via email.

In the late 1980's, when computer viruses first became a serious problem, very little was known. Viruses spread on diskettes, which became infected when used on an infected computer and which could spread the infection when used on other computers. But little was understood about their global spread. In 1998, Peter Norton, later of Norton AntiVirus fame, was alleged to have said that computer viruses were an urban myth, "[...] like the story of alligators in the sewers of New York. Everyone knows about them, but no one's ever seen them."

2.1   Getting It Wrong

In 1991, Tippett asserted that the spread of computer viruses was like that of bacteria in a Petri dish – that without outside intervention their growth would tend to be exponential [2]. Though there was not a rigorous model behind these statements, they were based on the well-known fact that many population models exhibit exponential growth in their early phases. The reason for this is easy to see. The first infected individual might spread the infection to two other individuals, who in turn spread it to four more, and so on. The spread will be approximately exponential until a large fraction of the population is infected, at which time the infection will continue to spread, but more slowly due to the lack of uninfected targets. Assuming that everyone in the population is susceptible to the infection, the virus will ultimately infect 100% of the population.

Armed with this alarming prediction, Tippett and others called for emergency action, fearing that a worldwide pandemic was just months away. But as early data on worldwide virus infections became available, it became clear that there were problems with this model. Virus spread was nowhere close to exponential. In fact, it was surprisingly slow. Few viruses that were collected by anti-virus companies were ever seen in real-world infections, and even those that were took up to a year to become worldwide problems. Viruses never reached 100% of the population, even after a fairly long time. In fact, their prevalence would reach a peak of at most a few percent of the population, and then it would *decrease* [3].

2.2   Getting It Right

Two features of this simple model of infection are easily seen to be problematic. First, there is an assumption that infected individuals remain in the population indefinitely and continue to spread the infection. But infected computers do not stay infected forever. If the virus causes system problems, and most viruses did, users would be highly motivated to get rid of the virus. They might use anti-virus software, if it was clear that it was a virus. They might replace their boot records, which would have gotten rid of most boot viruses. They might have reformatted their hard drives and started over. Ultimately, users would have gotten rid of their computers and moved to new computers. Few of us are still using the computers that we used in 1990!

Second, there is an assumption that every individual is susceptible to infection. But, as the computer virus problem became worse, and more people started using anti-virus software regularly, this was no longer the case. Indeed, as anti-virus software gained the ability to actively prevent computer viruses from running on a system, and to stay up to date with the latest threats, many computers became immune to a virus before the virus could ever reach them.

A third feature of this simple model is perhaps more subtle. The model assumes that any infected individual has an equal chance of infecting any other individual. The model essentially assumes that the population is trapped in an elevator for several months, and that anyone sneezing has as much chance of infecting one of the individuals as another. In biological epidemiology, this is known as the "homogeneous mixing" assumption [4].

For rapidly-spreading diseases, such as influenza, in populations with a high degree of contact, such as cities, this is still a pretty good model. But computer users did not exchange diskettes in this pattern. They exchanged diskettes relatively infrequently, and often only within a group of close co-workers. Diskette exchanges between random people in the world occurred very infrequently. It turned out that the topology of how an infection may spread was a critical, and previously overlooked, feature of a successful model.

Kephart et al. described models of the epidemiology of computer viruses that had a rigorous basis and took these features into account [5, 6]. In these models, standard biological epidemiology was used to describe individuals who were susceptible, those who were infected and contagious, and those who were both cured and immune. Individuals who were susceptible could become infected, and could later become both cured and immune. The models supported standard epidemiological results such as epidemic thresholds: if the virus is killed off faster than it spreads, there is no epidemic. This was a likely explanation for the observation that most viruses were never seen in real-world infections. They were too inept at spreading or never got the chance. Similarly, epidemics in the model never reached 100% of the population. They were killed off by disinfecting infected computers or by preventative measures.

Instead of assuming homogeneous mixing, Kephart et al. modeled infections as spreading on a directed graph, in which the nodes were computers and the arcs denoted a pathway by which a particular computer could infect another. In very sparse graphs, which are likely the correct model for diskette-based virus spread, it was harder for an epidemic to start and easier for it to die off. In highly clustered graphs, representing more diskette sharing inside workgroups and less between them, viruses that were rampant in one part of the graph seldom leaked out to other parts of the graph, explaining the observation that some university computer labs had rampant, ongoing infections while more controlled environments rarely did.

It turned out that virus epidemiology in computer systems bore deep and striking similarities to the biological world. The same models could represent viruses in both worlds. The thing that distinguished the directed graph models from the "exponential growth" model was that it was not a case of reasoning by analogy. It had a rigorous mathematical basis and an explicit set of assumptions that could be validated in the real world. It was inspired by biology, but grounded in the actual system at hand.

3   A Digital Immune System

The mammalian immune system is very complex, and has evolved over millions of years to protect individuals against a very large and ever changing array of threats. It has a number of mechanisms, both innate and adaptive, to find and destroy foreign organic material that may pose a threat to the body.

The immune system is an obvious place to look for inspiration in combating cyberspace threats such as computer viruses. Before we do so, let us look at some of the mechanisms that it uses.

When viruses enter the bloodstream, some of them are engulfed and destroyed by macrophages (white blood cells), which then present antigens (proteins from the bacterium or virus) on their surface. Cells called T cells are capable of recognizing particular antigens by binding to them chemically. There are a vast number of T cells in the bloodstream, and collectively they are capable of recognizing a vast number of different antigens. When a particular T cell recognizes an antigen, it is stimulated to reproduce, so there are more T cells to find instances of that virus. It is also stimulated to produce antibodies that bind to the antigens on the surfaces of the virus. Viruses that are coated with antibodies are easier for macrophages to ingest. So, in response to an invading virus, the immune system produces a huge number of antibodies that help kill off that particular virus.

T cells that happen to recognize proteins found in the body are weeded out at an early stage in their lives, so the body does not (usually) produce antibodies against itself. Only T cells that might recognize viruses and do not recognize the body's cells (the "self") are allowed to circulate [7].

3.1   Getting It Wrong

We begin with the problem of detecting a computer virus in the first place.

Forrest *et al.* suggest a method for detecting computer viruses that is very strongly rooted in the mammalian immune system [8]. Given a set of files that they want to protect on a PC, they divide the files into a collection of bit strings of a fixed length, say 32 bits long. They then generate 32-bit "detector" bit strings at random and discard those that have a match to the strings that make up existing files on the PC. This is very much like the immune system creating T cells, and weeding out those that attach to proteins in the "self." Forrest *et al.* calculate the number of non-self detector strings that will be needed in order to detect new or changed files (i.e. non-self files) with a given probability.

A sufficient number of non-self detector strings is then generated, and the PC is scanned periodically to determine if any of the non-self strings are found within the files. This is very much like the immune system spreading T cells throughout the body, and reacting to any of them binding to non-self proteins.

So far, this is very plausible. It is a general method for detecting changes in the system, that is, files that have come to look different than they were to begin with. This could well indicate the presence of a computer virus.

Let us examine what it would take to implement this on a typical PC today. In doing so, we will make assumptions that more strictly parallel biology than Forrest *et al.* might advocate. The model that they report allows, for instance, only approximate matching of detector strings to strings in the files of the PC as a way of increasing its efficiency. Here we will assume exact matching.

In the experiments involving this method, the authors typically assume a rather high probability of failing to detecting a change. 0.02 is a typical probability that is used. We will set a stricter standard, as biology does. Let us suppose that we want to detect changes on a typical PC and we want the probability of failing to detect a single-bit change in one of the 32-bit strings in the files to be less than 2^{-32}. This is not an unreasonable bound, given that a typical PC with 100GB of storage has $\sim 2^{40}$ bits on it which, if we separate these into 32-bit strings for this method, yields 2^{35} such strings. If we randomly change all 2^{35}, we would only fail to detect 1000 of the changed strings.

Using the equations developed in [8], we estimate that we will need nearly 10^{11} detection strings that are each 32 bits long to achieve the required detection probability. If this were the mammalian immune system, that would be a small number of T cells. In a computer, however, that many detection strings would require nearly 400GB of storage, which is more than a typical PC has these days. Plus, scanning for the presence of 10^{11} detection strings would take quite some time!

Functionally, this is a method of determining if new files have been added to the PC, or if existing files have changed. Let us consider another method of accomplishing this goal. Suppose we calculate a 32-bit hash, or checksum, for each file on the computer, and store it away along with the path and filename of the file. This will allow us to detect changes in files with a failure rate of 2^{-32} per file. To be fair, the two detection methods are not functionally identical. The hash method can detect deleted files, whereas the detector method cannot. The detector method has a higher probability of detecting multiple-bit changes. Nonetheless, it is an instructive comparison.

If we keep 4 Bytes (32 bits) of hash per file, and ~32 Bytes of path and filename information, we need ~36 Bytes per file. A typical PC might have ~10^5 files on it, so we need less than 4MB of storage for our hash database. If all we want to do is detect changes to files on our PC, this is a much more economical way to do it.

This surprising economy is not available to the mammalian immune system. While it is easy to implement hash functions for files on a computer, it is difficult to think of a way that evolution could have provided a hash function for protein sequences, or even what such a hash function would look like. Biology has vast numbers on its side, so producing billions of T cells is a natural approach. Computing has much more strict limits on its resources, but much more flexibility in its computations.

A closer examination of the assumptions made by the detector model reveals a curiousity. It assumes that the makeup of the "self" that the method defends is constant. That is, it assumes that strings that initially matched strings in the "self" will match them in the future, and that strings that did not match strings in the "self" will not match them in the future. This is a good assumption in mammals, where the proteins that are expressed on the surfaces of cells are determined by the organism's genetic makeup, and do not vary over time.

It is not a good assumption, however, in computer files, which change all the time for valid, benign reasons. New files are created, existing files are updated, and old files are deleted. There is no static "self" in computers. Just because a file changes does not indicate the presence of a virus. Quite the contrary, the number of files that change due to viruses is much, *much* smaller than the number that change for benign reasons. In this case, the computer world is very different from the biological world.

In a subsequent paper based on this same approach [9], Somayaji *et al.* state:

> "Although we believe it is fruitful to translate the structure of the human immune system into our computers, ultimately we are not interested in imitating biology. Not only might biological solutions not be directly applicable to our computer systems, we also risk ignoring non-biological solutions that are more appropriate. A more subtle risk, however, is that through imitation we might inherit inappropriate 'assumptions' of the immune system."

This is the ongoing risk of biologically-inspired design.

3.2   Getting It Right

If we cannot rely on a distinction between self and non-self to recognize computer viruses, how can we recognize them? Perfect recognition of computer viruses – determining that an arbitrary program is a virus and never making a mistake – is equivalent to the halting problem [1, 10]. Nevertheless, there are a variety of heuristics that, in practice, turn out to be remarkably effective. Many viruses are variants of older, known viruses, and can often be found by scanning for strings that are found in known viruses but that are unlikely to be found in normal programs. Many viruses use a few common tricks, like self-encryption to attempt to hide from scanners, so noticing that a program uses one of these tricks may lead us to suspect it of being a virus.

Unfortunately, all of these heuristics have false positives – they occasionally accuse a perfectly normal program of being a virus. It would be bad if the system acted on this accusation without being sure, erasing the accused file or, worse, attempting to remove the "virus" from the file.

In a system described by Kephart *et al.* [11, 12], heuristics were used to identify files that might contain a virus, and a copy of these files was sent to a central virus analysis lab. Here, an important difference between biological and computing systems was exploited. In biological systems, lots of things replicate themselves: DNA, viruses, our body's cells and entire organisms. Self-replication is one of the most important capabilities of all life. In computing systems, however, almost nothing that is really useful undergoes self-replication. Almost without exception, if it self-replicates, it is a computer viruses, and hence it is undesirable. So the virus analysis lab isolated the suspect virus in a virtual machine and tried to make the virus self-replicate. If it did, it was indeed a virus.

Multiple replicas were gathered, so that the system could take into account any variation between them. The replicas were analyzed, and strings were extracted that detected all of the replicas but were very unlikely to be found in normal programs. The goal of this latter step was much the same as the goal of the immune system in producing T cells: create something that will recognize the virus but will not also recognize good cells/files. Because it would be infeasible to follow biology closely and test the string against every file that exists or will exist on the Earth, a statistical characterization of a large collection of normal programs was used to estimate the probability that the string would be found in any normal program. Only strings with extremely small probabilities were used. At the same time, an algorithm for disinfecting the file – for removing the virus and returning the file to its original state – was derived.

Once these detection strings and disinfection algorithms were extracted and tested, they were sent back to the infected system, which then used them as a highly specific way of finding and disinfecting that particular virus. At the same time, they were made available worldwide to protect computers that were not yet infected. In most cases, this was all done automatically, with quality that exceeded human analysis, and was complete from detection to cure in a few minutes.

While this process bears some resemblance to the way the mammalian immune system works, it is really very different. In fact, it bears more resemblance to an early 20th century theory of the mammalian immune system called "instruction theory," in which antigens themselves caused the formation of antibodies, but only after the antigen appeared and by somehow using parts of the antigen in antibody formation [13]. This theory was disproven shortly after it was proposed. But computers are not mammals, and mechanisms that work poorly in biology may be just the ticket in computing.

In computing, what constitutes "self" and "non-self" changes constantly, so observing a computer virus reproduce is one of the few sure ways to determine that it really is a virus and not just a normal program. Furthermore, crafting specific defenses for specific viruses works very well in computing system, where we cannot have billions of detectors for "non-self." Once again, we see how critical it is to understand the differences between biological and computing systems, as well as the similarities.

4   Self-Assembling Autonomic Systems

Since the first paper outlining the vision of autonomic computing [14], biology has been used as an analogy for how large computing systems should work. The autonomic nervous system plays an important role in regulating critical systems in the body – such as breathing, heartbeat, digestion, and eye focus – without involving our conscious minds. This lets our conscious mind focus on conceptual problems with fewer distractions. By analogy, autonomic computing seeks to create computing systems that are largely self-regulating, allowing system administrators to tell the systems what to do at a high level, and then have the systems themselves figure out how to do it.

The autonomic nervous system is one possible biological source of inspiration for autonomic computing. Let us examine another.

In the early stages of embryonic development in mammals, cells divide to form a blastocyst, a roughly spherical collection of cells that start out nearly identical. As development proceeds, these cells reproduce and differentiate to form structures, such as arms and a spine, based on their own genetic information and their local chemical environment. Remarkably, there is no central planning agent that tells the body how to develop.

Nevertheless, trillions of cells acting in their local environments manage to develop into extremely complex structures such as eyes, muscles and brains. Consider the circulatory system, which must carry blood to all parts of the body. How does the developing circulatory system know where to grow new capillaries? The answer, of course, is that it does not, at least in the sense that there is no centrally managed plan for where they should be. Rather, cells that are getting insufficient oxygen generate growth factors that stimulate nearby capillaries to grow. Thus cells in regions of the developing body that are not yet getting enough oxygen stimulate capillary development in that region until they are getting enough oxygen, at which time they stop [15].

The mammalian body has countless mechanisms that direct its resources to places and for purposes that most benefit the body. Mechanisms that enable distributed self-assembly of complex features are among the most powerful.

4.1   Getting It Wrong

Let us focus on one important aspect of self-assembly in computing systems: determining where in the system to put a new server that has become available. We have a large computing center, with many application environments. Each application environment is a collection of the computing resources needed for a particular application – for a web server, for instance, or a portfolio analysis application. We want to figure out into which application environment we should put our new server, and how best it can be used within that environment.

In the developing blastocyst, it does not matter where a new cell is placed. It develops according to what it senses of its local environment. Suppose we held slavishly to biology and did the same thing with our new server. There is no sense of "local environment" in our collection of application environments. Logically, they are all peers. So we let the server choose the first application environment that it finds in a directory of such things.

We will even credit the application environment with good sense about how to use the server. Perhaps it is asked to become a web server to handle more customer requests. Perhaps it becomes a host for that processor-intensive portfolio analysis to achieve more accurate results.

Of the biologically-inspired approaches that we have discussed so far, this one has the most obvious flaws. Clearly, choosing a random application environment into which to incorporate the server is unlikely to be the best choice. The chosen environment may be handling its traffic just fine, whereas another environment is starved for resources.

Servers are not cells. Cells reproduce, and their population can grow nearly limitlessly to serve the needs of the developing organism. Servers, on the other hand, are a highly constrained resource. Putting a server to work on one application often means that it is not available for another application.

This approach is *too* distributed. By not taking advantage of global information, in this case information about the value of an additional server to the various applications that might make use of it, we are stuck with a very suboptimal result.

4.2   Getting It Right

A traditional approach to allocating a new server is for system administrators to examine the various application environments in detail and plan out, quite a long time in advance, where that new server is most needed.

This can be made less burdensome for system administrators by allowing them to specify policies about how resources such as servers should be allocated. The web server application may be highly important for customer satisfaction, and the policy might be to allocate new servers to it until it is meeting its performance goals. Servers not needed for this application could be given to the less important but computationally intensive portfolio analysis application that can use as many servers as it can get.

Research is underway to imbue servers with the ability to incorporate themselves into an application environment, once the choice of environment is made. They can find the other resources that they need to operate and hook themselves up without the need for manual intervention by system administrators [16].

This idea can be extended to the dynamic operation of the system. Suppose, in our previous example, that the load on the web application varies, that it is high during the day and low at night. A global resource arbiter can be given a policy that instructs it to give as many servers as needed to the web application, but to move any servers that it does not need to the portfolio analysis application. We would see servers moved to the financial application in the morning, and then moved back to the computationally intensive application in the evening.

More generally, application environments can have a quantitative measure of the benefit that they could provide if given one or more additional servers. A global mechanism could then arbitrate between the environments to determine the best global allocation of all servers [17].

This keeps the best features of self-assembly while achieving globally optimal utilization of scarce resources. In large part, system administrators could be relieved of the burden of planning out, in detail, which environment should get which server at any given moment, and the burden of adding that server to that environment. Instead, administrators could set higher-level policies and let the system figure out how best to achieve them.

Again, this is not the way cells work in the body. Cells do not transform themselves from liver cells to brain cells when we are working on hard math problems, nor do kidney cells become muscles when we run. But principles like self-assembly from biological systems can be applicable to computing systems if we understand the differences between the systems.

5   Conclusions

In this paper we reviewed three areas in computing in which people have drawn inspiration from biology. In the first, computer virus epidemiology, we saw that simple analogies with biological virus spread do not capture essential features of computer virus spread, but that a rigorous and biologically-based model can. In the second, we saw that following the workings of the biological immune system too closely can result in an unwieldy and inaccurate technology for detecting computer viruses, whereas a deep understanding of how computers differ from biological organisms can lead us to a digital immune system that works extremely well. In the third, we saw that a simple analogy with self-assembling biological systems results in decisions about where to place a new server in a data center that are clearly wrong, while an understanding of how global information differs between biological systems and our data center helps us use the best features of biological self-assembly and avoid suboptimal solutions.

Biology does things for its own reasons. In the mammalian body, development must be consistent with evolution and the mechanisms available to it. We cannot grow a hand without growing an arm at the same time. And it must work with the materials available to it – cells but not electronic circuitry.

In engineering, we face different constraints. We are able to harness incredible computational power, but we do not get access to trillions of self-reproducing parts. Hence the solutions that we adopt in engineering will often be very different from the solutions adopted by biology.

Reasoning by analogy is dangerous. It tempts us to ignore the underlying assumptions that make a technique work in one field but fail in another. Instead, we must know the assumptions that are being made in both computing and biological systems. We must have a rigorous underlying model, preferably a mathematical model, of the systems that we are building. And we must know when a computing system does not behave like a biological system. In many cases, this knowledge can help us find a solution that is even better than those used in biological systems.

We can be inspired by biology. Indeed, we should be. Biology is very inspiring and can often lead to new ways of thinking about computing systems. But we must avoid the temptation of letting it dictate our designs.

6   Acknowledgements

The author would like to thank Jeffrey O. Kephart and David M. Chess for many insightful conversations.

7   References

1. F. Cohen, Computer Viruses, Ph.D. thesis, USC (1985)

2. P.S. Tippett, The Kinetics of Computer Virus Replication: A Theory and Preliminary Survey, Safe Computing: Proceedings of the Fourth Annual Computer Virus and Security Conference, New York, NY, March 14-15, 1991, p. 66-87

3. J.O. Kephart, S.R. White, Measuring and Modeling Computer Virus Prevalence, in Proceedings of the 1993 IEEE Computer Society Symposium on Research in Security and Privacy, Oakland, CA, May 24-25, 1993, p. 2-14

4. N.T.J. Bailey, The mathematical theory of infectious diseases and its applications, second edition, Oxford University Press, New York, 1975

5. J.O. Kephart, S.R. White, Directed-Graph Epidemiological Models of Computer Viruses, in Proceedings of the 1991 IEEE Computer Society Symposium on Research in Security and Privacy, Oakland, CA, May 20-22, 1991, p. 343-359

6. J.O. Kephart, S.R. White, D.M. Chess, Computers and epidemiology, Spectrum, IEEE, Vol. 30, Issue 5, May 1993, p. 20-26

7. R.A. Goldsby, T.J. Kindt, B.A. Osborne, Kuby Immunology, fourth edition, New York: W.H. Freeman, 2000

8. S. Forrest, A.S. Perelson, L. Allen, R. Cherukuri, Self-Nonself Discrimination in a Computer, in Proceedings of the 1994 IEEE Symposium on Research in Security and Privacy, Los Alamitos, CA: IEEE Computer Society Press, 1994

9. A. Somayaji, S. Hofmeyr, S. Forrest, Principles of a Computer Immune System, in Proceedings of the 1997 New Security Paradigms Workshop, Langdale, Cumbria, UK, 1997

10. F. Cohen, Computer Viruses: Theory and Experiments, in Minutes of the 7th Dept. of Defense / NBS Computer Security Conference, September 24-26, 1984

11. J.O. Kephart, G.B. Sorkin, M. Swimmer, S.R. White, Blueprint for a Computer Immune System, in Proceedings of the Seventh International Virus Bulletin Conference, San Francisco, CA, October 1-3, 1997

12. S.R. White, M. Swimmer, E.J. Pring, W.C. Arnold, D.M. Chess, J.F. Morar, Anatomy of a Commercial-Grade Immune System, in Proceedings of the Ninth International Virus Bulletin Conference, September/October 1999, p. 203-228

13. A.M. Silverstein, Darwinism and immunology: from Metchnikoff to Burnet, Nature Immunology, Vol. 4, No. 1, p. 3-6, 2003

14. P. Horn, Autonomic Computing: IBM's Perspective on the State of Information Technology, October 2001, http://www.research.ibm.com/autonomic/manifesto/autonomic_computing.pdf

15. B. Alberts, A. Johnson, J. Lewis, M. Raff, K. Roberts, P. Walter, Molecular Biology of the Cell, fourth edition, Garland Science, New York, Chapter 22

16. D.M. Chess, A. Segal, I. Whalley, S.R. White, Unity: Experiences with a Prototype Autonomic Computing System, in Proceedings of the First International Conference on Autonomic Computing (ICAC'04), May 17-18, 2004, New York, NY, p. 140-147

17. G. Tesauro, R. Das, W.E. Walsh, J.O. Kephart, Utility-Function-Driven Resource Allocation in Autonomic Systems, Proceedings of the Second International Conference on Autonomic Computing (ICAC'05), June 13-16, 2005, Seattle, WA, p. 342-343

On Building Maps of Web Pages with a Cellular Automaton

H. Azzag[1], D. Ratsimba[3], D. Da Costa[1], C. Guinot[1,2], and G. Venturini[1]

[1] Laboratoire d'Informatique de l'Université de Tours,
École Polytechnique de l'Université de Tours - Département Informatique
64, Avenue Jean Portalis, 37200 Tours, France.
Phone: +33 2 47 36 14 14, Fax: +33 2 47 36 14 22
{hanene.azzag,venturini}@univ-tours.fr
david.dacosta@etu.univ-tours.fr
[2] C.E.R.I.E.S.,
20 rue Victor Noir, 92521 Neuilly sur Seine Cedex.
christiane.guinot@ceries-lab.com
[3] Laboratoire ERIC, Université de Lyon2, Bat. L, 5 avenue Pierre Mendés-France
69676 Bron Cedex
dratsimb@club-internet.fr

Abstract. We present in this paper a clustering algorithm which is based on a cellular automaton and which aims at displaying a map of web pages. We describe the main principles of methods that build such maps, and the main principles of cellular automata. We show how these principles can be applied to the problem of web pages clustering: the cells, which are organized in a 2D grid, can be either empty or may contain a page. The local transition function of cells favors the creation of groups of similar states (web pages) in neighbouring cells. We then present the visual results obtained with our method on standard data as well as on sets of documents. These documents are thus organized into a visual map which eases the browsing of these pages.

1 Introduction

The aim of web pages visualization is to present in a very informative and interactive way a set of web documents to the user in order to let him or her navigate through these documents. In the web context, this may correspond to several users' tasks: displaying the results of a search engine, or visualizing a graph of pages such as a hypertext or a surf map. In addition to web pages visualization, web pages clustering also greatly improves the amount of information presented to the user by highlighting the similarities between the documents [1]. These similarities take into account the content of the pages. Several systems have been designed with the double aim of creating groups among web pages and of visualizing such groups. If one considers the visual models of topic maps [2][3], and compared to graph displaying models such as (Kartoo, Mapstan, TouchGraph, GoogleBrowser) and to other plot based vi-

Please use the following format when citing this chapter:

Azzag, H., Ratsimba, D., Da Costa, D., Guinot, C., Venturini, G., 2006, in IFIP International Federation for Information Processing, Volume 216, Biologically Inspired Cooperative Computing, eds. Pan, Y., Rammig, F., Schmeck, H., Solar, M., (Boston: Springer), pp. 33–42.

sualization [4], then the advantages of topic maps are the following: they may represent an important number of documents and of created clusters, they may provide a global view which can be easily zoomed, and most importantly, they use a cartographic metaphor which manipulation is easily learned by the user. We consider in this work a set of n web pages that we would like to represent as a topic map in order to let the user browse these pages. This problem can be instantiated in several ways: the automatic construction of a hypertext, the visual presentation of search engines results, the automatic creation of web sites maps. The map must represent these pages in such a way that thematic clusters will clearly appear. To build such a map, one must be able to measure the similarity between pages, to detect groups among the pages, to visualize such groups and the neighbourhood relationships between the pages (similar pages must be displayed together on the map). By reaching this goal, one overcomes the traditional limitations of text-based interfaces: In the case of search engines, a greater number of results can be explored. In the case of hypertext construction, the discovered neighbourhood relationships will naturally act as hyperlinks.

In the remaining of this paper, Section 2 describes the main principles of the methods that visually cluster web pages, as well as the main properties of cellular automata. Section 3 present our algorithm, a new method for visual clustering with cellular automata. In Section 4, we present the results obtained by our method on benchmark data and on web pages. We conclude by presenting the limits of our method as well as the perspectives which can be derived from this work.

2 Principle of documents maps and cellular automata

2.1 Documents visual clustering and maps

In order to solve the problem at hand, we must study the methods that cluster documents into a visual map [2][3]. Kohonen maps are one of the most well known examples [5][6]. Other similar methods have been recently applied to the generation of document maps: it is the case for instance of a biomimetic approach which uses artificial ants to sort objects (i.e. documents) on a 2D grid [7].

The main characteristics of these visual representations are the following: the map is built from the set of documents by calling a clustering algorithm the results of which can be directly visualized. These results are organized in a 2D plan. Documents which are close to each other on the plan should be similar from their content point of view (thus a correlation should appear between the location of the documents on the grid, and their textual similarity). Documents represented on the map can be annotated with text labels in order to let the user better understand the clusters which have been found. These labels can be the title of documents, or keywords extracted from the documents, and also colours which indicate the density of documents in a given area of the map. In conclusion, these maps must achieve the following properties: to create groups of documents (with informative neighbourhood relationships that are representative of the textual similarity between documents), to inform the user on the size of groups, the thematic content of a group (by displaying for instance common keywords in documents that belong to this group), to zoom and provide additional details about a document (title, opening of the document).

2.2 Principles of cellular automata and application in visual clustering

Among all the methods related to clustering [8], researchers have developed models which are inspired by biological systems. As far as we know, no clustering algorithm making use of cellular automata has been defined yet. However, the cellular automata model is known since many years and has many interesting properties such as those which can be found in the popular game of life [9]: the emergence of complex behaviours that result from local and simple interactions. We show in the following that this model, which has been used in numerous domains [10], can make valuable contributions to the visual clustering problem and to the building of web pages maps.

We remind here the reader of basic principles used in cellular automata (CA). A CA is defined by a 4-tuple denoted by (C, S, V, δ). $C = \{c_1, , c_{NCell}\}$ represents the set of cells where $NCell$ remains constant over time. $S = \{s_1, , s_k\}$ is the finite set of states that each cell will be able to take. The state of a cell c_i is denoted by $c_i(t)$. V denotes the neighbourhood between cells which gives a spatial structure to the cells. For each cell c_i, we denote by $V(c_i)$ its set of neighbouring cells. In this work, we are interested in a 2D structuration of the cells which are thus placed on an $N \times N$ matrix or grid (as a consequence the number of cells is $NCell = N^2$). The neighbourhood of a given cell is a square with an edge of size v and which is centered on the cell. This neighbourhood is such that the grid is toroidal (top connected to bottom, left side connected to right side). The neighbourhood of a cell is thus a set of v^2 cells. The local transition function denoted by δ determines the next state of a given cell as a function of its neighbouring cells. Finally, we call configuration of the CA at time t the state vector $CA(t) = (c_1(t), ..., c_{NCell}(t))$. A CA evolves from $CA(t)$ to $CA(t+1)$ by applying δ to each cell, either in a synchronous way (parallel mode) or in an asynchronous way (parallel or sequential mode).

The main principle of our method is to consider that the states of the CA can be the documents themselves. Then the next step is to adapt the local transition function in such a way that states representing similar documents appear in close location on the grid. Once a stable configuration has been obtained in which similar documents become located close to each other, it is straightforward to create a map from this grid, and we will show in section 4.3 that these results check the desired properties mentioned in the previous section.

3 A CA model for documents visual clustering

In the following, the n documents (or data) to be clustered are denoted by $d_1, ..., d_n$ and $Sim(i, j) \in [0, 1]$ denotes the similarity between two documents d_i and d_j. We have considered a 2D CA where the $NCell$ cells are structured on a squared grid.

The set of possible cells states is equal to $S = \{empty, d_1, ..., d_n\}$. In other words, each cell will be either empty or may contain one (and only one) document or data. At each simulation step, the states of cells will be possibly modified according to local transition rules which will aim at letting similar states (documents) appear at close locations on the grid.

The size of the grid has been empirically determined as in [11] and is computed with the function $N = E(\sqrt{3n}) + 1$. This size is supposed to give enough space (N^2 cells but n data only) to the spatial organization of the clusters. The size of the neighbourhood described in the previous section is the edge v of the square centered on each cell and is empirically determined by the following formula: $v = E(N/10) + 1$.

We use the following definition in our algorithm: a cell is isolated if its immediate ($v = 1$) neighbourhood contains less than 3 non empty cells. We have decided to obtain non overlapping clusters: thus a state d_i may appear in one cell at a time. Therefore, we use a list of states denoted by L which represents the list of documents which do not appear on the grid and that remain to be placed. Initially, L contains all the documents and the states of cells are all empty.

The local rules for evolving the states of cells are the following, firstly for an empty cell C_{ij}:

- R1 : If C_{ij} is isolated Then (with probability $1 - P' = 0.25$) $C_{ij}(t + 1) \leftarrow d_k$, where d_k is a randomly selected document of L (and provided that $\overline{Sim}_{d'_k \in V(c_{ij})}(d_k, d'_k) > Threshold(t)$)
- R2 : If C_{ij} is not isolated Then $C_{ij}(t + 1) \leftarrow d_k$, where d_k is either a randomly selected document of L (with probability $P = 0.032$), or (with probability $1 - P$) the document of L which is the most similar to the document represented by C_{ij} neighborhood, (and provided that, in both cases, $\overline{Sim}_{d'_k \in V(c_{ij})}(d_k, d'_k) > Threshold(t)$).

For a cell C_{ij} that contains a document d_k (i.e. $C_{ij}(t) = d_k$), the transition rules are the following:

- R3 : If C_{ij} is isolated, Then $C_{ij}(t+1) \leftarrow empty$ with a probability $P' = 0.75$ (d_k is placed back in L).
- R4 : Else if $\overline{Sim}_{d'_k \in V(c_{ij})}(d_k, d'_k) < Threshold(t)$, Then $Cij(t + 1) \leftarrow empty$ and d_k placed back in L

In all other cases, the cell state remains unchanged ($C_{ij}(t + 1) \leftarrow C_{ij}(t)$). One can notice that the values of P and P' thresholds have been obtained experimentally.

In order to apply these rules to cells and in order to avoid conflicts when assigning on the grid the data of L, we have considered that one cell will evolve at a time (sequential evolution of the CA). We have tested several ways of selecting the cell to which the rules are applied at the current time step: we have kept a randomly selected order, once for each run of the algorithm (a permutation of the N^2 cells is randomly generated at the beginning of the algorithm).

In the rules, we mention a threshold $Threshold(t)$ which evolves over the simulation steps t. This threshold is initialized to the maximum similarity value observed in the data set, and then slowly decreases through the run. Initially, the documents located close to each others on the grid are thus very similar to each others, thus forming highly similar "seeds" for the future clusters. At each time step, $Threshold(t)$ is decreased of a constant quantity (equal to 1/200 of the standard deviation observed in the similarity values). This decreasing is also such that the algorithm converges because documents will be very unlikely to be removed from the grid once $Threshold(t)$ becomes low.

4 Results

4.1 Standard data

In order to validate the clustering abilities of our algorithm, we have applied it first on standard benchmark databases from the Machine Learning Repository [12]. The similarity measure that we have used is based on an *Euclidean* distance.

We have used the same set of parameters for all tested databases. Our first experiments have consisted in performing numerous tests in order to determine an average and satisfying set of parameters. We have run our algorithm on the 13 mentioned databases. Each parameters set has been tested over 20 runs. More than 1500 parameters sets have been tested. The obtained conclusions are the detection of correlations between parameters and the obtaining of a satisfying set of parameters with a low error rate (Rand measure), a high purity and a good number of found clusters (close to the real number of clusters).

The visual results presented in figure 1 illustrate the clusters found for some databases (see table 1 for the complete results). One must notice that the layout of the clusters corresponds to known properties of the databases, like for instance in the cases of the Iris and Wine. The execution times were measured on a PC AMD Athlon64 792MHz with 500Mo of RAM, and an implementation in a Java Applet (the execution is therefore slower than in a C implementation for instance).

A quantitative analysis of the results is presented in table 1. The performances of our CA are quite correct compared to the ascending hierarchical clustering (AHC) which is a widely used clustering algorithm.

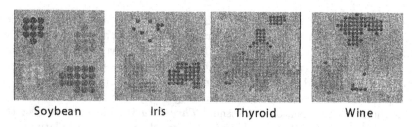

Soybean   Iris   Thyroid   Wine

Fig. 1. Visual results obtained (the colors indicate the real classes)

Table 1. Results obtained on standard databases (C_F represent the number of found clusters, P_R the purity , E_C the error measure and T_{Exe} the execution time

Databases	Cellular automata				AHC			
	C_F	P_R	E_C	T_{Exe}	C_F	P_R	E_C	T_{Exe}
Art1	6.25 [1.26]	0.87 [0.09]	0.15 [0.03]	4.3s	5	0.84	0.15	0.92s
Art2	6.35 [1.39]	0.97 [0.04]	0.20 [0.09]	28s	3	0.98	0.14	23.73s
Art3	7.70 [1.38]	0.92 [0.06]	0.20 [0.05]	59s	3	0.89	0.16	32.34s
Art4	6.25 [1.04]	1.00 [0.00]	0.29 [0.04]	1.2s	3	1.00	0.13	0.11s
Art5	8.65 [1.31]	0.63 [0.19]	0.14 [0.03]	7.5s	10	0.78	0.08	14.25s
Art6	4.75 [0.62]	1.00 [0.002]	0.02 [0.01]	8.0s	5	1.00	0.03	0.91s
CE.R.I.E.S.	5.80 [1.2]	0.75 [0.18]	0.18 [0.02]	3.5s	3	0.56	0.24	0.25s
Glass	5.50 [0.92]	0.56 [0.16]	0.36 [0.05]	3.7s	3	0.49	0.43	0.14s
Iris	4.75 [1.18]	0.95 [1.00]	0.15 [0.05]	0.8s	3	0.88	0.13	0.05s
Pima	5.50 [1.48]	0.67 [0.08]	0.47 [0.03]	70s	3	0.48	0.48	9.52s
Soybean	3.95 [0.28]	0.96 [0.11]	0.02 [0.05]	0.4s	6	1.00	0.08	0.00s
Thyrod	4.80 [0.6]	0.85 [0.12]	0.33 [0.07]	2.2s	5	0.84	0.35	0.14s
Wine	4.70 [0.66]	0.90 [0.1]	0.13 [0.04]	2.6s	6	0.84	0.20	0.06s

Table 2. Textual databases tested

Databases	Size (# of documents)	Size (Mb)	# of real classes
CE.R.I.E.S.	259	3.65	17
AntSearch	332	13.2	4
WebAce1	185	3.89	10
WebAce2	2340	19	6

Table 3. Results obtained on textual databases

Databases	Cellular automata			AHC		
	E_C	C_F	P_R	E_C	C_F	P_R
AntSearch	0.35 [0.06]	4.2 [0.6]	0.59 [0.21]	0.17	6,00	0.79
CERIES	0.62 [0.12]	3.6 [0.9]	0.27 [0.10]	0.36	3,00	0.29
WebAce1	0.48 [0.10]	3.8 [0.9]	0.36 [0.21]	0.28	4,00	0.27
WebAce2	0.15 [0.07]	8.0 [0.6]	0.81 [0.27]	0.29	3,00	0.79

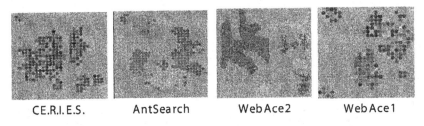

| CE.R.I.E.S. | AntSearch | WebAce2 | WebAce1 |

Fig. 2. Results on the textual data bases

4.2 Textual data

We have applied our algorithm on textual databases (see table 2). In this case, the similarity measure is computed with specific algorithms. The CE.R.I.E.S. database contains 258 texts dealing with healthy human skin [13]. The AntSearch database contains scientific documents dealing with several different subjects (73 documents about scheduling problems, 84 about image processing and pattern recognition, 81 about network and Tcp-Ip, and finally 94 about 3D and VRML courses). We have used a search engine to extract these documents from the web. The WebAce databases contain web pages extracted from Yahoo! categories [14].

We use the *cosinus* measure in order to compute the similarity between documents. Each document is represented as a vector of word count but weighted according to the *tf-idf* scheme [15]. The resulting clusters are analysed with the same methodology as the previous numeric databases.

We present in figure 2 the obtained clusters (see table 3 for the complete results). We a priori know that the Webace1 and CE.R.I.E.S. databases are rather difficult for many clustering algorithms because the similarity is not very informative. So the poor results are not surprising. However, we wish to check if the generated map makes sense (because the found clusters are representative of the similarities, but the similarities are not representative of the expert a priori clustering). With the Webace2 and Antsearch databases, the obtained maps look now much better and one may clearly distinguish the original clusters on the obtained 2D grid.

4.3 Map generation

From the previously created grid, we have generated a " browsable " map in the following way: the 2D positions of the documents are respected and the grid is converted into an HTML table. Each cell of the table contains one document and is annotated using the beginning of the document's title. Then, with JavaScript commands, we may add interactions to the map. Clicking on a cell opens the corresponding document. Zooming the map is possible directly with the browser using the mouse wheel. The resulting map thus represents the similarities between documents, the title of documents and the possibility to zoom and open documents. It is possible to visually evaluate the size of clusters, and also to perform an information retrieval task by exploring the set of documents by their content.

We present in figures 3 and 4 a complete map generated from the Antsearch database and a specific zoom on figure 4. Generating the keywords is very simple (and fast) but gives a basic explanation about the clusters. The beginnings of titles are complementary to each others and provide a good idea of the topic a given area of the map deals with. When one observes the titles, one may notice that these titles have many significant keywords in common. A simple and straightforward extension of this work would consist in extracting the keywords commonly found in every group of 9 cells (the considered cell to be annotated and its 8 neighboors) and to use these keywords for annotation.

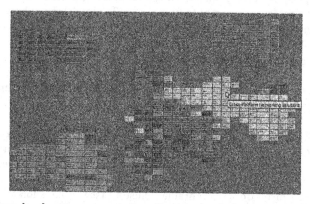

Fig. 3. Example of a map generated on the Antsearch databases (319 documents) with annotations

5 Conclusion

We have presented in this paper a new algorithm for visual clustering which makes use of cellular automata. We have experimentally shown that this algorithm is able to cluster in a relevant way standard numeric and textual data-bases.

The main limitations of our method are the followings: 1) the annotation of cells is simple, 2) zooming on the map makes the user loose the global context of the map which is confusing when dealing with several thousands of documents, 3) some clustering errors remain. For keywords extraction, we have mentioned in the previous section a method which consists in extracting common keywords to groups of 9 cells. In order to avoid the loss of context, we propose to use a semantic zooming which establishes several hierarchical levels in the map: starting from the initial grid, one may easily group together the cells (by groups

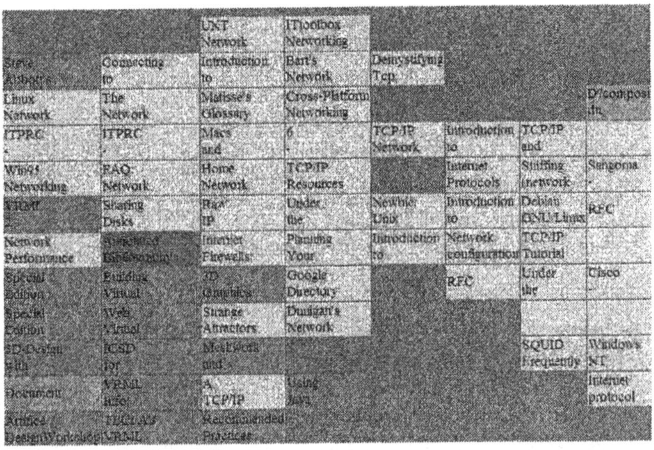

Fig. 4. Zoom on a part of the Antsearch map

of 3×3 cells) and thus make several levels in the visualization. The annotations provided at an upper level could be derived from the previous lower level. This semantic zoom would allow the user to easily go from one level to the other and to keep a good perception of the global context of the map. Finally, as far as visualization is concerned, we could represent each document using visual attributes that are more informative than a colored cell: one could use for instance thumbnail views of the documents, or other visual attributes indicating the size, type, etc, of documents.

From the clustering point of view, we think that our algorithm can be further improved with respect to clustering errors but also to its complexity. In the first case, we wish to use a local threshold for each data, rather than a global one. This will avoid that some data get too easily placed on the grid at the end of runs. For improving the algorithm complexity, one may consider that after a given number of time steps, some cells do not evolve anymore and that they should not be considered anymore. The number of cells to processed would thus decrease with time. Finally, we also want to prepare a comparison between our method and similar visual clustering algorithm like the SOM [2].

References

1. Zamir O, Etzioni O (1999). Grouper : a dynamic clustering interface to Web search results Computer Networks (Amsterdam, Netherlands : 1999), 31(11-16) :1361-1374.
2. Kohonen T (1998). Self-organization of very large document collections: State of the art In: Niklasson, Lars; Bodén, Mikael; Ziemke, Tom (Eds): Proceedings of ICANN98, the 8th International Conference on Artificial Neural Networks Conference: Skövde, Sweden, September 2-4 Springer (London) 1998 p 65-74.

3. Wise, J. A: The Ecological Approach to Text Visualization In: Journal of the American Society for Information Science (JASIS), 50 (1999) 13, p 1224-1233.
4. Cugini, J (2000). Presenting Search Results: Design, Visualization and Evaluation In: Workshop: Information Doors - Where Information Search and Hypertext Link. San Antonio, TX, May 30.
5. Roussinov D, Tolle K, Ramsey M, McQuaid M, and Chen H (1999). Visualizing Internet Search Results with Adaptive Self-Organizing Maps. Proceedings of ACM SIGIR, August 15- 19, Berkeley, CA.
6. Chen H, Schuffels C, Orwig R (1996). Internet categorization and search: a self-organizing approach In: Journal of visual communication and image representation, p 88-102.
7. Handl Julia, Bernd Meyer. Improved ant-based clustering and sorting in a document retrieval interface. In Proceedings of the Seventh International Conference on Parallel Problem Solving from Nature, Vol. 2439 of Lecture Notes in Computer Science (pp. 913-923). Berlin, Germany: Springer-Verlag.
8. Jain AK, Murty MN, Flynn PJ (1999). Data clustering: a review, ACM Computing Surveys, 31(3), pages 264-323.
9. Gardner M (1970). Mathematical Games: The fantastic combinations of John Conway's new solitaire game 'life' Scientific American, pages 120-123, Octobre.
10. Ganguly N, Sikdar BK, Deutsch A, Canright G, Chaudhuri P (2003). A Survey on Cellular Automata Technical Report Centre for High Performance Computing, Dresden University of Technology, December.
11. Lumer E, Faieta B (1994). Diversity and adaption in populations of clustering ants In Proceedings of the Third International Conference on Simulation of Adaptive Behaviour: From Animals to Animats 3, pages 501-508 MIT Press, Cambridge.
12. Blake CL, Merz, CJ (1998). UCI Repository of machine learning databases http://wwwicsuciedu/mlearn/MLRepositoryhtml] Irvine, CA: University of California, Department of Information and Computer Science.
13. Guinot C, Malvy DJM, Morizot F, Tenenhaus M, Latreille J, Lopez S, Tschachler E, et Dubertret L (2003). Classification of healthy human facial skin Textbook of Cosmetic Dermatology Third edition.
14. Han Eui-Hong, Boley Daniel, Gini Maria, Gross Robert, Hastings Kyle, Karypis George, Kumar ipin, Mobasher Bamshad, Moore J (1998). Webace : a web agent for document categorization and exploration In AGENTS '98 : Proceedings of the second international conference on Autonomous agents, pages 408-415, New York, NY, USA, ACM Press.
15. Salton G, Yang CS, Yu CT (1975).A theory of term importance in automatic text analysis Journal of the American Society for Information Scienc, 26(1):33-44.
16. Azzag H, Picarougne F, Guinot C, Venturini G (2004). Un survol des algorithmes biomimétiques pour la classification Classification et Fouille de Données, pages 13-24, RNTI-C-1, Cépaduès.
17. Mokaddem F,Picarougne F, Azzag H, Guinot G, Venturini G (2004). Techniques visuelles de recherche d'informations sur le Web, à paraître dans Revue des Nouvelles Technologies de l'Information, numéro spécial Visualisation en Extraction des Connaissances, Pascale Kuntz et Franois Poulet rédacteurs invités, Cépaduès.
18. Von Neumann J (1966). Theory of Self Reproducing Automata, University of Illinois Press, Urbana Champaign, Illinois.

Completing and Adapting Models of Biological Processes

Tiziana Margaria[1], Michael G. Hinchey[2], Harald Raffelt[3], James L. Rash[2], Christopher A. Rouff[4], and Bernhard Steffen[3]

[1] Chair of Service and Software Engineering, Universität Potsdam (Germany), margaria@cs.uni-potsdam.de
[2] NASA Goddard Space Flight Center, Information Systems Division, Greenbelt, MD, USA, michael.g.hinchey, james.l.rash@nasa.gov
[3] Chair of Programming Systems, Universität Dortmund (Germany), harald.raffelt,steffen@cs.uni-dortmund.de
[4] SAIC, Advanced Concepts Business Unit, McLean, VA 22102 rouffc@saic.com

Abstract. We present a learning-based method for model completion and adaptation, which is based on the combination of two approaches: 1) R2D2C, a technique for mechanically transforming system requirements via provably equivalent models to running code, and 2) automata learning-based model extrapolation. The intended impact of this new combination is to make model completion and adaptation accessible to experts of the field, like biologists or engineers. The principle is briefly illustrated by generating models of biological procedures concerning gene activities in the production of proteins, although the main application is going to concern autonomic systems for space exploration.

1 Motivation

A formal approach to Requirements-Based Programming, provisionally named R2D2C ("Requirements to Design to Code"), was developed at NASA [1] as a general-purpose method to mechanically transform system requirements into a provably equivalent model. This is a central need for ultra-high dependability systems like those developed at NASA for space exploration. The R2D2C approach provides mathematically tractable round-trip engineering for system development, rigorously based on formal modelling and formal reasoning techniques. In this paper we complement this method with a learning-based method for model completion and adaptation in order to make model completion and adaptation accessible to experts of the field, like biologists or engineers.

Before discussing the technical background and the biological application, we briefly sketch the standard areas of application.

Application Areas The work described below is motivated by the need for requirements-based programming for *ultra-high dependability* systems which are *remote*, *embedded*, and increasingly *autonomic*.

Please use the following format when citing this chapter:

Margaria, T., Hinchey, M.G., Raffelt, H., Rash, J.L., Rouff, C.A., Steffen, B., 2006, in IFIP International Federation for Information Processing, Volume 216, Biologically Inspired Cooperative Computing, eds. Pan, Y., Rammig, F., Schmeck, H., Solar, M., (Boston: Springer), pp. 43–54.

Sensor Networks An example of a sensor network for solar system exploration is the Autonomous Nano Technology Swarm mission (ANTS) [2], which is at the concept development phase. This mission will send 1,000 pico-class (approximately 1 kg) spacecraft to explore the asteroid belt. The ANTS spacecraft will act as a sensor network making observations of asteroids and analyzing their composition. Embedded sensors in space applications are a challenge along several research dimensions: large signal propagation delays in communications with Earth; unavailable or blocked communications paths between the spacecraft and mission control on Earth for variable (perhaps long) intervals of time; and operations under extremes of dynamic environmental conditions.

Due to the complexity of these systems as well as their distributed and parallel nature, they will have an extremely large state space and will be impossible to test completely using traditional testing techniques. R2D2C helps by converting the scenarios into a formal model that can be analyzed for concurrency-related errors, consistency and completeness, as well as domain-specific errors.

Robotic Operations We have been experimenting with generating code to control robots, but more interesting is the use of this approach to investigate the validity and correctness of procedures for complex robotic assembly or repair tasks in space, which rely heavily on the support of embedded controllers. Exploratory work here concerns providing an additional means to validate procedures from the Hubble Robotic Servicing Mission (HRSM) – for example, the procedures for replacement of cameras on the Hubble Space Telescope (HST).

Communication Systems The learning based approaches have fared quite promisingly for the test-based discovery of models of legacy communication systems, thus outperforming prior approaches based on trace combination [3]. As shown in [4, 5], the test-based model generation by classical automata learning is very expensive. It requires an impractically large number of queries to the system, each of which must be implemented as a system-level test case. Key towards the tractability of observation based model generation are powerful optimizations exploiting different kinds of expert knowledge in order to drastically reduce the number of required queries, and thus the testing effort. Recent studies have brought to a thorough experimental analysis of the second-order effects between such optimizations in order to maximize their combined impact [5], and to the development of a mature toolset for experimentation [6], which is used here. As shown in [7], our learning method is coherent with the usual notions of conformance testing.

In the specific R2D2C context, we investigate the possible application of the combined approach to the specification of communication mechanisms described in the previous application domains. This can be completed by a test-based or monitoring-based validation once those systems are operational.

In the following, we sketch the principles on which the R2D2C approach works and the effects of the learning-enhanced method.

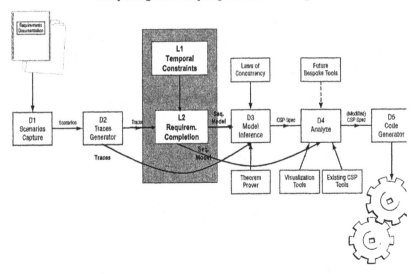

Fig. 1. The enhanced R2D2C Approach with Requirement Completion

2 How R2D2C Works

The R2D2C approach involves a number of phases, which are reflected in the system architecture described in Figure 1 and described below.

D1 Scenarios Capture: Engineers, end users, and others write scenarios describing intended system operation. The input scenarios may be represented in a constrained natural language using a syntax-directed editor, or may be represented in other textual or graphical forms.

D2 Traces Generation: Traces and sequences of atomic events are derived from the scenarios defined in D1.

D3 Model Inference: A formal model, or formal specification, expressed in CSP is inferred by an automatic theorem prover – in this case, ACL2 [8] – using the traces derived in phase 2. A deep[1] embedding of the laws of concurrency [9] in the theorem prover gives it sufficient knowledge of concurrency and of CSP to perform the inference. The embedding will be the topic of a future paper.

D4 Analysis: Based on the formal model, various analyses can be performed, using currently available commercial or public domain tools, and specialized tools that are planned for development. Because of the nature of CSP, the model may be analyzed at different levels of abstraction using a variety of possible implementation environments. This will be the subject of a future paper.

---

[1] "Deep" in the sense that the embedding is semantic rather than merely syntactic.

D5 Code Generation: The techniques of automatic code generation from a suitable model are reasonably well understood. The present modeling approach is suitable for the application of existing code generation techniques, whether using a tool specifically developed for the purpose, or existing tools such as FDR [10], or converting to other notations suitable for code generation (e.g., converting CSP to B [11] and then using the code generating capabilities of the B Toolkit).

According to this full cycle, developing a system that will have a high level of reliability requires the developer to represent the system as a formal model that can be proven to be correct. Through the use of currently available tools, the model can then be automatically transformed into code with minimal or no human intervention to reduce the chance of inadvertent insertion of errors by developers. Automatically producing the formal model from customer requirements would further reduce the chance of human error insertion.

In this paper we focus on a specific, new aspect of the R2D2C approach, the completion of the requirements given as a set of traces as generated by D2. This needs a short introduction into automata learning.

3 Automata Learning

Machine learning deals in general with the problem how to automatically generate a system's description. Besides the synthesis of static soft- and hardware properties, in particular invariants [12], [13], [14], the field of *automata learning* is of particular interest for soft- and hardware engineering [15], [16], [17], [18], [19].

Automata learning tries to construct a deterministic finite automaton (see below) that matches the behavior of a given target automaton on the basis of observations of the target automaton and perhaps some further information on its internal structure. [3, 20, 21] explain our view on the use of learning. Here we only summarize the basic aspects of our realization, which is based on Angluin's learning algorithm L^* from [22].

L^*, also referred to as an *active* learning algorithm, learns a finite automaton by *actively* posing *membership* queries and *equivalence* queries to that automaton in order to extract behavioral information, and refining successively an own hypothesis automaton based on the answers. A membership query tests whether a string (a potential run) is contained in the target automaton's language (its set of runs), and an equivalence query compares the hypothesis automaton with the target automaton for language equivalence, in order to determine whether the learning procedure was (already) successfully completed and the experimentation can be terminated.

3.1 Learning-Based Model Completion and Adaptation

Specifications in terms of individual traces are by their nature very partial and represent only the most prominent situations. This partiality is one of the major problems in requirement engineering. It often causes errors in the system design that are difficult to fix. Thus techniques for systematically completing and later on adapting such partial requirement specifications in cooperation with the application expert are of major practical importance.

We therefore propose a method for requirements completion and adaptation, based on automatic (active) automata learning. In essence, the method

- *initializes* the learning algorithm with the set of traces constituting the requirement specification and with the model needing adaptation (this model may well be empty), and
- constructs a *consistent behavioral model* by establishing predefined consistency and well-foundedness conditions. The details of how to do this have been explained in [20] its practical handling in [4, 5], and a library-based toolset for experimentation in [6].

In this fashion, we arrive at a finite state behavioral model, which is an *extrapolation* of the given requirement specification: it comprises *all* 'positive' traces of the specification, and rejects all forbidden traces. All the other potential traces are consider as 'don't cares', in order to construct a corresponding state minimal hypothesis automaton. In particular, although the learning procedure by its nature will only investigate finitely many traces, the constructed hypothesis automaton will typically accept infinitely many traces, as the extrapolation process introduces loops.

For this method to work, a number of membership queries need to be answered. Both, establishing closure of the model, as well as establishing the consistency of the abstraction of reaching words into states (i.e., of the characterization from above introduced in the previous section) can only be effected on the basis of additional information about the intended/unknown system.

3.2 Requirement Completion in R2D2C

Fig. 1 shows the R2D2C scenario including the new requirement completion components. As indicated by the arrows representing the potential flow of R2D2C processes, our new components introduce the following new options, which complement the original R2D2C process here indicated by the arrow bypassing the requirements completion module L2:

- Most powerful is the integrated mode of use, where the requirement completion component L2 is added to the original process. Its role is here simply to support the evaluation of the given set of requirement traces, and to hint at underspecified portions which may be successively completed. This option strengthens the original R2D2C process.

– Alternatively, one may replace the model inference component D3 by our requirements completion component L2, meaning that the subsequent component D4 and D5 directly work on the model produced by L2. Currently, this means that we restrict ourselves to sequential models. However, we are investigating how to overcome this restriction in the future.

The next section presents a non-standard application of our technology to the description of biological processes.

4 Application: Generating and Verifying Complex Biological Scripts and Procedures

Finding patterns in biological sequences has the goal of identifying parts that have a biological meaning [23, 24, 25]. There are several approaches to this problem. Bioperl [26] provides a collection of perl modules used for the development of perl scripts for use in Bioinformatics applications.

The Bioperl [27, 28] Project is an international association of developers of open source Perl tools for bioinformatics, genomics and life science research, with strongly increasing relevance over the almost 10 years. Bioperl relies on a large number of scripts to access, steer, and orchestrate a growing number of bioinformatic tools and databases. These scripts are becoming increasingly complex and intertwined, so that their correctness has become a legitimate concern of the community.

The application of software validation techniques to Bioperl is attempting to provide an ongoing, systematic testing of the Bioperl basis, with patches and validated new code being added to the public codebase. The goal is to establish user confidence that software components will work as described. R2D2C is a comprehensive software validation method that has been already successfully applied to problems in this domain.

We consider here again the application example already handled with R2D2C in [29] and solve the model creation problem with the combined methodology, using the requirement completion in replace mode.

4.1 From Scenarios to CSP

Let us consider again the same example from [30] (pp. 146-147). The problem is described in the form of a scenario:

– Gene *GeneOne* produces protein *ProteinOne* in t1 units of time; *ProteinOne* dissipates in time u1 and triggers condition *cone*.
– Gene *GeneTwo* produces protein *ProteinTwo* in t2 units of time; *ProteinTwo* dissipates in time u2 and triggers condition *ctwo*.
– Once produced, *ProteinTwo* positions itself in *GeneOne* for u2 units of time preventing *ProteinOne* from being produced.

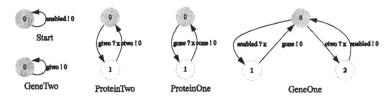

Fig. 2. Learned models of the single actors

The scenario represents a process that is expressed and implemented in Bioperl using a Perl script. However, it is also possible to express this scenario using a formal model based on CSP [31]. *GeneOne, ProteinOne, GeneTwo, ProteinTwo* can be considered as separate processes with timing constraints implicitly included. (Timing constraints may be explicitly handled by using Timed CSP, a variant of CSP which extends the semantics of CSP with time [32].) The implicit pre-condition that *GeneOne* must be enabled is handled by the *Start* process. The events and conditions describing protein production are represented as messages *gone, cone, gtwo, ctwo,* and *enabled.* The resulting R2D2C input scenario is (D1):

```
Start sends enabled.
GeneOne receives enabled then sends gone.
ProteinOne receives gone then sends cone.
GeneTwo sends gtwo.
ProteinTwo receives gtwo then sends ctwo.
GeneOne receives ctwo then sends enabled.
```

and the corresponding system description in CSP (after Phase D2):

```
channel cone, ctwo, enabled, gone, gtwo : T ;
Start = enabled ! 0 -> Start ;
GeneOne = enabled ? x -> gone ! 0 -> GeneOne ;
ProteinOne = gone ? x -> cone ! 0 -> ProteinOne ;
GeneTwo = gtwo ! 0 -> GeneTwo ;
ProteinTwo = gtwo ? x -> ctwo ! 0 -> ProteinTwo ;
GeneOne = ctwo ? x -> enabled ! 0 -> GeneOne ;
System =
     GeneOne [| {| |} |]
     GeneTwo [| {| |} |]
     ProteinOne [| {| |} |]
     ProteinTwo [| {| |} |]
     Start ;
```

4.2 Learning and Adapting the Models

Instead of analyzing the CSP model, as in [29], we have here used our learning technique to fully automatically produce automata models for each system component (see Fig. 2), as well as for the model of the whole system (Fig. 3).

These graphs show in a very intuitive way the global behaviour of the system. It is thus very direct also for someone unfamiliar with CSP and its tools to validate the behaviour by inspection.

A frequent mistake in implementing these requirements is in fact the omission of constraints, either due to their implicit presence in the requirements, or due to errors in code development. For example, omitting *Start* sends *enabled* (which makes explicit an implicit precedence) nothing prevents *GeneOne* from constantly generating *ProteinOne* and ignoring *ProteinTwo* inhibition. The corresponding erroneous system of [29] has also been learnt with our method, resulting in the global behaviour of Fig. 4(4).

This inspection could then be used to revise the requirements before developing the Bioperl code, even before carrying out a formal analysis at D4.

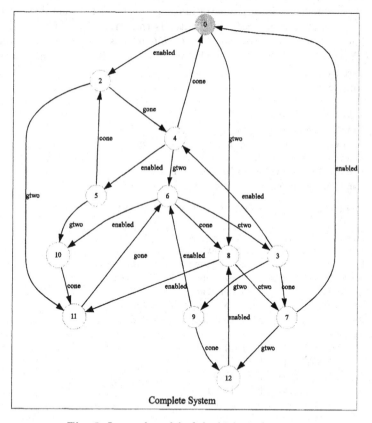

Complete System

Fig. 3. Learned model of the biological system

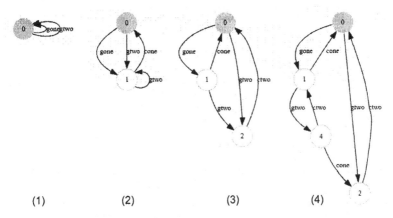

(1)   (2)   (3)   (4)

Fig. 4. Stepwise learned model of the incorrect biological system

4.3 Successive Refinement

The erroneous system could be learned in only four iterations. Fig. 4 illustrates the concrete learning process starting from the initial hypothesis along the application of the algorithm.

To learn this model from scratch we initialize the learning algorithm with no information about the system except for the alphabet of symbols. No initial trace is provided, no hints on possible symmetries or independent actions.

1. After processing the queries of length 0 and 1 with these outcomes

()	*acc*
gone	*acc*
gtwo	*acc*
ctwo	*nonacc*
cone	*nonacc*

   the learning algorithm generates the hypothesis model depicted in Figure 4(1): there is at least one state, which accepts *gone* and *gtwo* and rejects *cone* and *ctwo*. In the picture we show only the accepting traces: the automata are incomplete in the sense that all the absent symbols lead to a single nonaccepting state.

2. By model checking an expert-given corresponding property we find out that *gone.gone* is not an accepting sequence, thus the model (1) is not yet accurate and must be refined. We refine it starting from this counterexample, and reach a new hypothesis shown in Fig. 4(2). Here, the counterexample sequence leads to the discovery of a second state, state 1, and we have distinguished further behaviours.

3. Due to expert knowledge, we find out that *gtwo.gtwo* is another trace that must be rejected. This leads to the further refinement of state 1 and by completion we reach a new hypothesis as in Fig. 4(3).

4. After also rejecting *gone.gtwo.ctwo.gone* in a similar fashion, we arrive at
   the automaton shown in Fig. 4(4), which satisfies all our expectations.

In order for this method to scale, and to limit the required expert-interaction, we
provide a number of optimizations that exploit other sources of expert knowledge, like prefix closure of the language, symmetry between certain components
(genes always behave like genes), and the independence of certain observations.

5 Conclusions and Perspectives

We have presented a learning-based method for model completion and adaptation, which is based on the combination of two approaches: 1) R2D2C, a technique for mechanically transforming system requirements via provably equivalent models to running code, and 2) automata learning-based model extrapolation. The intended impact of this new combination is to make model completion
and adaptation accessible to experts of the field, like biologists or engineers.

Currently, we are investigating the power of our method. Until now, we
used it for an initial model completion, as a support for the creation of the first
model. We are currently carrying out case studies that concern model evolution
and change, in this case continuously updating the model of biological processes
according to new information.

We are also building and adapting models of servicing procedures for space-
crafts, and adaptive control procedures for remote autonomic systems. These
are the application areas that in our opinion are going to profit enormously of
the combined completion-adaptation technique.

References

1. Michael G. Hinchey, James L. Rash, Christopher A. Rouff: *A Formal Approach
   to Requirements-Based Programming,* Proc. ECBS 2005, 12th IEEE Int. Conf. on
   the Engineering of Computer-Based Systems, Greenbelt (MD), 2005, IEEE, pp.
   339–345.
2. S. A. Curtis, J. Mica, J. Nuth, G. Marr, M. L. Rilee, and M. K. Bhat. ANTS
   (Autonomous Nano-Technology Swarm): An artificial intelligence approach to
   Asteroid Belt resource exploration. In *Proc. Int'l Astronautical Federation, 51st
   Congress,* October 2000.
3. A. Hagerer, H. Hungar, O. Niese, and B. Steffen. Model Generation by Moderated
   Regular Extrapolation. *Proc. of the 5th Int. Conf. on Fundamental Approaches
   to Software Engineering (FASE 2002),* LNCS 2306, pp. 80–95.
4. H. Hungar, T. Margaria, B. Steffen: *Test-Based Model Generation for Legacy
   Systems,* IEEE International Test Conference (ITC), Charlotte, NC, September
   30 - October 2, 2003.
5. T. Margaria, H. Raffelt, B. Steffen: *Analyzing Second-Order Effects Between Optimizations for System-Level Test-Based Model Generation,* Proc. IEEE International Test Conference (ITC), Austin, TX (USA), November 8 - 10, 2005, IEEE
   Computer Society Press.

6. H. Raffelt, B. Steffen, T. Berg: *LearnLib: A Library for Automata Learning and Experimentation*, Proc. FMICS 2005, 10th ACM Workshop on Formal Methods for Industrial Critical Systems, Lisbon, Sept. 2005.

7. T. Berg, O. Grinchtein, B. Jonsson, M. Leucker, H. Raffelt, B. Steffen: *On the Correspondence Between Conformance Testing and Regular Inference*, Proc. FASE 2005, 8th Int. Conf. on Fundamental Approaches to Software Engineering, Edinburgh, UK, April 2005, LNCS N.3442, pp. 175–189, Springer Verlag, 2005.

8. M. Kaufmann and Panagiotis Manolios and J Strother Moore. *Computer-Aided Reasoning: An Approach*. Advances in Formal Methods Series. Kluwer Academic Publishers, Boston, 2000.

9. M. G. Hinchey and S. A. Jarvis. *Concurrent Systems: Formal Development in CSP*. International Series in Software Engineering. McGraw-Hill International, London, UK, 1995.

10. *Failures-Divergences Refinement: User Manual and Tutorial*. Formal Systems (Europe), Ltd., 1999.

11. M. J. Butler. *csp2B : A Practical Approach To Combining CSP and B*. Declarative Systems and Software Engineering Group, Department of Electronics and Computer Science, University of Southampton, Feb. 1999.

12. M. D. Ernst, A. Czeisler, W. G. Griswold, D. Notkin. Quickly detecting relevant program invariants In proceedings of the 22nd *International Conference on Software Engineering* (ICSE 2000), 449–458, June 2000.

13. J. W. Nimmer, M. D. Ernst. Automatic generation of program specifications In Proceedings of the 2002 *International Symposium on Software Testing and Analysis* (ISSTA 2002), 232–242, July 2002

14. Y. Brun, M. D. Ernst. Finding latent code errors via machine learning over program executions Proc. 26th *Int. Conf. on Software Engineering* (ICSE'04), pp. 480–490, May 2004

15. J. E. Cook, A. L. Wolf Discovering Models of Software Processes from Event-Based Data ACM Trans. on Software Engineering and Methodology (TOSEM) pp. 215–249, 1998

16. L. Mariani, Mauro Pezzè. A technique for verifying component-based software Proceeding of the *Int. Workshop on Test and Analysis of Component Based Systems*, TACOS 2004, Barcelona, March 2004

17. T. Xie, D. Notkin Mutually Enhancing Test Generation and Specification Inference. In Proceedings of 3rd *International Workshop on Formal Approaches to Testing of Software* (FATES 2003), LNCS Vol. 2931, Springer, pp. 60–69, Oct. 2003.

18. D. Peled, M. Y. Vardi, M. Yannakakis Black Box Checking Formal Methods for Protocol Engineering and Distributed Systems, (FORTE/PSTV), pp. 225-240, 1999, Kluwer.

19. J. E. Cook, Z. Du, C. Liu, A. L. Wolf. Discovering Models of Behavior for Concurrent Systems Tech. rep. New Mexico State University, Dept. of Computer Science, Aug. 2002

20. B. Steffen and H. Hungar, Behavior-based model construction. In S. Mukhopadhyay and L. Zuck, editors, *Proc. 4th Int. Conf. on Verification, Model Checking and Abstract Interpretation*, LNCS 2575, Springer 2003.

21. T. Margaria, O. Niese, H. Raffelt, and B. Steffen Efficient Test-based Model Generationfor Legacy Reactive Systems. To appear in Proceedings of International High Level Design Validation and Test Workshop, 2004 Sonoma, California.

22. D. Angluin. Learning regular sets from queries and counterexamples. *Information and Computation*, 2(75):87–106, 1987.

23. D. E. Krane and M. L. Raymer. Fundamental Concepts of Bioinformatics. Benjamin Cummings, San Francisco, 2003.

24. S. A. Krawetz and D. D. Womble. Introduction to Bioinformatics: Theoretical and Practical Approach. Humana Press, Totowa, New Jersey, 2003.

25. A. M. Lesk. Introduction to Bioinformatics. Oxford University Press, Oxford, UK, 2002.

26. J. Stajich and E. Birney. The Bioperl project: motivation and usage. SIGBIO Newsl., 20(2):1314, 2000.

27. P. van Heusdan. Applying software validation techniques to Bioperl. In 2004 Bioinformatics Open Source Conference, Glasgow, UK, 2930 July 2004. Abstract.

28. Stajich JE, Block D, Boulez K, Brenner SE, Chervitz SA, Dagdigian C, Fuellen G, Gilbert JG, Korf I, Lapp H, Lehvaslaiho H, Matsalla C, Mungall CJ, Osborne BI, Pocock MR, Schattner P, Senger M, Stein LD, Stupka E, Wilkinson MD, and Birney E: *The Bioperl toolkit: Perl modules for the life sciences.* Genome Res 2002 Oct; 12(10) 1611-8. PubMed HubMed [bioperl2002]

29. J. Rash, M. Hinchey, D. Gracanin, C. Rouff: *An Approach to Generating and Verifying Complex Scripts and Procedures*, 4th IEEE-CS Computational Systems Bioinformatics, CSB Workshops, Stanford, Aug. 2005, pp. 305–313.

30. J. Cohen. Bioinformaticsan introduction for computer scientists. ACM Comput. Surv., 36(2):122158, 2004.

31. C. A. R. Hoare. Communicating Sequential Processes. Prentice Hall International Series in Computer Science. Prentice Hall International, Englewood Cliffs, NJ, 1985.

32. S. Schneider, J. Davies, D. M. Jackson, G. M. Reed, J. Reed, and A. W. Roscoe. Timed CSP: Theory and practice. In Proc. REX, Real-Time: Theory in Practice Workshop, volume 600 of LNCS, pages 640-675. Springer-Verlag, 3–7 June 1991.

The Utility of Pollination for Autonomic Computing

Holger Kasinger and Bernhard Bauer

University of Augsburg
Universitaetsstrasse 14
86135 Augsburg, Germany
kasinger|bauer@informatik.uni-augsburg.de

Abstract. From the biology's point of view, pollination is an important step in the reproduction of seed plants. From our point of view, pollination is a promising and novel, biological paradigm for future dependable and self-managing computing systems. This estimation is based on the characteristics the pollination process between plants and insects implies inherently.

To utilize pollination as a paradigm for self-managing and thus autonomic computing systems, this paper identifies the useful properties that emerge by the collaborative behavior of insects and plants during the pollination process. Based on this process the paper presents an artificial pollination system that implements these properties by adapting the natural architecture and behavior. Furthermore, the paper illustrates the practical value of this system by an application in aviation. Finally open issues and an outlook on future work are presented.

1 Introduction

Imagine sitting in an aircraft and looking out of the window whilst waiting for departure, you may see a buzz of activity: Dozens of baggage trains carrying innumerable pieces of luggage, catering trucks transporting fresh meals and drinks, service cars taking cabin crews to their aircrafts, or fueling vehicles pumping kerosene into the aircrafts' wings. In spite of this hectic overall picture, all activities seem to be intended and coordinated, what is the achievement of the ground control, a central facility at an airport. This institution is responsible for the coordination and management of all activities on the apron of an airport, in particular for every aircraft handling. In addition the ground control has to cope with any conceivable disturbances, e. g. absent ground vehicles, accidents on the apron, delayed or different typed aircrafts, unavailable passenger bridges, occupied ramps (the places for embarking and disembarking) due to delay, or other activities not finished properly.

However, in face of their valuable work, these centralized ground controls will become a bottleneck and single point of failure to airports in future, as the total passenger traffic world wide will continue its trend of the last decades and rise constantly. For example, Atlanta International Airport handled almost 76

Please use the following format when citing this chapter:

Kasinger, H., Bauer, B., 2006, in IFIP International Federation for Information Processing, Volume 216, Biologically Inspired Cooperative Computing, eds. Pan, Y., Rammig, F., Schmeck, H., Solar, M., (Boston: Springer), pp. 55–64.

millions of passengers in 2001, while in 2004 it have been almost 84 millions [1]. This results in an increased flight density at airports which causes the latter to expand in the same manner. This in turn boosts the management efforts of centralized ground controls more and more. Thus, ground control is clearly in need of new management approaches to cope with these future challenges.

Limiting management and administration efforts for computing systems also is the vision of Autonomic Computing (AC) [2]. Future autonomous computing systems are supposed to feature system-level self-managing capabilities, i. e. they ought to be self-configuring, self-optimizing, self-healing, and self-protecting (also referred to as self-* properties). But in spite of the many prospective approaches in various fields that delivered a couple of contributions to future autonomic computing systems in recent years (for an overview see [3]), this vision is not procurable easily. A remaining research challenge is that elements of an autonomic system have to share a set of common behaviors, interfaces and interaction patterns that are demonstrably capable of engendering system-level self-management [4].

To meet this challenge, it might be a good idea to throw a glance at nature. The adaptation of self-organizing biological systems [5] is a common method for the solution of artificial problems. For example, Swarm Intelligence [6] uses the collective behavior of biological systems (e. g. ant colony foraging, bird flocking, or termite mound construction) as paradigm for solving optimization problems. Also Autonomic Computing already makes use of biological paradigms in various fields (e. g. [7, 8, 9]), even the AC initiative [10] itself is based on a biological paradigm: the autonomous nervous system. Thus, looking for biological paradigms engendering autonomy at system-level and adapting their architecture and behavior will be a promising way for building future autonomous systems.

In this paper we present such a novel, biological paradigm: pollination of plants. From the biology's point of view [11], pollination is an important step in the reproduction of seed plants. Thereby pollen grains – the male gametes – are transfered from the anther of a flower to the carpel of a flower, i. e. the structure that contains the ovule – the female gamete. Pollination is not to be confused with fertilization, which it may precede. From our point of view, pollination can evolve into an important biological paradigm for future autonomic computing systems. This estimation is based on the self-* properties the pollination process between plants and insects implies inherently. Thereby system-level autonomy is not a result of one homogeneous but of two heterogeneous organizations, plants and insects.

The rest of the paper is organized at follows: Section 2 provides some background information on Autonomic Computing as well as on the biological pollination process. Section 3 identifies the emerging self-* properties of this process, that make pollination useful for AC, and presents an artificial pollination system that implements these properties by adaptation. In section 4 we illustrate the practical value of the artificial pollination system by applying it as a new management approach to the initial scenario presented above. Section 5 concludes and presents open issues as well as an outlook on future work.

2 Background

This section provides some needful background information on Autonomic Computing as well as on the natural pollination process between plants and insects.

2.1 Autonomic Computing

The Autonomic Computing initiative was founded by IBM in 2001. For its vision of self-managing systems, IBM proposes a reference architecture for autonomic computing systems [12], that consists of four levels: On the lowest level *managed resources (MR)* are located, e. g. HW/SW-components like servers, databases or business applications, together forming the entire IT infrastructure. So-called *touchpoints* on the next level provide a manageability interface for each MR – similar to an API – by mapping standard sensor and effector interfaces on the sensor and effector mechanisms of specific MRs, e. g. commands, configuration files, events or log files. The next higher level is composed of so-called *touchpoint autonomic managers (TAM)* directly collaborating with the MRs and managing them through their touchpoints.

Generally an *autonomic manager (AM)* implements an intelligent control loop (closed feedback loop) called *MAPE loop*. The latter is composed of the components *monitor* (collects, aggregates, filters and reports MR's details), *analyze* (correlates and models complex situations), *plan* (constructs actions needed to achieve goals) and *execute* (controls execution of a plan). Additionally, a knowledge component provides the data used by the four components, including policies, historical logs and metrics. Together with one or more MRs, an AM represents an *autonomic element (AE)*.

A TAM also provides a sensor and an effector to *orchestrating autonomic managers (OAM)* residing on top level. The latter are responsible for system-wide autonomic behavior, as TAMs are only responsible for an autonomic behavior of their controlled MRs.

2.2 The natural pollination process

In nature pollination involves different components and sub-process.

Pollination components Normally two components are involved in the pollination process, plants – more precisely the flowers of a plant as pollen source and pollen sink – and pollination vectors – agents carrying pollen from the source's anther to the sink's stigma (the receptive part of the carpel). Admittedly, there are a few plants that can self-pollinate, but as this results in inbreeding, most species rely on cross-pollination by some kind of pollination vector to accomplish pollination. The pollination vector not essentially has to be an insect or an animal, also wind and water come into operation. However, many plant species do not bank on random pollination by wind or water, thus insects and animals are the preferred pollinators of most species. In some cases, the evolutionary link between a species and its pollinator has become so tight that each is dependent on the other's efforts for its continued survival.

Attraction process During bloom the flowers of a plant need to attract pollinators that pick up and deliver pollen (grains) respectively to accomplish pollination. For the attraction, flowers provide certain attraction cues that might be visual or olfactory.

Showy petals or sepals with obvious shape, size, and color for the vectors' vision are important visual cues. Of course not every pollinator is attracted by the same colors, e. g. butterflies and birds are only attracted to red and yellow colors. Additionally, there might be color patterns (e. g. bull's eyes or nectar guides) that form a high-contrast exhibit to make the flowers stand out against a background of green foliage. Such cues assist a pollinator to "see" the flowers and in beginning to concentrate its visits only on those with the same certain colors. However, some vectors have limited visual capabilities but an extensive ability to find a flower by its fragrance. Thus, flowers produce volatile chemicals that diffuse and are carried by air movements through the environment. A vector that is able to recognize such a fragrance and fly up the concentration gradient, can easily find the next flower of a particular species. Flowers over time have evolved a wide array of fragrances which results in efficient pollinator attraction too. Again, different pollinators have different sensitivities to certain fragrances, e. g. flowers specialized in attracting flies are famous for their fetid aroma.

Not until a successful fertilization succeeds the pollination, a flower ceases to attract pollinators, as there is no need of further pollen grains.

Rewarding process Nevertheless, attracting pollinators is not fruitful on its own, as pollinators usually are intelligent enough to avoid the energy waste of behaviors that do not result in some kind of reward. Thus, a flower needs to reward an attracted pollination vector so that it will perceive the reward as a result of its visit. The vector's intelligence will then allow it to decide to visit similar flowers nearby to obtain additional rewards. This is the reason why vectors visit only one flower species on a trip.

While collecting its reward the vector unconsciously picks up and delivers pollen grains by its underside. Vectors collect rewards as long as they have had enough or they can not find anymore. This remarkable vector behavior ensures an effective pollination. The vector's reward can be either nectar, pollen, behavior, or some combination of these. *Nectar* is a carbohydrate rich droplet that is used as an energy source for vectors. Hummingbirds, for example, must consume vast quantities of nectar to continue their high-energy method of flight. Bees collect nectar and evaporate it down to make honey for winter supplies. The *pollen* itself contains protein, starch, oil, and other nutrients. It is far richer than nectar in vitamins and minerals too. For bees, the collection and consumption of pollen is critical as it is their basic protein supply. Fortunately, pollinators on this account are not very careful in cleaning off sticky pollen that cling to their bodies. *Behavior* can also be a reward that gets a repeat visit by a vector. The vector must like the experience while visiting and come back for more.

3 An artificial pollination system

3.1 Pollination process properties

Over the past millions of years plants and insects have evolved a natural, autonomous system that exhibits various useful properties for AC:

Self-configuration: The evolutionary link between a species and its pollinator is responsible for a seamless incorporation of new plants and pollination vectors. A plant is incorporated as soon as a linked vector scents its fragrance, while as soon as a vector scents a linked fragrance, it is incorporated itself.

Self-optimization: Vectors carrying pollen faster will collect more reward. In addition, flowers providing higher reward will be visited more often. Both speeds up the pollination process by different strategies within the components.

Self-healing: The loss of pollination vectors yields (to a certain extent) to no significant disturbance of the pollination process, as other pollinators will pick up and deliver pollen grains instead of. The reason is, that flowers produce pollen as long as they are fertilized (or their bloom is over before respectively).

Self-protection: Reward is only provided to vectors that pick up or deliver pollen during its visit. Flowers are that structured, that no intruders can receive any reward without picking up or delivering pollen as a trade-off.

Self-adaptation: A plant (species) not adapting its attracting and rewarding to the available pollination vectors over the long run will finally die out. Vice versa, a vector (species) not adapting its behavior to the specific characteristics of the available plants will become extinct either.

Self-organization: Pollination exhibits all required aspects [13] for a self-organizing system: It exposes an *increase in order* – evoked by the attracting and rewarding –, is *autonomous* – it has no external control –, is *adaptable and robust w.r.t. changes* – it has no single point of failure – and is *dynamical.*

3.2 System architecture

The adaptation of the natural architecture and behavior requires some premises necessary for an efficient exploitation of the above pollination process properties: (1) A single artificial pollination system represents a finite, natural pollination environment, e. g. a grassland or a piece of forest. The representation of the entire nature as a huge, single, and closed pollination system would be absurd. (2) Sun, wind and rain come not into operation within the artificial pollination system, neither as pollination vectors nor as influencing quantities. Thus, pollination is based on "living" vectors only. (3) The attraction of artificial vectors is based on olfactory cues (fragrances) only, as volatile chemicals are representable, see pheromones [14] for example. Visual cues would be nonsensical in the scope of autonomic computing systems. (4) The rewarding of artificial vectors is based on nectar rewards only. It would be counterproductive if vectors are allowed to consume picked up pollen. Defining an exiting behavior for software components is absurd either.

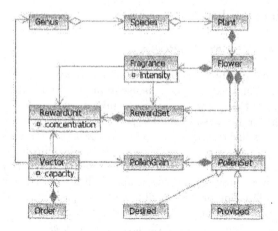

Fig. 1. Meta model of the artificial pollination system

Figure 1 depicts the meta model of the system architecture of the artificial pollination system (APS), that takes the above premises into consideration. **Plants** within the APS are defined by its **genera** and **species**. The scientific classification of natural plants into genera (e. g. roses or tulips) and species (e. g. Redleaf Rose, Gooseberry Rose, . . .) goes back to Linnaeus [15] and is adapted here as well. According to Linnaeus, a genus consists of one or more species, whereas a species consists of a plenty of entities (plants). A species may be subdivided into subspecies, races, . . . , but this refinement is not mandatory here. Linnaeus regarded genera and species as disjunctive sets, what is reasonable for biology (a rose is a rose and not a rose and a tulip at the same time). But for the APS this disjunction would hold some disadvantages. Thus, without loss of generality, we admit a plant to be a member of one or more species, as well as a species to be a member of one or more genera at the same time – which represents evolution. As a consequence, a natural pollination environment can be considered as a special case of the APS. For zoology Linnaeus specified a scientific classification too. For the APS we only adapt the hierarchical term of order. In this case the natural disjunction remains, i. e. a **vector** belongs to exactly one **order** at the same time. Due to the fact that the system represents a finite pollination environment, the system boundaries are clearly defined and the number of plants and vectors is determinable at any time.

In contrast to the entire plant a **flower** is only allowed to be of a single genus and single species at the same time. From the fertilization's point of view the allocation of a flower to a species is not essential in either case. Sometimes it is sufficient, if the pollen grain a flower is pollinated with emanates from a flower of the same genus, independent of its species, and vice versa.

A **pollen grain** within a **pollen set** is of the same species and genus as the flower it is produced by. Note, a pollen grain includes no more information, in particular no hint on the flower serving as addresser or addressee for it.

A flower possesses a **provided** and a **desired** pollen set, each including a dynamically changing quantity of pollen grains. This diverges from nature in one aspect: A natural flower does not know about the quantity of provided and desired pollen grains. The reason for this divergence is the representation of fertilization, as the moment of fertilization is responsible for the cessation of attracting and rewarding vectors. The APS represents this moment by the time a flower provides and desires no more pollen grains. On this account the divergence has no effect on the overall process.

A **reward unit** within the **reward set** of a flower corresponds to a nectar drop. As experiments (see [16, 17]) have pointed out, that e. g. honey bees do not only determine a good food source by the quantity but also by the quality of the reward, more precisely by the sugar concentration of the nectar, the **concentration** is attributed to a reward unit. To cover the quantitative aspect, we additionally define the constraint that *"per picked up or delivered pollen grain a vector will receive one reward unit"*. Thus, the size of the provided reward set of a flower is always equal to the current quantity of provided and desired pollen grains. Furthermore, a change of concentration affects all reward units within a reward set in the same way.

A **fragrance** propagates the current reward conditions of a flower and therefore consists of all the information vectors need to decide to visit the flower: The genus, the species, the reward concentration, and the quantity of reward units (for pick up as well as delivery of pollen grains) provided by the flower. Additionally, an **intensity** is attributed to a fragrance, what ensures two natural aspects: Firstly, the temporal volatility of a fragrance, and secondly, the route guide for a vector. Note, like in nature a fragrance consciously includes no information on the identity of the emitting flower. A vector follows a fragrance because it wants to receive an adequate reward, no matter from which flower of a certain species or genus. If the vector scents on its way to this flower another fragrance with better conditions, the vector may follow this new fragrance.

A vector is a pollinator for only one or a few genera and can only pick up or deliver pollen grains from flowers of these genera. This represents the natural fact that not all vectors serve as a pollinator for every genus, but only for elected ones – flies will not pollinate roses for example. Furthermore, a vector's **capacity** limits its ability to collect innumerable quantities of reward units (and pollen grains) – just like in nature. There, a bee, for example, that is full of nectar, has to fly back to its hive and deliver the collected nectar as honey before being able to collect further nectar. As hives are not directly part of the APS, we define the constraint that *"per delivered pollen grain a vector may consume two reward units"* to free its capacity again. This coerces a vector with no available capacity, first to deliver a few or all of its picked up pollen grains and to consume the respective amount of reward units, before picking up any further pollen grains. As the genus and species of the first collected reward unit of a vector predefine the only species to be visited on the trip (like in nature), the end of a trip is represented by the moment a vector has collected no more reward units. This is the time when all picked up pollen grains are delivered.

4 An autonomous aircraft handling system

To illustrate the utility of pollination for Autonomic Computing, we use the artificial pollination system for an autonomous aircraft handling system, that may help to reduce the ground control management efforts at airports in future. Therefore, consider the model depicted in figure 2, which represents an instance of the meta model in figure 1, and visualizes the mapping between APS elements and real aircraft handling entities at an airport.

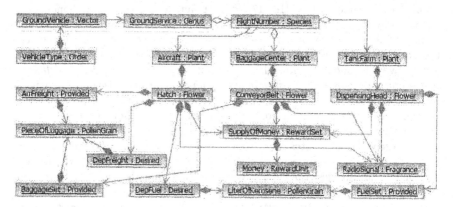

Fig. 2. Instance model of an autonomous aircraft handling system

To simplify matters, this instance model shows a flattened aircraft handling, where only two ground services, baggage handling and fueling, are required. Thereby each *ground service* is mapped on a genus. *Flight numbers* of arriving aircrafts, e. g. LH 457, AC 874, ..., each are mapped on a species, whereas the *aircrafts* themselves become a plant. Aircraft facilities, here the *baggage center* and the *tank farm*, are mapped on plants too. Flowers (*hatches, conveyor belts,* and *dispensing heads*) emit *radio signals* as fragrances, that attract *ground vehicles* (mapped on vectors) of a certain *vehicle type* (mapped on orders), e. g. here baggage trains or fueling vehicles. Just like in nature, such an attracted vector carries the *pieces of luggage* or *liters of kerosene* (mapped on pollen grains) from the provided pollen sets of flowers (here the freight by arrival *ArrFreight*, the *baggage set* and the *fuel set*) to the desired pollen sets (here the freight by departure *DepFreight* and the fuel by departure *DepFuel*) and hence are rewarded by the flowers with *money* (mapped on reward units) of the provided reward sets (mapped on the *supply of money*) of every flower.

Beneath this theoretical mapping, the AC reference architecture has to be applied, to make the autonomous aircraft handling work. Thus, every real entity (airport facilities, aircrafts, vehicles, ...) is represented as a managed resource and equipped with a touchpoint as a management interface. On top of these touchpoints autonomic managers, e. g. software agents, are placed, that assume the corresponding role and behavior that are assigned to each resource by the mapping above. By these mappings and applications the aircraft handling proceeds in the same autonomous manner as the pollination process in nature and thus can make use of all the self-* properties identified in subsection 3.1, what may reduce the management efforts by ground controls.

5 Conclusion, open issues and outlook

This paper pointed out, that pollination is not only an important step in the reproduction of seed plants in nature, but also serves as a biological paradigm for future autonomic computing systems due to its properties implied inherently. This was accomplished by an adaptation of the natural pollination process between plants and insects as well as the corresponding sub-processes. The resultant artificial pollination system and its meta model respectively now enable the exploitation of these natural properties for the self-management of future systems, in particular the self-configuration, self-optimization, self-healing and self-protection of these systems. The future practical value of this paradigm was demonstrated by an example application for an autonomous aircraft handling system.

Nevertheless, the presented meta model provides no blueprint for all kinds of future autonomic computing systems. A domain-specific application requires a possible mapping of plants, flowers, fragrances, pollen grains and vectors on appropriate entities that are desired to run or perform a task autonomously. Beneath autonomous aircraft handling, one can think of autonomous manufacturing control, where robots (vectors) carry workpieces (pollen grains) to product machines (plants), or high rack warehouses with a similar behavior, for example. Of course these application scenarios already today run automatically, but not inevitably autonomously. By virtue of these versatile applications, a mid-term objective will be to expand the pollination system to an autonomic middleware for suchlike application domains.

However, this objective brings several open issues about. One issue is the management of the global system behavior by high-level policies. This requires knowledge about the correlations between the global system behavior and the local behavior of single components, in particular how to control emergence. Further issues are novel and enabling technologies supporting the intended APS behavior, like Semantic Web and Semantic Web Services, Grid, P2P, or multi-hop ad-hoc sensor networks.

Thus, the next step will be the implementation of an APS simulation. This may shed light on alterable system parameters, as the optimal relationship between the number of plants, flowers, and vectors, a flower's fragrance emitting frequency and the intensity (decrease) of a fragrance as well as the reward unit concentration adjustment. This enables an evaluation of the scalability, efficiency, robustness and low-latency of the APS and may help to meet some open issues.

References

1. Airports Council International: Passenger traffic 2000 – 2004 final. (Available at http://airports.org)
2. Kephart, J.O., Chess, D.M.: The vision of Autonomic Computing. Computer **36** (2003) 41–52
3. Sterritt, R.: Autonomic Computing. Innovations in Systems and Software Engineering **1** (2005) 79–88
4. Kephart, J.O.: Research Challenges of Autonomic Computing. In: 27th International Conference on Software Engineering. (2005) 15–22
5. Camazine, S., Deneubourg, J.L., Franks, N.R., Sneyd, J., Theraulaz, G., Bonabeau, E.: Self-Organization in biological systems. Princeton Studies in Complexity. Princeton University Press (2001)
6. Bonabeau, E., Dorigo, M., Theraulaz, G.: Swarm Intelligence: From natural to artificial sytems. Santa Fe Institute Studies on the Sciences of Complexity. Oxford University Press (1999)
7. Anthony, R.J.: Emergence: A paradigm for robust and scalable distributed applications. In: First International Conference on Autonomic Computing. (2004) 132–139
8. Birman, K.P., Guha, R.M.S.: Scalable, self-organizing technology for sensor networks. In: Advances in Pervasive Computing and Networking. Kluwer Academic Press (2004)
9. Saffre, F., Blok, H.R.: "SelfService", a theoretical protocol for autonomic distribution of services in P2P communities. In: First International Conference on Autonomic Computing. (2004) 326 – 327
10. IBM: Autonomic computing: IBM's perspective on the state of information technology. (Available at http://www.research.ibm.com/autonomic/manifesto/ autonomic_computing.pdf)
11. Pollination: The Columbia Encyclopedia. 6th edn. Columbia University Press, New York (2001-04)
12. IBM: An architectural blueprint for autonomic computing. (Available at http://www-03.ibm.com/autonomic/pdfs/ACBP2_2004-10-04.pdf)
13. Wolf, T.D., Holvoet, T.: Emergence versus self-organisation: Different concepts but promising when combined. In: Engineering Self-Organising Systems. (2004) 1–15
14. Dorigo, M., Maniezzo, V., Colorni, A.: The Ant System: Optimization by a colony of cooperating agents. IEEE Transactions on Systems, Man, and Cybernetics Part B: Cybernetics **26** (1996) 29–41
15. Linnaeus, C.: Systema naturae per regna tria naturae, secundum classes, ordines, genera, species, cum characteribus, differentiis, synonymis, locis. 10th edn. L. Salvii, Stockholm (1758)
16. Camazine, S., Sneyd, J.: A model of collective nectar source selection by honey bees: self-organization through simple rules. Journal of Theoretical Biology **149** (1991) 547–571
17. Seeley, T.D., Camazine, S., Sneyd, J.: Collective decision-making in honey bees: how colonies choose among nectar sources. Behavioral Ecology and Sociobiology **28** (1991) 277–290

Towards Distributed Reasoning for Behavioral Optimization

Michael Cebulla

Technische Universität Berlin, Fakultät für Elektrotechnik und Informatik,
Institut für Softwaretechnik und Theoretische Informatik,
Franklinstr. 28/29, 10587 Berlin
mce@cs.tu-berlin.de

Abstract. We propose an architecture which supports the behavioral self-optimization of complex systems. In this architecture we bring together specification-based reasoning and the framework of ant colony optimization (ACO). By this we provide a foundation for distributed reasoning about different properties of the solution space represented by different viewpoint specifications. As a side-effect of reasoning we propagate the information about promising areas in the solution space to the current state. Consequently the system's decisions can be improved by considering the long term values of certain behavioral trajectories (given a certain situational horizon). We consider this feature to be a contribution to *autonomic computing*.

1 Introduction

The main target of our research consists in the definition of an architecture which supports the integration of reasoning and optimization thus enabling autonomic systems behavior. We take our starting point in the introduction of concepts for the knowledge-based fuzzy specification of various systemic aspects (extending our results from [1]). We show how it is possible to inexpensively check the conformance of these properties by traversing the solution space. These traversals of the solution space are performed by ant colonies. Areas of the solution space which are promising w.r.t. to a certain specification are marked with numerical information (frequently called *trail*). This information is propagated to the current state where it can be exploited for the optimization of behavior. Since there are multiple aspects of systems behavior which are examined by ant colonies different sorts of trail have to be evaluated in the process of decision making. As we will see this task is performed by an entity referred to as the *queen*.

In this paper we propose a hybrid architecture which integrates knowledge-based modeling [2], automata-based techniques of reasoning [3] with ant colony algorithms [4] in order to enable intelligent behavior of complex systems. In order to give specific support for robustness of reasoning and behavior we rely on fuzzy concepts for knowledge representation and reasoning.

Please use the following format when citing this chapter:

Cebulla, M., 2006, in IFIP International Federation for Information Processing, Volume 216, Biologically Inspired Cooperative Computing, eds. Pan, Y., Rammig, F., Schmeck, H., Solar, M., (Boston: Springer), pp. 65–74.

After firstly giving a brief introduction to our usage of fuzzy description logics (in Section 2) we discuss a simplified application scenario (Section 3). The semantic and algorithmic aspects of reasoning are described in Section 4 and 5. The architectural integration is discussed in Section 6.

2 Fuzzy Description Logics

For the fuzzification of description logics fuzzy sets [5] are introduced into the semantics instead of the crisp sets used in the traditional semantics (cf. [2]). For more detailed discussion of these issues cf. e.g. [6, 7].

If C is a concept then $C^{\mathcal{I}}$ will be interpreted as the *membership degree function* of the fuzzy concept C w.r.t. $\mathcal{I}$. Thus if $d \in \Delta^{\mathcal{I}}$ is an object of the domain $\Delta^{\mathcal{I}}$ then $C^{\mathcal{I}}(d)$ gives us the degree of being the object d an element of the fuzzy concept C under the interpretation $\mathcal{I}$ [6]. For some selected constructors which were considered for description logics the interpretation function $\cdot^{\mathcal{I}}$ has to satisfy the following equations:

$$\top^{\mathcal{I}}(d) = 1$$
$$\bot^{\mathcal{I}}(d) = 0$$
$$(C \sqcap D)^{\mathcal{I}}(d) = min(C^{\mathcal{I}}(d), D^{\mathcal{I}}(d))$$
$$(C \sqcup D)^{\mathcal{I}}(d) = max(C^{\mathcal{I}}(d), D^{\mathcal{I}}(d))$$
$$(\neg C)^{\mathcal{I}}(d) = 1 - C^{\mathcal{I}}(d)$$
$$(\exists R.C)^{\mathcal{I}}(d) = sup_{d' \in \Delta^{\mathcal{I}}}\{min(R^{\mathcal{I}}(d, d'), C^{\mathcal{I}}(d')\}$$
$$(\exists T.C)^{\mathcal{I}}(d) = sup_{d' \in \Delta^{\mathcal{I}}}\{min(T^{\mathcal{I}}(d, o), C^{\mathcal{I}}(o)\}$$
$$(qR.C)^{\mathcal{I}}(d) = \{d | d \in \Delta^{\mathcal{I}}, |\{d' | R(d, d') > 0\}| \geq q\}$$
$$(mod_q R.C)^{\mathcal{I}}(d) = \{d | d \in \Delta^{\mathcal{I}}, mod(|\{d' | R(d, d') > 0\}|) \geq q\}$$
$$(\langle q_1, \ldots, q_n \rangle R.C^{\mathcal{I}}(d) = \{d | d \in \Delta^{\mathcal{I}}, \forall i \in \{1, \ldots, n\}, \#_i(R(d, d')) \geq q_i\}$$

Remarks. In addition to roles we also support functional roles T which are needed for the integration of fuzzy concrete domains Δ_D (with $o \in \Delta_D$). We support a very simple style of quantifications allowing the use of positive rational numbers q or fuzzy modifiers mod (defined by piecewise linear membership functions). In addition we support a construct of tuple-valued cardinality which will be used to represent quantification concerning different aspects. As we will see such tuples contain global numerical information from different sources (commonly referred to as *trail*).

From Subsumption to Conformance. Deviating from common approaches based on description logics we do not focus on model-based reasoning about equivalence or subsumption. This is the reason why we do not rely on tableaux-based reasoning and thus do not have to face the resulting computational complexity (cf. [2]). In contrast we propose a syntax-directed approach for reasoning about the conformance of specifications. Specifications concerning different aspects of systems behavior are compared with the specification of the solution space. As we will see this is done by colonies of artificial ants. The requirements related to conformance are represented by sets of constraints describing *morphisms*. This approach is heavily influenced by [8].

3 Fuzzy Specifications

In this section we describe a simple example which we use to illustrate some characteristics of our approach. We apply fuzzy terminologies to the description of *locations* in sensor networks (cf. [9]). We use this concept as a high-level abstraction since in many cases it does not make sense to address the individual components of a sensor network explicitly. Alternatively such systems provide the transparent access to data from interesting places (without having to mention individual components). Similar arguments and more details about sensor networks can be found in [10].

A terminological description of a location is shown in the following (simplified example):

$$\text{loc-wl-xyz} \doteq 1.0 \text{ contains.Sensor1} \sqcap 0.7 \text{ contains.Sensor2} \sqcap$$
$$0.6 \text{ contains.Sensor3}$$
$$\text{Sensor1} \doteq \exists \text{energy.}_{=.7} \sqcap \exists \text{water-level.}_{=8.5}$$
$$\text{Sensor2} \doteq \exists \text{energy.}_{=.8} \sqcap \exists \text{water-level.}_{=9.1}$$
$$\text{Sensor3} \doteq \exists \text{energy.}_{=.6} \sqcap \exists \text{water-level.}_{=8.9}$$

As an example we introduce a terminological description of a simple location which contains three individual sensor components. The containment relation *contains* is quantified by a relevance value of the specific sensor component in the actual location. Note that this value is taken from the interval $[0,1]_\mathbb{Q}$. For the sake of our example sensor components contain data describing the current energy level and data concerning the water level. Note that the relations *energy* and *water-level* have to be treated as functional roles containing objects which represent concrete domain values (cf. Section 2).

Scenario. For the sake of this presentation we assume that the system has to decide which location it prefers in order to retrieve information in a given situation. Thus the solution space in this scenario contains various behavioral alternatives which each corresponds to the choice of an individual location. Obviously the quality of a solution is determined by parameters like *relevance* and *energy-level*. In our approach ant colonies have the task to retrieve this information (related to these two different aspects) and to mark the trajectories which conform best to their viewpoint specifications.

Viewpoint Specifications. In order to gain interesting information about the current situation different viewpoint specifications are checked throughout the solution space. These specifications may concern different aspects like availability of energy, like relevance or like flooding.

$$
\begin{aligned}
\text{high-energy} &\doteq \text{Most contains.energy(High)} \\
\text{high-relevance} &\doteq \text{Most contains.Sensor} \\
\text{flooding} &\doteq \text{Most contains.water-level(High)}
\end{aligned}
$$

Each of these three viewpoint specifications describe a criteria whose value is important for the systems decision making. Note that in such specifications we can use fuzzy terms like *most* and *high*. While *most* is defined in terms of fuzzy role quantification *high* is defined on concrete domain values of energy. Note that we are able to formulate less restrictive (and more robust) constraints using fuzzy concepts. In our framework such specifications are associated with colonies of ants which traverse the solution space (within a certain horizon) and check accessible paths for their conformance w.r.t. a certain specification.

4 Semantics

In the following we will extensively use the fact that we can consider specifications as tree-like term structures. For example both the systems specification as well as the viewpoint specifications can be represented in such a way (cf. Figure 1). We propose a syntax-directed approach for reasoning about *fuzzy conformance* which is based on the concurrent traversal of trees. Note that the promising paths in the solution space are marked with their value of conformance as a side-effect of reasoning.

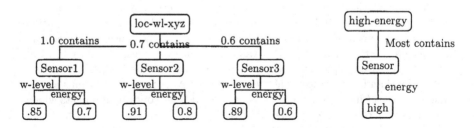

Fig. 1. Tree-like Representations of Specifications

Observations and Experiments. Intuitively, we say that two specifications are conform (to a certain degree) if they support similar observations and experiments. Observations and experiments on fuzzy specifications are described by fuzzy transition systems (FTS).

signature FTS
obs: $X \times T \to [0,1]_{\mathbb{Q}}$
next: $X \times T \times X \to [0,1]_{\mathbb{Q}}$

In the signature of the transition system we can see that the observation and transitions functions are multi-valued. In fact we are interested in observations (whose content is represented by a fuzzy terminological concept) which hold to a certain degree. On the other hand we want to know which costs are coupled with a certain state transition (triggered by a terminological role). Thus the application of the transition function $next$ yields a result which corresponds to the (fuzzy quantification) of the role term which is used as parameter (frequently referred to as $costs$).

Fuzzy Morphisms. In order to get a foundation for the notion of fuzzy conformance we rely on the notion of fuzzy morphism (cf. [11]).

Definition 1 (Fuzzy Morphism on FTS). *A fuzzy morphism f between two fuzzy transitions systems A_1 and A_2 is given by: $obs_2(T) \leq obs_1(f(T))$, and $next_2(X_2, T, X_2') \leq next_1(f(X_2), f(T), f(X_2'))$,*

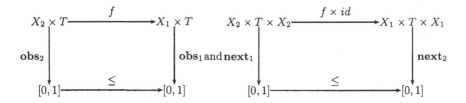

Fig. 2. Fuzzy Homomorphism on Signatures

Note that we sometimes assume (in Figure 2 and elsewhere) that both specifications use the same terminology T. We interpret positive differences between observations as conformance values (e.g. $obs_2(T) - obs_1(T)$). As a side-effect of reasoning the solution space is annotated with these values. In the following we heavily rely on an operational interpretation of these morphisms. For more details concerning this approach cf. [12].

5 Reasoning

In this section we heavily use the argument that morphisms can be mapped on bisimulations between automata (cf. [13]). We construct an automaton whose purpose is to recognize such bisimulations between two fuzzy tree automata. Such an automaton is called tree tuple automaton [3]. For the description of transition rules we use concepts from membrane computing (cf. [14]).

Membrane-Based Tuple Tree Automaton. Intuitively the automaton checks whether the systems description D supports the same experiments and observations as a certain viewpoint specification S. If there are multiple experiments necessary copies of the automaton are created for every experiment.

We exploit the characteristics of membrane computing and its computational properties for the creation and handling of multiple copies of tree automata. In our proposal the automaton for the recognition of bisimulation is implemented as a rewriting P-system (on structured objects) (cf. [14]). In this formalism we can use embedded membranes in order to articulate the tree-like structure of a term. In addition membranes contain multisets of terminal symbols or other information (e.g. trail). Consequently we can define transition rules for the processing of expressions using the paradigm of multiset rewriting. While (atomic) concept expressions are represented by molecules role expressions (and their cardinalites) are encoded in membrane labels. In order to deal with fuzzy expressions we support rational cardinalities of multisets. For more details on our usage of P-systems cf. [12].

Definition 2 (P-system for Bisimulation). *A P-system for bisimulation is defined as a tuple* $P_{BS} = \langle T, \mu, w1, \ldots, w_m, R_1, \ldots R_m \rangle$*, where T is a terminology and $\mu = [_0[_D]_D[_S]_S]_0$ is the initial configuration (of the membrane structure).*

While the membrane $[_D]_D$ represents the systems description $[_S]_S$ contains a viewpoint specification. Intuitively in each step of the simulation the necessary observations and experiments are drawn from the viewpoint specification (by obs_S and $next_S$) and then applied to the systems description (by obs_D and $next_D$). For simplicity we assume that both automata (and both specifications) use the same terminology T.

The behavior of the automaton is defined by the following rewriting rules:

1. Atomic Concepts $A \in T$:

$$[[_DX]_D[_SA[_Q\alpha]_Q]_S] \rightarrow [[_DX, \mathbf{t_i^d}]_D[_S[_Q\alpha]_Q]_S], \text{when } \mathbf{obs}_D(A) \geq \mathbf{obs}_S(A)$$

Note that a molecule representing the conformance value d is introduced into the systems specification per side-effect. Intuitively the molecule t (for *trail*) is related to the ith viewpoint specification and represents a rational conformance value d.

2. Basic Roles $Q \in T$:

$$[[_DX]_D[_S[_Q\alpha]_Q]_S] \rightarrow [[_D\mathbf{ann\text{-}lbl}(\mathbf{t_i^d})]_D[_S\alpha]_S],$$
$$\text{when } \mathbf{next}_D(Q) \geq \mathbf{next}_S(Q)$$

These rules describe a test concerning the costs of transitions. Thus by a call to $next_S$ we can retrieve the transitions which have to be supported by the system's description D in order to stay conform to the specification. Again trail is left when conformance is detected. We use the operation *ann-lbl* to introduce the molecule representing the trail information into the tuple-valued quantification of the membrane-label (not explicitly shown in the rules).

3. For the treatment of the constructors from fuzzy description logics the following rules can be used (selected examples). Note that the operators have to be treated according to fuzzy semantics (cf. Section 2).

$$[[_DX]_D[_sA \sqcap B]_S] \rightarrow [[\sqcap[[_DX]_D[_sA]_S]][_DX]_D[_sB]_S]]\sqcap]$$
$$[[_DX]_D[_s\exists Q.C]_S] \rightarrow [\sqcup_{i \in \{1,...,k\}}[i[\sqcap[_D\mathbf{next}^i]_D[_sQ]_S \\ [_D\mathbf{next}^i]_D[_sC]_S]\sqcap]_i],$$

In the rules for the processing of quantified role expressions (involving atomic roles) the terms labeled with i have to be created for each $i \in [1, k_T]$ where k_T is the branching factor of the tree. Intuitively this corresponds to the creation of a copy of the automaton for each role filler of Q. $\mathbf{next}^i$ are procedures for the explicit navigation in trees (retrieving the ith subtree of the current node). As we will see the fuzzy semantics of the operators controls the propagation of trail.

4. The treatment of numeric quantification is similar to the treatment of quantification described above. For each role filler a copy of the automaton is created.

$$[[_DX]_D[_sqQ.C]_S] \rightarrow [\sqcup_{i \in \{1,...,k\}}[i[\sqcap[_D\mathbf{next}^i]_D[_sQ]_S \\ [_D\mathbf{next}^i]_D[_sC]_S]\sqcap]_i] \text{ when } \#_DQ \geq q$$
$$[[_DX]_D[_smod_qQ.C]_S] \rightarrow [\sqcup_{i \in \{1,...,k\}}[i[\sqcap[_D\mathbf{next}^i]_D[_sQ]_S \\ [_D\mathbf{next}^i]_D[_sC]_S]\sqcap]_i] \text{ when } mod(\#_DQ) \geq q$$

Example. While comparing the specifications from our example the situation in Figure 3 is constituted at some point. On the left hand side of the transformation we see that experiments concerning *most contains* are prescribed by the specification. Since there are three such experiments possible on the system's description three copies of the automaton are created. Then the experiments concerning *contains* are initiated concurrently (as shown at the right hand side of the rule). For this mechanism we rely on the fact that *membrane division* is a common and inexpensive operation in membrane computing (cf. [14]).

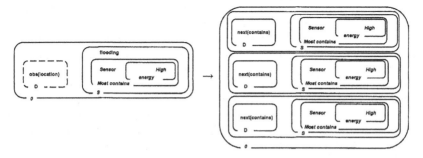

Fig. 3. Example: Behavior of Tuple Tree Automaton

Trail Propagation. In the final phase of reasoning about the conformance of a viewpoint specification the information represented by the trail is propagated. For this sake the numerical information is treated like a *synthesized*-attribute in attributed grammars (cf. [15]). Intuitively the information about promising locations in the solution space is *propagated* to the the current state thus increasing the quality of the system's decisions. Again we exploit some characteristics of membrane computing for the reactive propagation of this information.

Fig. 4. Example: Trail Propagation

In the example transition in Figure 4 we can see how trail information is propagated bottom-up through the membrane hierarchy. The rules for the propagation are determined by the semantics of the operators (in this case ⊓). According to Zadeh's logic the value of f is defined as the minimum of i, j, k.

6 Distributed Reasoning

We propose an architecture for the integration of high-level modeling, automated reasoning and ant-colony optimization. Our goal is to propagate information about valuable places in the solution space in order to support decision making in the current state. Generally we propose that systems rely on solutions found by ant colonies during normal situations while they have to depend on default values for their decision in highly dynamic situations (represented by so-called myopic heuristic information, cf. [4]).

Integration. In order to collect additional information about the long-term values of behavioral alternatives ant colonies iteratively traverse the accessible trajectories. A given ant colony is embodied by a fuzzy tuple tree automaton as discussed in the previous sections. Note that tree automata are copied into multiple instances while examining different branches of a tree thus keeping the correspondence to the metaphor of ant colonies. Since we use fuzzy morphisms in our framework we assume that ants leave large amounts of *trail* on traces in the systems state space where the conformance to their specification is strong. The global choice between these solutions is performed by the queen. Note that the marked traces in the systems behavior can be considered as trajectories in an n-dimensionary hypercube. Unfortunately we cannot discuss the issue of *trail evaporation* [4] due to space limitations.

Example. In a simplified example we consider the situation that the system (represented by the queen) has to choose between two locations. Obviously at first sight it is not possible to decide which group of sensors to use (since heuristic information about the costs – as represented by attribute *def* – are equal concerning both alternatives).

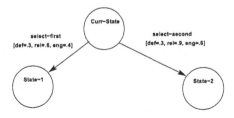

Fig. 5. Example Situation

We assume that the ants examinations (concerning relevance and energy) resulted in the values shown in Figure 5. Consequently it is the queen which has to infer the best alternative from the available information. For this sake we define the queen as a tree tuple automaton which performs a simple version of multi-criteria optimization: the queen always selects the behavioral alternative which is marked with the greatest global value (depending on environmental parameters). Note that for simplicity we assume a non-fuzzy decision behavior of the queen always resulting in the choice of exactly one behavioral alternative.

$$[_{\langle \alpha,\beta \rangle}[_{\langle s_0,s_1,s_2 \rangle A_1}]_{\langle s_0,s_1,s_2 \rangle A_1}[_{\langle t_0,t_1,t_2 \rangle A_2}]_{\langle t_0,t_1,t_2 \rangle A_2}]_{\langle \alpha,\beta \rangle} \rightarrow [_{A_1} \cdots]_{A_1}$$
$$\text{when } max_{1,2}(s_i) > max_{1,2}(t_i) \text{ and } \alpha > \beta$$
$$[_{\langle \alpha,\beta \rangle}[_{\langle s_0,s_1,s_2 \rangle A_1}]_{\langle s_0,s_1,s_2 \rangle A_1}[_{\langle t_0,t_1,t_2 \rangle A_2}]_{\langle t_0,t_1,t_2 \rangle A_2}]_{\langle \alpha,\beta \rangle} \rightarrow [_{A_1} \cdots]_{A_1}$$
$$\text{when } s_0 > t_0 \text{ and } \beta > \alpha$$

For the sake of example we give two rules which describe the queen's decision making in our scenario. We encode the information about trail into membrane labels. The first rule describes how behavioral alternative A_1 is selected on the basis of trail information (represented by t_1, t_2, s_1, s_2). The global parameter α denotes the weight of trail information (during normal environmental conditions) while β contains a high value when the situation is highly dynamic. This case is described by the second rule where also A_1 is selected but this time on the basis of heuristic information (contained in s_0, t_0). Remember that trail information tends to be useless in the presence of environmental changes.

7 Conclusion

Our motivation in this paper is directed towards an architectural integration of high-level knowledge-based modeling, of automated reasoning and of techniques for local optimization in order to support context-aware behavior in

74   Michael Cebulla

autonomic systems. For this reason we propose to use colonies of artificial ants
for the exploration of the solution space of complex systems. In this framework
we support distributed and robust reasoning about high-level specifications.
Knowledge about the systems properties is diffusing through the solution space
thus supporting decentral and distributed forms of decision-making and control.

References

1. Peter Pepper, Michael Cebulla, Klaus Didrich, and Wolfgang Grieskamp. From
   program languages to software languages. *The Journal of Systems and Software*,
   60, 2002.
2. Franz Baader and Werner Nutt. Basic description logics. In Franz Baader, Diego
   Calvanese, Deborah McGuinness, Daniele Nardi, and Peter Patel-Schneider, editors, *The Description Logic Handbook*. Cambridge University Press, Cambridge,
   U.K., 2003.
3. H. Comon, M. Dauchet, R. Gilleron, F. Jacquemard, D. Lugiez, S. Tison,
   and M. Tommasi. Tree automata techniques and applications. Available on:
   http://www.grappa.univ-lille3.fr/tata, 1997. release October, 1rst 2002.
4. Marco Dorigo and Thomas Stützle. The ant colony optimization metaheuristic:
   Algorithms, applications, and advances. In Fred Glover and Gary A. Kochen-
   berger, editors, *Handbook of Metaheuristics*. Kluwer Acad. Publ.: Boston et.al,
   2003.
5. Lofti A. Zadeh. Fuzzy sets. *Information and Control*, 8(3):338–353, 1965.
6. Umberto Straccia. Reasoning with fuzzy description logic. *Journal of Artificial
   Intelligence Research*, 14:137–166, 2001.
7. Steffen Hölldobler, Hans-Peter Störr, and Tran Dinh Khang. The fuzzy description
   logic ALC_{FH} with hedge algebras as concept modifiers. *International Journal of
   Advanced Computational Intelligence and Intelligent Informatics*, 7(3):294–305,
   2003.
8. Dusko Pavlovic, Peter Pepper, and Douglas Smith. Specification engineering. *to
   appear*, 2006.
9. David Culler, Deborah Estrin, and Mani Srivastava. Overview of sensor networks.
   IEEE Computer, 37:41–49, August 2000.
10. S. Madden, R. Szewczyk, M. Franklin, and D. Culler. Supporting aggregate
    queries over ad-hoc wireless sensor networks. In *IEEE Workshop on Mobile Com-
    puting Systems and Applications*, 2002.
11. George J. Klir and Bo Yuan. *Fuzzy Sets and Fuzzy Logic. Theory and Applications*.
    Prentice Hall, Upper Saddle River, N.J., 1995.
12. Michael Cebulla. Reasoning about knowledge and context awareness. In *Proc. of
    FLAIRS'06*, 2006.
13. Jan Rutten. Automata and coinduction (an exercise in coalgebra). Technical
    report, Centrum voor Wiskunde en Informatica, Amsterdam, 1998.
14. Gheorghe Păun. *Membrane Computing. An Introduction*. Springer, Berlin, 2002.
15. Donald E. Knuth. Semantics of context-free languages. *Theory of Computing
    Systems*, 2(2):127–145, June 1968.

Ant Based Heuristic for OS Service Distribution on Ad Hoc Networks

Tales Heimfarth and Peter Janacik

Heinz Nixdorf Institut, University of Paderborn
Fuerstenallee 11, 33102 Paderborn, Germany
{tales,pjanacik}@upb.de

Abstract. This paper presents a basic and an extended heuristic to distribute operating system (OS) services over mobile ad hoc networks. The heuristics are inspired by the foraging behavior of ants and are used within our NanoOS, an OS for distributed applications. The NanoOS offers an uniform environment of execution and the code of the OS is distributed among nodes.
We propose a basic and an extended swarm optimization based heuristic to control the service migration in order to reduce the communication overhead. In the basic one, each service request leaves pheromone in the nodes on its path to the service provider (like ants leave pheromone when foraging). An optimization step occurs when the service provider migrates to the neighbor node with the higher pheromone concentration. The proposed extension takes into account the position of the node in the network and its energy.
Realized simulations have shown that the basic heuristic performs well. The total communication cost in average is just 40% higher than the global optimum. In addition, both heuristics have a low computational requirement.

1 Introduction

Distributed systems running on MANETs (mobile ad hoc networks) open a new spectrum of applications but also bring new challenges. Many interesting applications in this domain consist of collaborative distributed tasks among geographically dispersed nodes. However, for a good resource utilization and for an adequate development of such distributed applications, the support offered by an operating system (OS) is important. The OS manages the hardware resources and offers a common system call interface in each node simplifying the application development.

The objective of this paper is to introduce a basic and extended heuristic for service distribution used in our OS. NanoOS is a complex, innovative OS for resource constrained embedded devices able to establish an ad hoc network. The code of the OS is distributed among the wireless nodes in order to fit into the small nodes.

Please use the following format when citing this chapter:

Heimfarth, T., Janacik, P., 2006, in IFIP International Federation for Information Processing, Volume 216, Biologically Inspired Cooperative Computing, eds. Pan, Y., Rammig, F., Schmeck, H., Solar, M., (Boston: Springer), pp. 75–84.

As the OS components (services) are distributed, adapting automatically to dynamically changing conditions by changing the distribution of functionality across the ad hoc network is an important issue in our system. This adaptation should also help to reduce the overhead and the energy consumption. For this propose, we develop an distribution and migration algorithm based on swarm intelligence which tries to reduce the communication among different nodes of the system. As processing speed usually is orders of magnitude higher than communication speed, this also affect positively the global performance of the system.

2 Related Work

The academic system called MagnetOS [1] offers a distributed Java virtual machine that provides an automatic migration of elements of the system trying to maximize total application lifetime by utilizing power more efficiently. The migration mechanisms have some similarities with our ant-based migration algorithm but different from our approach, it neither considers the resource availability in the nodes nor the link quality.

Our problem of placement and migration of the OS services to different nodes is very similar to a global scheduler that decides where the processes will be executed in a distributed system.

The static scheduler makes the decisions just with information available at compilation time. There are several theoretical analysis of the task assignment problem. Some approaches consider a graph formed by system nodes together with tasks as vertices and communication costs together with execution costs as edges without considering a multi-hop network topology ([2, 3, 4]). Other research deals with multi-hop networks with a complex topology ([5, 6, 7, 8]).

In our approach, we are using a dynamic distributed non-cooperative scheduling strategy, i.e., the current state of the system is used in order to drive the migration. Moreover, each service is an autonomous agent that decides itself when to migrate and to which node.

In the area of dynamic distributed scheduling algorithms, there are a lot of approaches that try to share the load of networked nodes among them ([9, 10]).

Although the algorithms are distributed, they do not take in account the topology of the network. Moreover, movement of nodes is not considered.

3 Overview of the NanoOS

Our system is composed of three main components: the hardware, the OS and the application running on top of it (see Fig. 1). The hardware platform consists of a set of distributed mobile nodes, each one with small processing unit, limited memory and wireless adapter. Our *NanoOS* runs on top of such an architecture and provides the adequate set of services to the application. Besides the traditional OS services , the NanoOS provides a set of special services to support the distributed processing, like migration and distributed synchronization.

In our OS, each application is composed by a set of tasks. The OS provides a uniform and remotely available system call environment even with movement of nodes (and connections being broken).

For the purpose of reducing the per node OS footprint and to enable the execution of a rather complex OS in very hardware constrained nodes, the NanoOS distributes the services among the nodes. Each node of the system has just a small part of the services of the complete OS; a group of nodes together form an instance of the OS. At any instant of time one node may connect and use a service residing in another node using a remote method invocation (RMI).

The Figure 1 presents an overview of the system. The tasks from applications use services of the OS. In order to reduce the resource requirement in each node, the services are shared among different application tasks executed in other nodes.

The services and tasks can migrate in order to optimize communications. Moreover, the same migration mechanisms used by the OS services are also offered for application level tasks. Applications' tasks can offer services to others and may also automatically migrate. For sake of simplicity, we will speak from here on simply about migration of services. The main contribution of this paper is the algorithm presented that is responsible to assign dynamically the OS services (or tasks offering services) to nodes trying to minimize the communication overhead.

4 Service Distribution Using Swarm Optimization

After a service discovery phase (not described here), a communication between the node of the application task and the node hosting the service is set up. We now assume a situation where tasks distributed in the system are communicating with services which are distributed as well. A single path routing is responsible for finding a good route between the nodes.

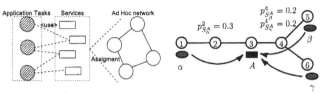

Fig. 1. System overview

Fig. 2. Pheromone based service distribution

The objective of the service distribution is to change the location where the services (and mobile tasks) are executed (migrating them) during runtime trying to minimize the communication overhead.

There are possible constraints to the movement of the objects: only to a direct neighbor (1 hop); within a neighborhood (k hops); or unbounded (infinity hops). In this paper we are just considering 1 hop movements.

4.1 Load and Communication Models

To support the migration/reconfiguration process, the load of the hardware and the communication pattern are important information and have to be exposed to the OS. For this paper, a simplified load model, just considering the amount of local free memory is used.

In order to model the communication, we create a link metric called *virtual distance* and is represented by $D(u,v)$ (d and v are nodes). It ranges from Γ to $\Gamma + A$:

$$D(u,v) = \Gamma + A \cdot (1 - (s_{(u,v)}^{\alpha} \cdot l_{(u,v)}^{\beta} \cdot d_{(u,v)}^{\gamma} \cdot e_{(u,v)}^{\zeta})^{\frac{1}{\alpha+\beta+\gamma+\zeta}}) \qquad (1)$$

The used metrics are the error rate: $e_{(u,v)} \in [0,1]$ (0 means 100% of error rate), the live time: $l_{(u,v)} \in [0,1]$ (this metric varies according the relapsed time of the link, 0 means new link), the delay (correlated with queue): $d_{(u,v)} \in [0,1]$ (0 means maximum delay, 1 means minimum delay) and the RSSI (received power): $s_{u,v)} \in [0,1]$ (0 means no reception signal).

α, β, γ and ζ define the weight of each metric in the geometrical mean.

4.2 Basic Heuristic for Service Distribution

In our approach we are optimizing the position of the services of the system through *migration*, i.e., we try to find the optimal configuration where the communication overhead caused by the remote requests is minimized. In order to solve this online discrete optimization problem, we decide to use an ant inspired algorithm that is described in this section. It is relatively simple and has shown good performance.

The system is represented by the graph $G = (V, E)$ with nodes V and bidirectional links E. The nodes correspond to the physical devices and the links to the wireless connections. The links are weighted with the *virtual distance* metric. Additionally, each service instance $i \in I$ is of a type $p \in P$. A task $a \in A$ has no type. We will use the word service and task to denote a service instance and task instance. Each requester $r \in \{I \cup A\}$ (requester can be services or tasks) of a service $i \in I$ has a service state S_r^i. A node $v \in V$ has a pheromone table $P_v = [p_{S_r^i}^v]_{r \in \{I \cup A\}, i \in I}$. This pheromone level represents the request rate (and traffic) made by the requester r to the service i that are crossing the node v. In our approach, all nodes are responsible for service distribution, since each node's evaluation is based on its *local* view. Moreover, the needed information is constantly changing, due to frequent pheromone updates so that transferring the decision to just certain nodes would incur an high additional communication overhead without efficiency gains.

Using an analogy with the ant foraging behavior [11], the services in our approach are the equivalent of the food source. The calls made by the requesters are the agents (or ants) and the requesters are the nests. The wireless links form the paths which the ants can use for movement. While the requests are being routed to the destination service, they leave pheromone on the nodes.

The pheromone tables in each node are updated according to the equation $p_{S_r^i}(t+1) = \frac{p_{S_r^i}(t)+\delta p(h)}{1+\delta p(h)}$, where the $\delta p(h)$ is the variation of the pheromone and it is a function of the size of the packet.

In defined time intervals, each service evaluates whether it should migrate to another node in order to improve the communication (reduce the overhead). This neighbor is selected using the following method.

Let $v \in V$ be the local node of the service $i \in I$, $d \in V$ is the destination node of the service and $N_v, v \in V$ is the set of neighbors of v.

$$b_{v \to d}^i = \frac{\sum_{x \in \{I \cup A\}} p_{S_x}^d}{\sum_{y \in N_v} \sum_{x \in \{I \cup A\}} p_{S_x}^y} \quad (2) \qquad e_i = max(b_{v \to d}^i), d \in N_v \quad (3)$$

$b_{v \to d}^i$ (eq. 2) represents a force between $[0,1]$ that the service i migrates form node v to node d. The selection of the final destination node $e_i \in V$ of the service i is made simply using the expression 3.

The migration process is initialized when the sum of pheromones of some neighbor exceeds a threshold value Θ.

In Fig. 2, a scenario with six nodes is shown. In this scenario, node 1 has the task α that accesses the service A in node 3. At the same time, tasks β and γ, located in the nodes 5 and 6 respectively, are also using the service A. Let's assume that the pheromone related to the connection $\alpha \to A$ in the node 2 is $p_{S_\alpha^A}^2 = 0.3$, the pheromone of the connection $\beta \to A$ in the node 4 is $p_{S_\beta^A}^4 = 0.2$ and the pheromone of the connection $\gamma \to A$ is $p_{S_\gamma^A}^4 = 0.2$. According to equation 2, the force attracting this service to the node 2 is $b_{3 \to 2}^A = \frac{0.3}{0.3+0.2+0.2} = 0.428$ whereas the force attracting to node 4 is $b_{3 \to 4}^A = \frac{0.2+0.2}{0.3+0.2+0.2} = 0.571$. This means that the service A will migrate to the node with higher total pheromone level, i.e., node 4.

Direction Extension In this section, an identified problem caused by the greedy nature of the presented algorithm is described and a solution is proposed. The problem occurs when more than one nearly located tasks request the same service, but due to the routing algorithm, the requests use different paths. An example of such situation is depicted in Fig. 3. This situation can only occur if there are more than two requesters using the same service. It is more likely to occur when the service is located in a node-dense area of the network.

In Fig. 3, the tasks α, β and γ are accessing the service A in node 3. The total communication cost C can be calculated using the eq. 4, where A is the

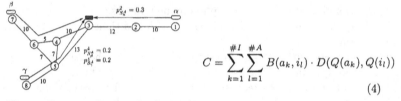

$$C = \sum_{k=1}^{\#I} \sum_{l=1}^{\#A} B(a_k, i_l) \cdot D(Q(a_k), Q(i_l))$$

(4)

Fig. 3. Instance that results in wrong migration

set of application tasks: $A = \{a_1, a_2, ..., a_m\}$ and I the set of service (instances) of the system $I = \{i_1, i_2, ..., i_n\}$.

The function $B(a_m, i_n) \geq 0$ gives the average bandwidth utilization by the requests made by the task a_m to the service i_n. The function $Q : A \cup I \to V$ maps the tasks and services to the hosting node. The objective function of the service distribution heuristic is to find the assignment function Q that minimizes the communication cost C (and therefore minimizes the energy consumption, assuming that communication is a major energy consuming operation). Our problem is a special instance of the QAP (*Quadratic Assignment Problem*), where instead of Euclidean distance between points, the sum of the virtual distances of the routed path is used ($D(v, w)$, where $v, w \in V$) and the cost is given by the bandwidth utilization ($B(a, i)$, where $a \in A$ and $i \in I$). It is known that the QAP is an NP-hard problem [12].

Returning to our example (Fig. 3), as the average bandwidth utilization is proportional to the pheromone deposited in a node inside the used path, the total communication cost in this case is 16.2 (calculated using eq. 4). As the pheromone in the node 2 is higher than in the nodes 4 and 5, the next step of the basic algorithm would be to migrate the service A to node 2. Here, the communication cost is 17.4. This result shows that the heuristic selects the wrong node to migrate to, increasing the total communication cost. This happens because of the lack of information over not directly connected parts of the network. The main idea of the improvement is to migrate the service not to the neighbor with the biggest amount of requests (requests we call also flow) but to the neighbor whose flow (request traffic) is crossing near to nodes that are in flows from other requests to the same service. If the defined metric (virtual distance) has (geographical) norm properties, this will be equivalent to migrating the service to the geographical *direction* where the highest amount of requests is coming from. Two requests coming from task α and β (see Fig. 3) are transversing neighboring nodes in order to reach A, thus, they should attract the service instead of γ.

In addition, the new migration heuristic is based not just on the pheromone level to drive the migration of the services, but also on a "potential goodness" of each node to receive highly loaded services and the energy level of the nodes. The "potential goodness" η_{vi} measures how appropriate it is for node v to receive service i, i.e., whether the node is central in the network and the service i is a highly required one. If the complete network would be known by each node, the centrality could be measured by the sum of the distances to every other node. The idea of the potential goodness is that services with high flow are coupled with high probability to locations with good connections to others. Just using this rule, it is possible to obtain good (but not optimal) placement of the services in the network [11].

Definitions and heuristic description:

Like in basic heuristic, each node has just local information, we define η_{vi} where $v \in V$, $i \in I$ and $0 \le \eta_{vi} \le 1$ in eq. 5.

$$\eta_{vi} = [1 - \sum_{g \in N_v} \frac{D(v,g)}{(\#N_v)^\delta \cdot D_{max}}] \cdot h(i) \quad (5) \qquad b^i_{v \to d} = \frac{[\tau^i_{v \to d}]^\alpha \cdot [\eta_{di}]^\beta \cdot [E_d]^\gamma}{\sum_{x \in N_v} [\tau^i_{v \to x}]^\alpha \cdot [\eta_{xi}]^\beta \cdot [E_x]^\gamma} \quad (6)$$

where $N_v, v \in V$ the set of neighbors of v and $\delta \ge 1$ gives the importance of the number of neighbors, and D_{max} gives the maximum allowed virtual distance. $h(i) : I \to [0,1]$ returns the current request load (how much traffic) that service i is currently serving (where 0 means the service is idle and 1 means full load). The energy of the node is given by E_v and $0 \le E_v \le 1$, where 1 means full and 0 empty.

In addition to the already presented pheromone table P_v that stores the rate of requests that are crossing the node v, there is a second table F_v that stores the information about the flows that are occurring in the neighbor nodes. $F_v(S^i_r) : \{I \cup A\} \times I \to \{0,1\}$ return 1, iff some direct neighbor of the node v is routing a request from the requester r to the service i.

The idea is that neighboring communications (like the S^A_β and S^A_γ in the figure) can be recognized as coming from the same network "direction" by the service A.

The table N_v is filled without the necessity of any direct exchange of messages between the node v and the neighbors. Each node just hears the communication originating from neighboring nodes to fill the table. If the node v has a directed connection to the node u where the service i is located, it ignores all the neighboring communication going to to the service i (i.e., for $\forall r \in \{I \cup A\}$, $F_v(S^i_r) = 0$). This avoids the problem that near the sink (service i) all nodes can hear each other, resulting on a false interpretation that all requests are coming from a similar direction.

Each request r to the service i now carries the information collected in the nodes about which requests to the service i are occurring in neighbor nodes (i.e., it collects the N_v information of the nodes when traveling to service i). $F(S^i_{r_1}, S^i_{r_2}) : \{I \cup A\} \times \{I \cup A\} \times I \to \{0,1\}$ return 1 iff r_1 and r_2 are neighboring requests (flows).

In the original heuristic, the "force" attracting the service i from node v to node d ($b^i_{v \to d}$, see eq. 2) does not take into account the requests coming from near areas of the network. The new $b_{v \to d}^i$ is calculated now in two steps. In the first, the $\tau_{v \to d}^i$ take in account the pheromone (and neighboring flow information) and rate the attractiveness of node d (eq. 7).

$$
\tau_{v \to d}^i = \frac{\displaystyle\sum_{x \in \{I \cup A\}} p_{S_x^i}^d + \sum_{x \in \{I \cup A\}} \sum_{z \in \{I \cup A\}} \sum_{g \in N_v - \{d\}} p_{S_z^i}^g \cdot \lceil p_{S_x^d}^d \rceil \cdot F(S_z^i, S_x^i)}{\displaystyle\sum_{y \in N_v} [\sum_{x \in \{I \cup A\}} p_{S_x^i}^y + \sum_{x \in \{I \cup A\}} \sum_{z \in \{I \cup A\}} \sum_{g \in N_v - \{d\}} p_{S_z^i}^g \cdot \lceil p_{S_x^i}^y \rceil \cdot F(S_z^i, S_x^i)]} \tag{7}
$$

The first term is the same of the eq. 7, that means, the sum of all requests coming to service i through node d. The second term of the numerator is the sum of the pheromone from flows that are neighbors of the ones traveling through d. As already explained, the F function tests whether S_z^i and S_x^i are neighbor flows, and the ceiling $\lceil p_{S_x^i}^d \rceil$ checks whether the connection S_x^i exists in the node d (i.e. $p_{S_x^i}^d > 0$). The denominator normalizes τ ($0 \le \tau_{v \to d}^i \le 1$).

Finally, the eq. 6 returns the new $b_{v \to d}^i$ that is the force between $[0, 1]$ that the service i migrates from node v to node d. This combines the pheromone value (with direction concept, eq. 7) with the potential goodness of a location to some service and the available energy. The selection of the destination node of the migration is made, like the basic heuristic, using eq. 3.

Returning to the example shown in Fig. 3, and assuming that all the nodes have the same potential goodness and energy ($= 1$), for sake of simplicity and that $\alpha, \beta, \gamma = 1$, $\tau_{3 \to 2}^A = b_{3 \to 2}^A = \frac{0.3}{0.3+0.4+0.4} = 0.27$, $\tau_{3 \to 4}^A = b_{3 \to 4}^A = \frac{0.2+0.2}{0.3+0.4+0.4} = 0.36$ and $\tau_{3 \to 5}^A = b_{3 \to 5}^A = \frac{0.2+0.2}{0.3+0.4+0.4} = 0.36$. This result shows that the service A will migrate correctly to the node 4 or 5 instead of 2 when the basic version of the heuristic is used.

5 Results

A simulation environment to evaluate our basic ant-based service distribution heuristic was implemented in C++ using the *Boost* library for graph algorithms support. The routing of network traffic was idealized by using Dijkstra shortest path algorithm.

Instances of the ad hoc network were generated by random selection of nodes' position. Moreover, the task force and the services of the OS including also the usage (dependency) graph were also randomly generated.

The received signal strength (RSSI) was calculated using the free space model for an isotropic point source in an ideal propagation medium (free-space path loss with rx,tx unitary gain: $L_f = \frac{4\pi d^2}{\lambda}$). The limits of the RSSI were determined using two thresholds that have the meaning of maximum signal strength and no signal (unit disk graph). The *RSSI* was the only metric used to produce the *virtual distance* (see Equation 1).

As already said, the objective of the heuristic is to find the assignment function Q that minimizes the communication cost C (and therefore minimizes the energy consumption, assuming that the communication is the main energy consuming operation). We restrict the maximum number of services and tasks to one per node. This simulates a simplistic resource constraint per node.

We run 10.000 different problem instances and the presented basic heuristic is applied in the first assignment (randomly generated). Fig. 4 shows the results. The x-axis shows the number of optimization steps of the algorithm, where the y-axis shows the average communication cost among all the realized simulations. The two straight lines depict the average communication cost of the first random solution to the assignment and the optimal solution (calculated using Branch and Bound over the QAP). Figure 5 shows the cumulative distribution of the testing cases.

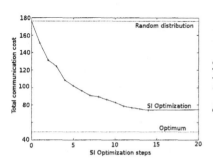 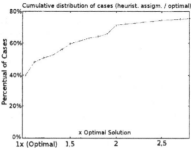

Fig. 4. Results of the simulations

Fig. 5. Cumulative distribution of the cases

6 Conclusions

In this paper we present the concept of the NanoOS for highly distributed applications running on ad hoc wireless networks. This OS allows the migration of application/OS services among nodes. The investigated objective was the minimization of the communication overhead between application tasks and services in an ad hoc network. We proposed ant-based heuristics. The problem was modeled in detail and the quality of our ant-based method was compared with the global optimum using simulations of a large number of problem instances.

The realized simulations of the basic heuristic have shown that it performs well in average (71.97 of cost compared with 50.16 that was the cost of the optimal distribution), i.e., the total communication cost is in average only about 40% higher than the global optimum obtained using Branch and Bound. The initial random distribution of services has an average cost of 176.6. Looking at the cumulative distribution of cases (Fig. 5), we see that for the majority of test cases (70%), the heuristic could find solutions that cost at most 2 times the optimal value. In 40% of the cases, the heuristic could find the optimum.

Moreover, our heuristics have an extremely low computational cost and a small information dependency, where just local communication is necessary for the migration decision. They are also adaptive to changes in the network and can be executed in a distributed manner where each entity tries itself to find a good assignment.

We are planning to simulate the extended version of the heuristic in order to compare it with the actual results. We also want to include movement into the simulation in our future work. Concluding, the results give yet another piece of evidence that principles encountered in the nature (like agents doing just local interactions helping to achieve global results) can be transferred to computers with satisfactory results.

References

1. Emin G Sirer, Rimon Barr, T. W. D Kim, and Lan Y Fung. Automatic code placement alternatives for ad-hoc and sensor networks. Technical report, Cornell University, Ithaca, NY, USA, 2001.
2. H. S. Stone. Multiprocessor scheduling with the aid of network flow algorithms. *IEEE Trans. Software Eng.*, SE-3:85 –93, 1977.
3. V. M. Lo. Heuristic algorithms for task assignment in distributed systems. *IEEE Trans. Comput.*, 37(11):1384–1397, 1988.
4. S. Ramakrishnan, I. H. Cho, and L. Dunning. A close look at task assignment in distributed systems. In *In IEEE INFOCOM 91*, pages 806 – 812, Miami, 1991.
5. Kenjiro Taura and Andrew A. Chien. A heuristic algorithm for mapping communicating tasks on heterogeneous resources. In *Heterogeneous Computing Workshop*, pages 102–115, 2000.
6. Nectarios Koziris, Michael Romesis, Panayiotis Tsanakas, and George Papakonstantinou. An efficient algorithm for the physical mapping of clustered task graphs onto multiprocessor architectures. In *Proc. of 8th Euromicro Workshop on Parallel and Distributed Processing (PDP2000)*, pages 406–413, Rhodes, Greece, 2000. IEEE Press.
7. M. Eshaghian and Y. Wu. Mapping heterogeneous task graphs onto heterogeneous system graphs. In *Proceedings of Heterogeneous Computing Workshop*, 1997.
8. R. F. Freund, M. Gherrity, S. Ambrosius, M. Campbell, M. Halderman, D. Hensgen, E. Keith, T. Kidd, M. Kussow, J. D. Lima, F. Mirabile, L. Moore, B. Rust, and H. J. Siegel. Scheduling resources in multi-user, heterogeneous, computing environments with smartnet. In *In Proceedings of Heterogeneous Computing Workshop*, 1998.
9. Christophe Lang, Michel Trehel, and Pierre Baptiste. A distributed placement algorithm based on process initiative and on a limited travel. In *PDPTA*, pages 2636–2641, 1999.
10. Shyamal Chowdhury. The greedy load sharing algorithm. *J. Parallel Distrib. Comput.*, 9(1):93–99, 1990.
11. Eric Bonabeau, Marco Dorigo, and Guy Theraulaz. *Swarm Intelligence: From Natural to Artificial Systems*. Oxford University Press, New York, NY, 1999.
12. Sartaj Sahni and Teofilo Gonzalez. P-complete approximation problems. *J. ACM*, 23(3):555–565, 1976.

An Artificial Hormone System for Self-organization of Networked Nodes

Wolfgang Trumler, Tobias Thiemann, and Theo Ungerer

Institute of Computer Science
University of Augsburg
86159 Augsburg
Germany
{trumler,ungerer}@email.address, thiemato@web.de

Abstract. The rising complexity of distributed computer systems give reason to investigate self-organization mechanism to build systems that are self-managing in the sense of *Autonomic* and *Organic Computing*. In this paper we propose the Artificial Hormone System (AHS) as a general approach to build self-organizing systems based on networked nodes. The Artificial Hormone System implements a similar information exchange between networked nodes like the human hormone system does between cells. The artificial hormone values are piggy-backed on messages to minimize communication overhead.
To show the efficiency of the mechanism even for large scale systems we implemented a simulation environment in Java to evaluate different optimization strategies. The evaluations show that local information is enough to meet global optimization criterion.

1 Introduction

State of the art computer and software systems raise the level of complexity to unexpected heights. Upcoming ubiquitous environments with their huge amount of different devices and sensors aggravate the situation even more. The need for self-managing systems, as proposed by IBM's *Autonomic Computing* [1] and the German *Organic Computing* [2] initiative, has never been more important than today. Future systems are expected to comprise attributes motivated by self-organizing natural systems as e.g. organisms or societies.

Self-organization seems to be embedded in biological systems in many ways. In the human body it arises at lower levels (e.g. the growth of an organism controlled by hormones) as well as at higher levels (the regulation of the homoeostasis by the autonomic nervous system).

We developed the AMUN middleware [3] to foster the development of ubiquitous computing environments such as Smart Office environments [4]. The aim of the middleware is to build service-oriented applications that can be distributed on networked nodes. The services which can be distributed and relocated between the nodes are monitored to collect information about their runtime behavior and resource consumption.

Please use the following format when citing this chapter:

Trumler, W., Thiemann, T., Ungerer, T., 2006, in IFIP International Federation for Information Processing, Volume 216, Biologically Inspired Cooperative Computing, eds. Pan, Y., Rammig, F., Schmeck, H., Solar, M., (Boston: Springer), pp. 85–94.

To implement the autonomic/organic goals within the AMUN middleware we propose a self-organization mechanism based on the human hormone system. The basic idea is to use the messages from services as containers for the information of our Artificial Hormone System like the hormones use the blood circuit in the human body. Each node locally collects information and packs its information onto outgoing messages. The important point is that no extra communication mechanism is used and no explicit messages are generated to exchange the information for the self-organization.

The remainder of the paper is structured as follows: In section 2 the human hormone system is described from an abstract point of view with focus on the mechanisms that were transferred to the Artificial Hormone System. Related work is presented in section 3. The model of the Artificial Hormone System is described in section 4 and evaluated in section 5. The paper closes with a conclusion and future work.

2 Human Hormone System

The human body contains different systems for information transport, depending on the speed of the stimulus transportation and the size of the affected area. The central nervous system is used for fast information transport of consciously given commands whereas the autonomic nervous system and the hormone system are mostly detracted from human's will. Together they regulate the human body to keep the inner environment as constant as possible, called homoeostasis.

The human hormone system differs from the autonomic nervous system in the way information is transported. The autonomic nervous system uses electrical impulses, whereas the hormone system uses chemical messengers (hormones). Beside the mostly known way to spread hormones through the blood circuit to trigger reactions in other parts of the body, a number of other kinds of messengers are known, which do not influence our Artificial Hormone System and therefore are not described here (see [5], [6], and [7] for further details).

The hormones spread to the blood circuit can theoretically reach every cell, but only act on those cells which possess the corresponding receptors. The hormones bind to the receptors and send their information to the inside of the cell on a chemical basis. The usage of receptors has two advantages. First the binding of a hormone can be shortened to designated cells, and second the same hormone can lead to different effects within different cells.

The reaction of the cells is controlled by the distribution of the activator and inhibitor hormones. In many cases the production of activator hormones lead to the production of inhibitor hormones to neutralize the reaction of the cells. This mechanism is called a negative feed-back loop because of the repressive effect of the inhibitors.

3 Related Work

In 1952 Alan Turing published "The Chemical Basis of Morphogenesis" [8]. Inspired by an invertebrate freshwater animal called hydra, he investigated the mathematical foundations for the explanation of the chemical processes during a morphogenesis. The hydra has the remarkable feature, that if it is cut in half, the head end reconstitutes a new foot, while the basal portion regenerates a new hydranth with a mouth and tentacles. During this process the available cells are reformed, moved, and redifferentiated to build new tissue without cell proliferation. One of the application areas of Turing's reaction-diffusion model is the generation of textures as described in [9].

The Digital Hormone Model [10] adopts the idea of hormone diffusion to the distributed control of robot swarms. The equations investigated by Turing combined with the limited wireless communication capabilities of robots can be mapped to the reaction-diffusion model known from tissues. The information of a robot can diffuse to the neighboring robots in vicinity. Simulations showed that such a distributed control algorithm can be used to control a robot swarm to fulfill different tasks. The challenges were to find and size targets, to spread and monitor a region, and to detour obstacles during mission execution.

For peer-to-peer and sensor networks so called Bio-Inspired approaches are currently investigated. In [11] an approach for a self-organizing peer-to-peer system in terms of load balancing is described. The authors show by simulation, that only local knowledge and the distribution of local information to randomly chosen nodes are sufficient to balance the load of the nodes nearly optimal. For sensor networks an approach exists that mimics the control loop for the blood pressure of the human body [12]. Information is disseminated in the network like hormones in the human body and a feedback loop is used to decide whether the requested task is already accomplished.

4 Model of the Artificial Hormone System

The AHS consists of four parts that can be directly mapped to their human counterparts. First we have metrics to calculate a reaction (transfer of a service in our case), which can be compared to the functions of the cells. Second, the hormone producing tissues of the human body are influenced by receptors which observe the environment to trigger hormone production. This behavior is modeled by monitors which collect information locally about the running services and piggy-back this information onto outgoing messages. Third, monitors for incoming messages collect the piggy-backed information and hand them over to the metrics, which is the same as the receptors of the cells does. And fourth, the digital hormone values carrying the information.

To further reduce the amount of information needed to exchange, we assume that the digital hormone value enfolds both, the activator as well as the inhibitor hormone. If the value of the digital hormone is above a given level, it activates while a lower value inhibits the reaction.

The AHS will be included into the AMUN middleware to implement the self-optimization. The services can be relocated during runtime to meet the optimization criterion of the self-optimization as good as possible. Thus the model of the AHS must take some requirements into account given by AMUN. In AMUN services run on the nodes and can be transferred to other nodes. The services consume resources and the optimization should distribute the services such that the resource consumption on all nodes is nearly equal. Resources can be CPU, memory, communication bandwidth, battery status, radio range or any other resource suitable for the optimization of an application.

The idea of the AHS is to define the resources used for the optimization process and a corresponding digital hormone value. The model assumes that the values of the hormone values are normalized to fit into an interval from 0 to 100. The hormone value describes the consumption of a resource. In combination this can be interpreted that the hormone value represents the percentage consumption of a resource. As mentioned above these values are calculated by the monitors which observe the services in the middleware. In the model we have to define these values initially for the simulation process.

4.1 Mathematical Model

Given k resources, the consumption of resource i for service s is characterized by $r_i(s)$, $1 \leq i \leq k$, which is normalized such that all resources i satisfy the condition $0 \leq r_i(s) \leq 100$. The allocated amount of a resource i for all services $s \in \mathcal{S}(n)$ (the set of running services on node n) is computed as follows:

$$R_i(n) = \sum_{s \in \mathcal{S}(n)} r_i(s) \tag{1}$$

$R_i(n)$ is the total consumption of resource i of all services on node n. In our model the maximum capacity for each resource i on every node n is always 100. So any time the inequation $0 \leq R_i(n) \leq 100$ holds for all resources i and all nodes n. The number of services assigned to one node is limited by the nodes capacity and must not be violated by a service transfer.

To balance the load within the network it is assumed that services can be transferred from one node to another. The cost for the transfer to another node is modeled as the service transfer cost $tc(s)$, $0 \leq tc(s) \leq 100$ which can be different for every service.

Simulation initialization The initial state of our simulation model is chosen randomly to ensures that our optimization strategies are evaluated under a great variety of start conditions.

To initialize a node, a random maximum capacity value between 0 and c_{max} is chosen for every resource of the node. Then services are created with random values for each resource. The maximum value for c_{max} of a node and the resources $r_{i_{max}}$ of a service are defined prior to the initialization of the simulation. Services are generated as long as the maximum capacity of the node's resources are not exhausted as defined by equation 1. If a node is filled with services the procedure is repeated for the next node until all nodes are initialized. Regarding the mean value of the nodes resource consumption, this guarantees that for l nodes we generate a total load of $\approx l\frac{c_{max}}{2}$ randomly distributed on all nodes.

On the other hand this assures that the number of generated services differ from every initialization depending on the number of nodes, the maximum initial capacity of the nodes c_{max}, and the maximum values given for the service resource parameters $r_{i_{max}}$.

Service communication model As the digital hormone values are piggybacked on the outgoing communication, it is important to model the communication paths between the services. The communication model relies on the assumption that certain services prefer to communicate with each other while others don't. This behavior can be observed by many systems where the usage dependencies between different modules or classes are given due to the structure of the application and the resulting method calls.

Hence each service is assigned a constant set of other services acting as its communication partners. In each step of the simulation a given number of services are chosen to be senders and for each of these services s_{send} a receiving service s_{rec} is randomly picked out of their communication partners. Assuming that service s_{send} is running on node n_{send} and service s_{rec} is running on node n_{rec} the information necessary for the optimization is piggy-backed on the message sent from n_{send} to n_{rec}.

If there is a node which had no services assigned during the initialization, it could not participate in the optimization process thus loosing the free capacity of this node. In a networked system this situation might occur if a node was not present during the initial resource allocation phase. Such nodes will connect other nodes of the network sooner or later which is modeled by a certain probability to choose empty nodes as sender nodes n_{send}. As these nodes do not have a predetermined set of receivers a receiver node n_{rec} is randomly chosen out of all other nodes.

4.2 Transfer Strategies

In the optimization process node n_{send} adds information about its resource consumption to a message sent by one of its services to node n_{rec}. Based on this information node n_{rec} uses a *Transfer Strategie* (TS) to decide whether to transfer one of its services to n_{send} or not. To avoid confusion it should be mentioned that the terms n_{send} and n_{rec} refer to the direction of message passing. However, a service is transferred in the opposite direction from n_{rec} to n_{send}. In the following we present different Transfer Strategies from very simple to more sophisticated ones. All TS have in common that they only have local knowledge and those information received from its communication partners. Furthermore there is no central instance to control the optimization process. Only the simulation environment has the possibility to check the state of the nodes after every simulation step to produce evaluation output.

Weighted Transfer Strategy The first TS is called *Weighted Transfer Strategy* because it uses weights for every resource to weight them in the decision process. The load of all resources multiplied by the corresponding weights are added and divided by the total amount of the weights. This value is the load value of a node. If all weights are one, all resources are treated equally, if one resource is weighted higher than the others evaluations show that the higher weighted resource is optimized better at the expense of the others.

If the node n_{rec} got a message from node n_{send} it subtracts the load value of n_{send} from its own. If the result is positive this means that the sender has a lower load than this node and that a service might be transferred to the sender. If the result is equal or less than zero, nothing will be done, as the sender's load is already equal or higher than the local load. To find a service for the transfer the loads of all services are compared to the half of the load difference and the service with the minimal distance to that value will be chosen for the transfer, as it best adjusts the load values of both nodes.

Transfer Strategy with Dynamic Barrier This TS uses a barrier to suppress the transfer of services. Evaluations showed, that the Weighted Transfer Strategy produces a high amount of service transfers beyond the estimated value. The TS with Dynamic Barrier continuously calculates the gain that could be obtained if a service would have been transferred. The dynamic barrier rises if the gain falls and vice versa.

The barrier can be calculated with a linear, an exponential, and a logarithmic function, while the latter produces the best results in terms of responsiveness due to load changes and attenuation behavior.

Transfer Strategy with Load-Estimator The problem of the Weighted TS is the missing knowledge about the total system load. If every node would know the load of all other nodes the mean load could be calculated and every node could trigger or prevent transfers depending on the load of the receiver and the sender node. With this TS a node keeps the last n load values of its sender nodes and calculates a mean load value. A service will only be transferred, if the senders' load is below and the local load above this value. A transferred service would not only optimize the load between the two nodes but also the overall load of the system, which is not always the case with the Weighted TS.

The TS with Load-Estimator is the best TS in terms of required service relocations. It nearly reaches the calculated theoretical optimal value. The drawback of this Strategy is the missing tolerance to dynamic service behavior. If the services change their load dynamically the strategy tries to further optimize the system and thus produces unwanted service relocations. The same applies for the Weighted TS.

Hybrid Transfer Strategy The fourth TS combines the advantages of the TS with Load-Estimator and the TS with Dynamic Barrier. At the beginning of the optimization process only the TS with Load-Estimator is used. If the change of the calculated estimated load is less than 10% within two consecutive steps, the TS with Dynamic Barrier is used additionally which results in an attenuated transfer behavior especially in case of dynamically changing service loads.

5 Evaluation

To evaluate the self-organization of the AHS we developed a simulation environment in Java. For the simulations we chose three resource parameters for the optimization. The different TS were simulated and the service transfers and the mean error of the average resource consumption have been measured. The simulator uses steps to perform the calculation and produces output after every step. We ran every simulation with 1000 nodes and 2000 steps a 100 times to take into account different starting conditions due to the random initialization process of the simulator. Thus we can show that the TS are independent of the initialization and produce good and stable results.

5.1 Service Transfers

Figure 1 shows the amount of service transfers of the different Transfer Strategies and the mean error of the average resource consumption. The mean error is the mean difference of a node's resource consumption from the expectation of the resource consumption. This value shows how good the algorithm reaches the theoretical optimum. The charts show that all four TS achieve good optimization results with a mean error ranging from 0.62 to 1.47 with varying amounts of service transfers. The Weighted TS needs about 5300 transfers, the Dynamic Barrier 3000, the Load-Estimator needs about 2300, and the Hybrid TS uses about 1750 transfers after 2000 simulations steps.

The mean resource consumption of a node for the simulations was 41,25. The lowest mean error reached with the TS with Load-Estimator is 0,62. This means that the optimization achieves 98,5% of the theoretical optimum. The least service transfers are generated by the Hybrid TS which achieves a mean error of 1,47 resulting in an optimization quality of 96,5% of the theoretical optimum. The Hybrid TS offers the best trade-off between service transfers and optimization quality.

With the amount of produced services during the initialization phase and the mean error at the beginning of the simulation the theoretical amount of service transfers needed to optimize the network can be calculated. For the above simulations this value is about 2300 service transfers. This implies that the TS with Load-Estimator produces the best result with the least error and that the Hybrid TS does not utilize all transfers as the dynamic barrier suppresses those transfers with a low gain.

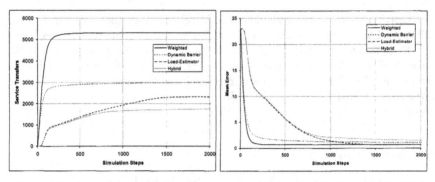

Fig. 1. Service transfers and the corresponding mean errors for the different TS.

Variation of Node Number To test the scalability of the systems we simulated networks with 100 to 5000 nodes. The number of services created is directly proportional to the number of nodes as expected from the initialization as described in section 4.1. Figure 2 shows that the service transfers increase only linear with the amount of nodes and services. The mean error remains nearly constant for all TS.

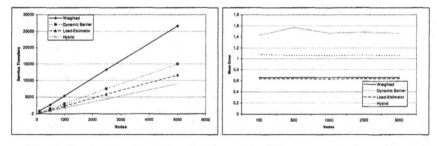

Fig. 2. Service transfers and mean error of the TS at varying node numbers.

Dynamic Services To evaluate the TS in a dynamic environment, we simulated a dynamic behavior of the services. Therefore a predefined amount of services change their resource consumption such that they raise or lower their resource consumption, hold that new value for a while and return to the initial value.

As expected the TS with Dynamic Barrier and the Hybrid TS tolerate the changes of the services' resource consumption while the other TS begin to oscillate resulting in a dramatic increase in service transfers. For both evaluations we defined 10% of the services to change their resource consumption up to 50% of the current value. The left chart of figure 3 shows the results if the change takes 10 simulation steps and 100 steps for the service to rest at its normal

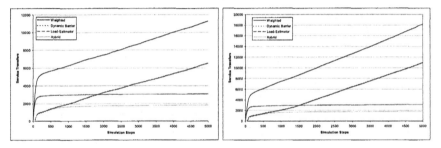

Fig. 3. Service transfers of the different TS with dynamic services.

level before the next change. The left chart shows the results for a 50 steps long change while the idle time is 100 steps which.

6 Conclusion and Future Work

In this paper we proposed the Artificial Hormone System for self-organization in networked systems. Derived from the human hormone system we developed a distributed algorithm that has neither a central control nor complete knowledge about the system. The organizational information is piggy-backed on top of the messages exchanged between the nodes of the networked system. The general approach of the AHS is described and implemented in a Java simulaton environment.

Evaluations showed that the AHS distributes services of networked nodes nearly optimal in terms of resource consumption and that the effort needed for larger networks increases only linear with the amount of nodes. Further evaluations regarding dynamic process behavior showed that the Hybrid Transfer Strategy tolerates load changes. The Hybrid Transfer Strategy is able to adapt the barrier to the mean load change, thus only few additional service transfers are produced due to dynamic process behavior.

Future work will be to implement and evaluate the AHS in AMUN and to further investigate the latencies produced by a service transfer and the corresponding costs for the optimization algorithm.

References

1. Horn, P.: Autonomic Computing: IBM's Perspective on the State of Information Technology. http://www.research.ibm.com/autonomic/ (2001)
2. VDE/ITG/GI: Organic Computing: Computer- und Systemarchitektur im Jahr 2010. http://www.gi-ev.de/download/VDE-ITG-GI-Positionspapier Organic Computing.pdf (2003)
3. et al., W.T.: AMUN - An Autonomic Middleware for the Smart Doorplate Project. In: UbiSys '04 - System Support for Ubiquitous Computing Workshop, Nottingham, England (2004)

4. Trumler, W., Bagci, F., Petzold, J., Ungerer, T.: Smart Doorplate. Personal and Ubiquitous Computing **7** (2003) 221–226

5. Silbernagl, S., Despopoulos, A.: Taschenatlas der Physiologie. Georg Thieme Verlag und Deutscher Taschenbuch Verlag, Stuttgart (2001)

6. Trepel, M.: Neuroanatomie Struktur und Funktion. Urban und Fischer Verlag, München,Jena (1999)

7. et al., F.H.: Biochemie des Menschen. Georg Thieme Verlag, Stuttgart (2002)

8. Turing, A.M.: The chemical basis of morphogenesis. In: Philosophical Trans. of the Royal Society of London. Volume 237 of Series B, Biological Sciences. (1952) 37–72

9. Witkin, A., Kass, M.: Reaction-diffusion textures. Computer Graphics **25** (1991) 299–308

10. Shen, W.M., Will, P., Galstyan, A., Chuong, C.M.: Hormone-inspired self-organization and distributed control of robotic swarms. Autonomous Robots **17** (2004) 93–105

11. et al., M.J.: A modular paradigm for building self-organizing peer-to-peer applications. In: Engineering Self-Organising Systems. Lecture Notes in Artificial Intelligence (2004) 265–282

12. et al., F.D.: Self-organization in sensor networks using bio-inspired mechanisms. In: ARCS'05: Workshop Self-Organization and Emergence. (2005) 139–144

A Biologically Motivated Computational Architecture Inspired in the Human Immunological System to Quantify Abnormal Behaviors to Detect Presence of Intruders

Omar U. Flórez-Choque[1] and Ernesto Cuadros-Vargas[2][3]

[1] Computer Science Department, National University of San Agustín. Arequipa, Perú. omarflorez19@gmail.com
[2] San Pablo Catholic University
[3] Peruvian Computer Society ecuadros@spc.org.pe

Abstract. In this article is presented a detection model of intruders by using an architecture based in agents that imitates the principal aspects of the Immunological System, such as detection and elimination of antigens in the human body. This model is based on the hypothesis of an intruder which is a strange element in the system, whereby can exist mechanisms able to detect their presence. We will use recognizer agents of intruders (*Lymphocytes-B*) for such goal and macrophage agents (*Lymphocytes-T*) for alerting and reacting actions.

The core of the system is based in *recognizing abnormal patterns of conduct* by agents (*Lymphocytes-B*), which will recognize anomalies in the behavior of the user, through a catalogue of Metrics that will allow us quantify the conduct of the user according to measures of behaviors and then we will apply *Statistic* and *Data Minig* technics to classify the conducts of the user in intruder or normal behavior. Our experiments suggest that both methods are complementary for this purpose. This approach was very flexible and customized in the practice for the needs of any particular system.

1 Introduction

Although the passwords, iris and retina readers as well as the digital signatures work well, a serious problem exists when these controls are overcome by stealing of the password, modification of the firmware or by stealing of the user's smart card. For intruders that masqueraded as valid users enter in the system and they carry out diverse actions that put in risk the integrity of the system [1]. Then, it arises the need of detecting those intruders, by knowing they have a different behavior pattern from the true user, with the result that it firstly is necessary to define a mechanism that allows us to measure each behavior of the user, so when comparing behaviors we will find a numeric value that allows to differ them.

Please use the following format when citing this chapter:

Florez-Choque, O.U., Cuadros-Vargas, E., 2006, in IFIP International Federation for Information Processing, Volume 216, Biologically Inspired Cooperative Computing, eds. Pan, Y., Rammig, F., Schmeck, H., Solar, M., (Boston: Springer), pp. 95–106.

In that sense it is admirable the way like the Immunologic System works. The Immunologic System is an important defensive system that has evolved in the vertebrate beings to protect them of microorganisms invaders (bacterias, virus, so on). In the moment when a wound appears, the white globules detect an antigen (intruder) in the human body through the sanguine torrent. Then appear two types of Lymphocytes among other agents, the *Lymphocyte-B* and the *Lymphocyte-T*. The Lymphocytes-B recognizes the antigen through proteins of complement (18 proteins that exist in the plasm and that are activated in a sequential way) and then these Lymphocytes produce Antibodies that can be able to face the identified intruding agent. The Lymphocyte-T is responsible for reactive functions destroying the strange substance, in view of each antibody is specific for each microorganism, the reaction of the Lymphocyte-T will vary according to the antigen recognized by the Lymphocytes-B.

It is remarkable the adaptability and the persistence of the information in the human body, since the white globules remember biochemically the analyzed antigen, so future answers will be quicker and more exact.

It is also interesting, and is the aim of this paper, to present the foundations of this mechanism of *detection and defense against intruders* toward a computational system.

The rest of this paper is organized as follows. In Section 2 is analyzed the architecture of the presented model by describing the hierarchical relationships between each one of the agents. In the Section 3 the functions of the used agents and their analogy with the Lymphocytes of the Human Immunologic System are described. In the Section 4 we define a catalog of metrics that will allow us to quantify the behavior of the user based on four behaviors: Effort, Memory, Trust and Special Requirements. In Section 5 we discuss the model of detection of intruders based on Statistical and Data Mining methods, which classify the vectors of behaviors in behaviors belonging to either intruders or normal users. In the Section 5 and 6 we discuss the obtained results. Section 7 briefly describes related works and specifies our contribution. And lastly, section 8 provides some conclusions.

2 Architecture of the model

The architecture is based on agents with different roles: Control-Reaction, Maintenance and Net, the model also includes databases that are organized in a distributed way.

According to the Figure 1, the *Control-Reaction Agents* are distinguished. They proactively read information of activity, find patterns and trigger alarms (through Lymphocytes-B) and they perform protection actions (through Lymphocytes-T). Besides, they control the use of resources wasted by the users, monitoring all their actions, in such a way this type of agents identifies profiles based on the account, resource and action that the user carried out. This type of agents are Lymphocytes-B and Lymphocytes-T.

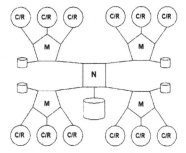

Fig. 1. Architecture of the Model based on agents

Then, we have the *Maintenance agents*, which create or delete Control-Reaction agents, and elimate redundant data, besides compression and local encoding of data is performed by this agent. This agent also maintains the database, where the profiles of activity and accounts of the users are stored, receiving the queries formulated by the Control-Reaction agents, execute them and return the results so that the Control-Reaction agents perform the necessary actions. There is one agent of this type for each authentication server because existis a single database inside this type of servers in the system. Lastly, the *Net Agent* creates or deletes Maintenance Agents. In view of this agent has a whole vision of network. It can detect other types of attacks, such as multi-host attack or *Denial for Service* (DOS), and besides it can realize the filter of packages on the net.

We use agents and not neural nets or other technology due to the heterogeneity presented in the problem: The *Lymphocytes-B* agents should learn that actions of the users change in the time and they should adapt their profiles according to these changes in view of each *Function of Behavior* is individual to each user. The *Lymphocytes-T* agents should learn how to trigger different security policies (resource denial, account elimination, lockout of account, restricted access) according to stored patterns of behavior. And the *Net agents* should learn how to recognize abnormal patterns of activity based on present information in the whole net to recognize multi-host distributed attacks . Therefore, when we use agents, we combine the necessity to use three great actors in the system.

3 Components of the architecture

3.1 Lymphocyte-B

These agents have the task of monitoring the actions of the user, identifying of this way the profiles, which store each action that the user carries out at one time in a certain resource. This information allows us to measure possible behavior changes in the account of the user and the later detection of an antigen in the system. It is possible to measure the behaviors of an user with metrics, which identify the behavior of the user in the system, according to this method a group of behaviors will define in a unique way the behavior of the user. Then, once obtained the vectors of user behaviors that began session, it is possible to compare the values of those vectors with the *Function of Behavior* of the user, and to foresee if there are abrupt variations in the behavior, which would reveal us an atypical and suspicious behavior, therefore the system will react.

The Lymphocyte-B agent has the particularity of requesting queries to the database that corresponds to it (there is one database for each authentication server), for example this agent requests information, creation, upgrading and elimination of profiles, but not carrying out them, for this, the Lymphocyte-B agent sends messages to the maintenance agents (wich are in charge of maintaining the database) and receives messages from agent of maintenance with the datasets of the query performed. In this type of agents, this information is necessary to be able to differ the behavior value calculated on relation to values of previous behaviors. For example, if the user gMoore@cisco.com usually uses its account to read information on internet, and then, in other session, the Lymphocyte-B agent monitors activities with a high usage of CPU due to compilation activities. It will compare this value with previous behaviors by formulating queries that will be executed in the database that stores the profiles and it will detect that this behavior changes is not normal, then the Lymphocyte-B will send a message to the corresponding agent so that it reacts because of this anomaly.

This mechanism resembles the recognition of a strange agent in the human body by the immunological system.

3.2 Lymphocyte-T

This type of agent has the task of reacting when an anomaly appears. Once detected the anomaly by the Lymphocyte-B agent, the Lymphocytes-T agent can give a message of alert, to expel the user, lockout the account, refuse an action to the user or ignore it depending on the case.

This mechanism resembles the reaction of the human body when a strange agent arises.

3.3 Maintenance Agent

This agent is the only agent allowed to manipulate the database, which stores the behavior information of each user. In fact, this agent executes the queries received from *Lymphocyte-B* and *Lymphocyte-T* agents to carry out them and returns datasets with the result of the query to the agent that requested it. If all the agents manipulated this database, the information would be outdated, and not synchronized, besides the traffic of net would be considerably increased since the use of the cache unit would be null. There is one *Maintenance* agent for each authentication server.

3.4 Net Agent

On the other hand, Mauro [2] filters all the packages of the net, so like a sniffer to read the headers of these packages and to see the executed command and starting from that to formulate the possible behavior of the user. This method has the advantage of not overloading the net considerably, however the presence of techniques of encryption could not make it appropiate, anyway, if this mechanism was implemented, this agent would be whom to implement it.

It is possible to take advantage of the geographic distribution of the system to achieve intrusion tolerance using the *fragmentation-redundancy-scattering* technique [3] by cutting all user sensitive data into fragments which are encrypted, stored and replicated among all the databases in the authentication servers. A high level of granularity in the data is obtained in view of several fragments together are not enough to disclose the information of the user. In fact, each *Lymphocyte-B* agent take a local decision to reject an intruder according changes on behavior which are locally stored, then this local decision is broadcasted to the other *Lymphocytes-B* agents and all the decisions, included the local decision, are locally voted and the rejection is locally trigged or not. This technique is called *majority voting* and ensures that false alarms can not be trigged.

4 The Vector of Behavior

If we want to transfer the mechanism of recognition of antigens, carried out by the Lymphocyte-B, by means of complement proteins toward a computational system we will need another mechanism that allows us to differ the intruders quantitatively since an user is a strange agent. In this article we propose a catalog of metrics that enables us to compare different user accounts independently of the operating system, programming language or implementation done, because they are based on changes of their behaviors.

Four behaviors of user can be identified in this discussion: *Effort*, *Memory*, *Trust* and *Special Requirements*. Each behavior reflects a great part of the way of behaving of the user into the system, for instance there will be user with great amount of work, user with low capacity of memory and users with special requierements like low display resolutions. Each aspects reflect a behavior of the user. This behavior is dynamic because it changea in the time. Therefore the total user behavior would be composed by a vector of behaviors, where each dimension of the vector is associated with a specific behavior.

Once we have all the dimensions from calculated behaviors, the value of behavior vector can be represented by a measure of distance to quantify the divergence among behaviors. Well known distances are Euclidean, Euclidean normalized, metric of Tchebycheff, Mahalanobis, and Tonimoto. We choose Euclidean distance because it exhibits some very interesting properties: it is variant to scale change and it depends on the relationships among the variables.

4.1 Behaviors

Effort This behavior reflects the quantity of work performed by an user, for example a high value of this behavior would mean that the user is using too much CPU time, maybe compiling a program, which in the worst case can be a *Troyan Horse* or a *port scanner*. Besides the user can be writing too much data on the hard disk, in the worst case it can reveal the presence of a virus in the System, on the other hand, if the user is producing plenty net traffic, it can reveal a typical DoS attack. Therefore, these aspects identify the quantity of effort of an user in the system. We show four metrics, which allow us to quantify this behavior:

1. $consumptionCPU = \frac{CPU\,time}{session}$
2. $readWriteDisk = \frac{Kbytes\,R/W\,in\,disk}{session}$
3. $trafficNet = \frac{Kbytes\,of\,data\,transferred\,in\,the\,net}{session}$
4. $durationSesion = Duration\,of\,the\,session$

Applying the *Euclidean distance*, the coefficients of the behavior of Effort are defined as:

$$Effort = \sqrt{consumptionCPU^2 + readWriteDisk^2 + trafficNet^2 + durationSesion^2} \qquad (1)$$

A considerable variation in the value of this behavior would involve that an user carries out activities that before he did not make which can be due to changes of departments, promotions in the work or the presence of an intruder masqueraded in the account. The system would detect this as an abnormal behavior for the user. A high value of this coefficient will also mean a great quantity of work carried out in the account of the user.

Memory This behavior reflects the amount of mistakes of the user due to the forgetfulness that he can experience, for instance the forgetfulness of the password, most of true users remember the password very well and they enter to the account in the first intent, however we should also consider elder users and, worse even, users with dyslexia that are not able to remember with easiness a password, in any way, this grade of forgetfulness defines an aspect of the behavior of the user.

We should also consider that when an intruder enters to the system, this intruder tries firstly to obtain information from the account by means of commands of information of the system [1], again, an average user will not need too much information about itself to begin to work normally. A similar case is when an user often uses a group of commands, while this user uses more this group of commands, less errors will happen when writing them, although we should consider users with low skill in the use of the keyboard and elder users with Parkinson disease [4].

Therefore we present three metric that qualify this behavior:

1. $wrongCommand = \frac{Commands\ written\ incorrectly}{session}$
2. $wrongLogin = \frac{Number\ of\ invalid\ logins}{session}$
3. $commandInformation = \frac{Number\ of\ times\ that\ information\ commands\ are\ executed}{session}$

Applying the *Euclidean distance*, the coefficients of the behavior of Memory are defined as:

$$Memory = \sqrt{wrongCommand^2 + wrongLogin^2 + commandInformation^2}$$
$$(2)$$

Trust This behavior reflects how reliable is an user in the system. There are users prone to be attacked [1], for example users that elect as password a word that is in the dictionary, without the use of uppercase, numbers or special characters; this makes the user to be not very reliable before a brute force attack. This is a subjective measure and we will say that a password with uppercase, numbers and special characters has a value of 0, an alphanumeric password has a value of 3 and a simple password has a value of 10. Then exist users that for curiosity or with purpose try to read, write or execute files and for obtaining information that does not correspond them, because they do not have the enough privileges to make it. Thereby, we can count the number of invalid accesses to define a feature of the user behavior that indicates if the user is not very reliable. Finally we can try to measure the fact that an user hides information through encryption of data. This last metric is relative, however most of hackers try to *hide their fingerprints* through encryption, so that the administrator of security can not examine the information that stores an account, although this fact is not so serious, however an excessive quantity of encrypted information is very suspicious.

Therefore, we present three metrics to quantify the trust of the system in a certain user:

1. invalidActions $= \frac{Number\ of\ invalid\ actions}{session}$
2. complexPassword = Complexity of password.
3. encryptedInformation = Amount of encrypted information stored in the account of a user.

Applying the *Euclidean distance*, the coefficients of the behavior of the Trust are defined as:

$$Trust = \sqrt{invalidActions^2 + complexPassword^2 + encryptedInformation^2}$$
$$(3)$$

Special Requirements This behavior reflects special needs that the user requires of the system, for example if an user is always connected by modem and then suddenly carries out a connection by wireless devices, this change of behavior appears suspicious for the system, then we assign a value of 0 if the connection is carried out on intranet, 3 if it is carried out by modem and 10 if it is carried out by wireless connection. It is also necessary to identify those users that are not authenticated by means of common mechanisms as their password, but through special devices as iris or retina readers, detection of faces, digital certificates, touch sensitive screens and so on. Whereby, if in the authentication process the password is introduced by keyboard, the values of 0 is assigned to this metric. If digital certificates are used, it is assigned a value of 3 and 10 in other cases. However we would keep in mind the possibility that an user changes the type of authentication, among other reasons the user suffers some temporary or permanent disability, for example, blindness which prevents to use iris readers, in this case the administrator would receive many warnings indicating a suspicious change of behavior. Lastly, we will try to quantify the fact that the user uses requirements of accessibility to work normally in the system [4]. Users without superior extremities will have difficulty to use the keyboard, for this is required a virtual keyboard on the screen, on the other hand users with astigmatism, myopia or permanent blindness require a magnificator screen, or a screen reader respectively. Then if an intruder changes these options, clearly it implies a change in the behavior of the user. This way if the user does not use any requirement of accessibility, a values of 0 is assigned to this coefficient, a value of 10 is assigned in other cases.

Then, we present three metrics to try to quantify special necessities of an user:

1. $typeConnection = Type\ of\ connection\ to\ the\ system.$
2. $typeAuthentication = Type\ of\ authentication.$
3. $reqAccessibility = Requirements\ of\ Accessibility.$

Applying the *Euclidean distance*, the coefficients of the behavior of the Trust are defined as:

$$\text{Special Requirements} = \sqrt{\text{typeConnection}^2 + \text{typeAuthentication}^2 + \text{reqAccessibility}^2} \quad (4)$$

5 Experimental results

We estimate our results over 200 registers, each register stores a behavior vector. We will use this method *5-fold cross validation* to estimate accuracy. The crossed validation is the standard method to estimate predictions on test data for Data Mining and Neural Nets [5]. We split the total of registers in 5 groups of same size. We use 4 groups for the training of the model (Training Set) and the remaining one for the evaluation of the model(Test Set), then we repeat the process 5 times leaving-one-out different partition in each cycle as test group. This procedure gives us a very reliable measure of accuracy of the model. Then we average the result of these 5 groups to recognize how the model was executed over the whole data. Then, we will use the *ROC curves* (Receiver Operating

Characteristics) to visualize the accuracy in the classification, the ROC curves are commonly used in the medicine for taking of clinical decisions and in recent years have been increasingly adopted by the communities of investigators of Data Mining and Learning Machines [6].

Given a classifier and one group of instances, there are 4 possible states in which the instance can be classified:

- True Positive (TP).- Intruder that is classified as Intruder by the system.
- True Negative (TN).- Normal User that is classified as Normal User by the system.
- False Positive (FP).- Normal User that is classified as Intruder by the system.
- False Negative (FN).- Intruder that is classified as Normal User by the system.

We are interested in the *rate of Intruders* detected by the model (*True Positive*) and in the rate of *"false alarms"* or Normal Users that are classified as Intruders (*False Positive*). To build the ROC curves we are interested in the following metrics:

- The rate of detected intruders: $\frac{PV}{TP+FN}$
- The rate of false alarms: $\frac{PF}{FP+TN}$
- The global accuracy: $\frac{TP+TN}{TP+TN+FP+FN}$

The results of the experiments are summarized in the Table 1.

Table 1. These are the results of classifying the behaviors of the user in the account gMoore@cisco.com organized by the type of used classifier. In spite of the method of Deviation Standard had the smallest rate of false alarms and the highest rate in Detection of Intruders, the method of Decision Trees detected different registers belong to *"true intruders"* which had not been detected by the Deviation Standard method.

Classifier	Deviation standard	Decision trees
True positive (TP)	77	68
True negative (TN)	73	61
False positive (FP) (PF)	7	14
False negatives (FN)	3	7
% Detection of Intruders	96.25 %	80.00 %
% False alarms	4.75 %	18.67 %
% Total accuracy	93.75 %	80.63 %

6 Discussion

Both considered approaches (Standard deviation, Decision trees) works very well in the detection of intruders, in spite of Decision trees had a lower value than Standard deviation, it detected different registers from intruders that those detected by Standard Deviation. This suggests that both classifiers can be mixed to define a stable and reliable method to implement intrusion detection schemes.

6.1 Statistic

In the Figure 2, we visualize the accuracy in the detection of intruders through techniques of Statistic and Data Mining. Both ROC curves are concave therefore they have a good exchange between detection and false alarms rates.

The classifier based in techniques of Statistic obtained the highest rate of *detection of intruder* due to this method is based in more recent behaviors of the user. Besides it adjusts by itself in the time in a learning way, based in the tendency of the behavior function in the time. This method also had the highest *global accuracy rate.*

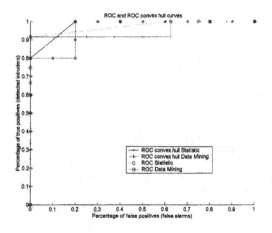

Fig. 2. ROC curves for the models of detection of intruders based on Statistical and Data Mining methods. Notice that curves generated by Deviation Standard have a higher detection of intruders rate regarding the curves generated by Decision Trees, although they intersect in a percentage of 92% in the detection of intruders for a percentage of false alarms of 14%.

6.2 Data Mining

The model of detection of intruder based on decision trees had the higher false alarm rate. In spite of having 80% in the *detection of intruders rate* the difference regarding the model based on Deviation Standard was 14%. The two models intersect in a *false alarms rate* of 14% with a *detection of intruders rate* of up to 90%.

7 Related works

An alternative approach is taken by Forrest et al. [7], who is focused to determinate normal behaviors for privileged process, that is, process that run as root (*sendmail* and *lpr*). However in this model is difficult to detect an intruder is masquerading as another user because of this approach is based in low level features (ports, system calls, processes). Our approach rely on more meaningful features (Effort, Memory, Trust and Special Requirements), which identify more exactly the behavior of the user into the system. These features are inherent to the user, therefore an user can not forget them and a intruder can not guess them. Besides we tried to emulate an architecture inspired in the principal functions of the Human Immulogical System through lymphocytes (B and T).

8 Conclusions

We believe the proposed model provides a base to implement a system capable to recognize intruders according to behaviors of the owner of the account, in that sense, we believe that an intruder can guess the *password* of an user, but difficultly , will be able to guess the *behavior* of the user. We showed that the model based on statistical techniques had the higher detection of intruders rate, 96.25%. Although the model based in techniques of Data Mining had the higher false alarm rate, 18.67%. Therefore we recommend mix both methods, these data can help to decide an security administrator to use one of the models or both, according the specific necessity of security. For example in an critic security environment, is more important to have a high grade of detection of intruders. On the other hand, in mail servers can be more important the availability of the service, in spite of this service do not be so exact, thereby a rate of false alarms of 18.67% can be acceptable.

Acknowledgements

The author wants to thank very especially the teachings and advices from the teachers of the National University of San Agustín at Arequipa Dr. Ernesto Cuadros-Vargas and Dr. Luis Alfaro Casas. Besides, I would like to express my deep gratitude to Dr. Rosa Alarcón Choque, University of Chile at Santiago, for her invaluable encourage.

References

1. K. Mitnick. The Art of Deception. *Wiley.* December, 2002.
2. A. Mauro. Adaptative Intrusion Detection System using Neural Networks. Conference of ACME! Computer Security Labs. November, 2002.

3. Y. Deswarte, L. Blain, and J. C. Fabre. Intrusion tolerance in distributed computing systems. In Proc. Symp. on Research in Security and Privacy, pp. 110-121,
   Oakland, CA, USA. 1991. IEEE Computer Society Press.
4. S. Burgstahler, Sheryl. Working Together: People with Disabilities and Computer. University of Washington. DO-IT. 2002.
5. R. Kohavi. A study of cross-validation and bootstrap for accuracy estimation and
   model selection. IJCAI. 1995.
6. T. Fawcett. ROC graphs : Notes and practical considerations for researchers.
   Technical report, HP Laboratories, MS 1143, 1501 Page Mill Road, Palo Alto
   CA 94304, USA. 2004.
7. S. Forrest, S. A. Hofmeyr. A. Somayaji, and T. A. Longstaff. A sense of self for
   Unix processes. In Proceedings of 1996 IEEE Symposium on Computer Security
   and Privacy, pp. 120-128 (1996).

Error Detection Techniques Applicable in an Architecture Framework and Design Methodology for Autonomic SoCs*

Abdelmajid Bouajila[1], Andreas Bernauer[2], Andreas Herkersdorf[1], Wolfgang Rosenstiel[2,3], Oliver Bringmann[3], and Walter Stechele[1]

[1] Technical University of Munich, Institute for Integrated Systems, Germany
[2] University of Tuebingen, Department of Computer Engineering, Germany
[3] FZI, Microelectronic System Design, Karlsruhe, Germany

Abstract. This work-in-progress paper surveys error detection techniques for transient, timing, permanent and logical errors in system-on-chip (SoC) design and discusses their applicability in the design of monitors for our Autonomic SoC architecture framework. These monitors will be needed to deliver necessary signals to achieve fault-tolerance, self-healing and self-calibration in our Autonomic SoC architecture. The framework combines the monitors with a well-tailored design methodology that explores how the Autonomic SoC (ASoC) can cope with malfunctioning subcomponents.

1 Introduction

CMOS technology evolution leads to ever complex integrated circuits with nanometer scale transistor devices and ever lower supply voltages. These devices operate on ever smaller charges. Therefore, future integrated circuits will become more sensitive to statistical manufacturing/environmental variations and external radiation causing so-called soft-errors. Overall, these trends result in a severe reliability challenge for future ICs that must be tackled in addition to the already well-known complexity challenges. The conservative worst case design and test approach will no longer be feasible and should be replaced by new design methods. Avizienis [1] suggested integrating biology-inspired concepts into the IC design process as a promising alternative to today's design flow with the objective to obtain higher reliability while still meeting area/performance/power requirements. Section 2 of the paper presents an Autonomic SoC (ASoC) architecture framework and design method which addresses and optimizes all of the above mentioned requirements. Section 3 surveys existing error detection techniques that may be used in our Autonomic SoC. Section 4 discusses implications on the ASoC design method and tools before section 5 closes with some conclusions.

* This work is funded by DFG within the priority program 1183 "Organic Computing".

Please use the following format when citing this chapter:

Bouajila, A., Bernauer, A., Herkersdorf, A., Rosenstiel, W., Bringmann, O., Stechele, W.,2006, in IFIP International Federation for Information Processing, Volume 216, Biologically Inspired Cooperative Computing, eds. Pan, Y., Rammig, F., Schmeck, H., Solar, M., (Boston: Springer), pp. 107–113.

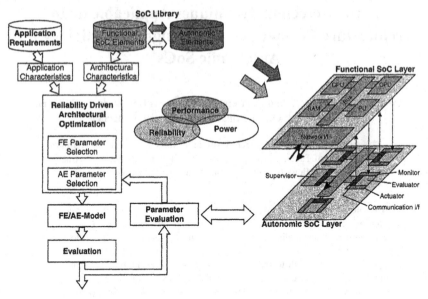

Fig. 1. Autonomic SoC design method and architecture [2]

2 Autonomic SoC Architecture and design method

Figure 1 [2] shows the proposed ASoC architecture platform. The ASoC is split into two logical layers: The functional layer contains the intellectual property (IP) components or Functional Elements (FEs), e.g. general purpose CPUs and memories, as in a conventional, non-autonomic design. The autonomic layer consists of interconnected Autonomic Elements (AEs), which in analogy to the IP library of the functional layer shall eventually represent an autonomic IP library (AE_lib). At this point in time, it is not known yet whether there will be an AE for each FE, or whether there will be one AE supporting a class of FEs.

Each AE contains a monitor or observer section, an evaluator and an actuator. The monitor senses signals or states from the associated FE. The evaluator merges and processes the locally obtained information originating from other AEs and/or memorized knowledge. The actuator executes a possibly necessary action on the local FE. The combined evaluator and actuator can also be considered as a controller. Hence, our two-layer Autonomic SoC architecture platform can be viewed as a distributed (decentralized) observer-controller architecture. AEs and FEs form closed control loops which can autonomously alter the behavior or availability of resources on the functional layer. Control over clock and supply voltage of redundant macros can provision additional processing performance or replace on-the-fly a faulty macro with a "cool" stand-by alternative.

Although organic enabling of next generation standard IC and ASIC devices represents a major conceptual shift in IC design, the proposed ASoC platform represents a natural evolution of today's SoCs. In fact, we advocate to reuse cores as they are and to augment them with corresponding AEs.

In order to study the feasibility of our ASoC framework, we already started looking in-depth into how to design such SoCs. We adopted a bottom-up approach in which we design autonomic building blocks and connect them to build an Autonomic SoC. The ultimate objective is to understand how to form an Autonomic IP library and, thus, how to design Autonomic SoCs in a systematic and well-established top-down design flow.

3 Existent CPU concurrent error detection techniques

The human body needs to sense the state of its different organs, e.g. pain or temperature, to let the immune system handle the problem or to try to ask for external help, e.g. medicines [1]. In analogy to the human body, the SoC needs to detect errors for example to allow a CPU to re-execute an instruction or to ask for a replacement CPU.

There are three main concurrent error detection techniques: hardware redundancy, information redundancy and time redundancy. In our survey, the efficiency of each technique is measured by 1) how many different types of errors can be detected (so we need to define a fault model and then to evaluate the fault coverage), 2) how much overhead (in terms of area, performance and power) the concurrent error detection technique induces, and 3) how feasible IP-reuse is, i.e. is it possible to achieve error detection in an already existent CPU by adding a separate monitor?

In [3], an (extended) fault model classification is presented. In fault-tolerant integrated circuits literature, faults are usually classified as permanent [4, 5], timing [6], transient [7] or design (logic) errors. The most widely used fault model is the single error fault, in which different errors don't occur simultaneously. The fault coverage [3] of a detection technique is given for a specific fault model. Fault coverage is either given by analytical (formal) methods or by simulation.

A. Hardware redundancy techniques: Hardware redundancy has good fault coverage (transient, timing and permanent errors). However, the area and power overheads are big. In the particular case of duplication, the monitor will be the duplicated circuit and the comparator. In spite of its big overheads, we could use this technique in our ASoC project because the percentage of logic parts in modern SoCs is less than 20%.

B. Information redundancy techniques: There are two different approaches using information redundancy. The first approach synthesizes HDL descriptions [4] to generate so-called path fault-secure circuits. The second approach tries to build self-checking arithmetic operators to achieve the fault-secure property [5]. The main drawback of the first approach towards our ASoC framework is the difficulty in separating between the functional and autonomic layers. Self-checking designs give fault-secure arithmetic operators for stuck-at faults (permanent faults) with low area overhead but their use requires redesigning existing IP-libraries.

C. Time redundancy technique: The time redundancy technique was proposed to detect transient errors. Transient errors can be modeled by SEU (Single Event Upset) and SET (Single Event Transient) [8].

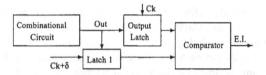

Fig. 2. Time redundancy technique [7]

The idea of Nicolaidis [7] is to benefit from the fact that a transient error will occur only for a short duration. Hence, if we sample a primary output at two successive instants separated by a duration larger than that of the SET pulse, we will be able—in theory—to detect all SETs. Figure 2 presents this scheme.

Simulations [9] on adders and multipliers showed that this scheme detects around 99% of SETs (an SET can escape from detection because of reconvergent paths). It also detects SEUs and timing errors. The area overhead depends on the circuit area per output parameter. Razor, a similar time redundancy technique for detection and correction of timing errors was suggested in [6].

These time redundancy techniques are very interesting for our ASoC framework and could be integrated in a systematic way to protect circuits against transient and timing errors. Also, the separation between the functional and autonomic layer is quite simple; for instance the monitor for Nicolaidis scheme (Fig. 2) will include the extra latch and the comparator.

D. Combination of Hardware and Time Redundancy: The Dynamic Implementation Verification Architecture (DIVA) [10] incorporates a concurrent error detection technique to protect CPUs. We can classify it either as a time redundancy and/or a hardware redundancy technique. The baseline DIVA architecture (Fig. 3a) consists of a (complex) processor without its commit stage (called DIVA core) followed by a checker processor (which consists of CHKcomp and CHKcomm pipelines, called DIVA checker) and the commit stage.

The DIVA checker checks every instruction by investigating in parallel (Fig. 3a) the operands (re-reading them)and the computation by re-executing the instruction. In case of an error, the DIVA checker, which is assumed to be simple and reliable, will fix the instruction, flush the DIVA core and restart it at the next program counter location. Physical implementation of a DIVA checker has an overhead of about 6% for area and 5% for power [11].

We believe that in very deep sub-micron technologies a checker which is reliable enough is difficult to achieve and could also result in a large area overhead. We suggest a modified version of DIVA in which both the DIVA core and checker re-execute an errant instruction, so that the checker no longer needs to be reliable.

The modified DIVA (Fig. 3b) only checks the CPU computation and protects the DIVA core/memory interface and the register file with error correcting codes (ECC). Therefore, the DIVA checker no longer needs to access the register file and data cache, eliminating structural hazards between the DIVA core and checker. The fault coverage of both DIVA versions includes transient, timing, permanent and logic errors. In both DIVA versions, it is mandatory that the error rate is bounded not to decrease perfor-

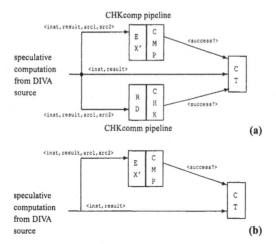

Fig. 3. DIVA architecture. (a) Baseline DIVA architecture [10], (b) Modified DIVA architecture

mance. DIVA cannot be inserted in a systematic way to protect existent CPUs because there are no standards in designing CPUs. Hence, a designer should study the CPU architecture and implementation and then separate the commit stage to be able to insert the DIVA checker. Nevertheless, we should mention that the separation between the functional layer and the autonomic layer is clear (the DIVA checker is the monitor). Also, DIVA enables us to re-use existent CPUs by identifying their commit stage.

We decided to use the modified version of DIVA to build autonomic CPUs because it allows us to separate functional and autonomic layers, permits IP-reuse and has the best fault coverage when compared to other detection techniques: it detects transient, timing, permanent and logic errors with a fault coverage close to 100%. The drawbacks of the other techniques are either big overheads (duplication, path fault-secure circuits), limited fault coverage (transient and timing-error detection oriented techniques (Nicolaidis and Razor), or restrictions to just stuck-at detection (Self-checking designs)).

4 Design Methodology and architecture for ASoC

A successful design of Autonomic SoCs needs a well-tailored design methodology that explores the effect of the AEs to cope with malfunctioning subcomponents. Our ASoC design methodology (Fig. 1) follows the established platform-based design approach, where a predefined platform consisting of a set of architectural templates is optimized for a given application with respect to several design constraints like area, performance and power consumption. In the context of this paper, the traditional process is extended by adding the autonomic layer to the platform model and considering reliability as an additional parameter. Therefore, the evaluation process now has to deal with the effects of the AEs—which include algorithms to support self-optimization—as well as with the AEs' relationship to system reliability. The evaluation process results in an optimized set of FE/AE parameters including provision of an a priori knowledge for the evaluators at the autonomic layer.

The design methodology will decide where and how many of the aforementioned error detection units the ASoC will need to meet the application's reliability requirements. The error detection units will be part of the AE_lib.

As the resulting ASoC will be able to change parts of its design during run time it will need design time information. In particular, the ASoC will need a priori knowledge about the application's behavior when an error occurs and, more importantly, about how the system has to self-modify to handle the error. The design methodology will gather this knowledge by injecting errors according to the error model into the application and architecture model and analyzing the consequences. The knowledge will be implemented distributed over the AEs in a self-organizing algorithm.

However, it won't be feasible to explore for all possible combinations of errors. For the explored error situations the self-organizing algorithm can react as given by the a priori knowledge. For the unexplored error situations it must be able to derive applicable measures but still meet the application constraints like temperature, timing and power consumption. The XCS classifier system presented by Wilson et al. [12] is capable to do this.

Registers attached to the error detection units will count the detected and corrected errors within a sliding time interval. When the counter exceeds some threshold, the self-organizing algorithm will take the necessary measures to correct for the error. It is also possible to provide a way to make the reliability information accessible to the application. With this, not only the hardware but also the application can adapt to varying reliabilities of some components, e.g. by rescheduling tasks to some more reliable CPU.

5 Conclusions and Outlook

This paper presented an Autonomic SoC architecture framework and design method. We are going to build an Autonomic CPU based on the LEON processor [13]. This will help us to evaluate the design effort, overheads and the gain of reliability achieved by our method. Later, we will build autonomic memory and autonomic interconnect; the ultimate objective is to get an ASoC architecture and design method integrating biology-inspired concepts.

References

1. A. Avizienis, Toward Systematic Design of Fault-Tolerant Systems, *IEEE Computer* **30**(4), 51–58 (1997).
2. G. Lipsa, A. Herkersdorf, W. Rosenstiel, O. Bringmann and W. Stechele, Towards a Framework and a Design Methodology for Autonomic SoC, in: 2nd ICAC (2005).

3. A. Avizienis, J.-C. Laprie, B. Randell and C. Landwehr, Basic Concepts and Taxonomy of Dependable and Secure Computing, *IEEE Trans. on Dependable and Secure Computing* **1**(1) (2004).

4. N. Touba and E. McCluskey, Logic Synthesis of Multilevel Circuits with Concurrent Error Detection, *IEEE Trans. CAD* **16**(7), 783–789 (1997).

5. M. Nicolaidis, Efficient Implementations of Self-Checking Adders and ALUs, in: Proc. 23rd Intl. Symp. Fault-Tolerant Computing, pp. 586–595 (1993).

6. D. Ernst, N. S. Kim, S. Das, S. Pant, T. Pham, R. Rao, C. Ziesler, D. Blaauw, T. Austin, T. Mudge and K. Flautner, Razor: A Low-Power Pipeline Based on Circuit-Level Timing Speculation, in: Proc. 36th Intl. Symp. Microarch., pp. 7–18 (2003).

7. M. Nicolaidis, Time Redundancy Based Soft-Error Tolerance to Rescue Nanometer Technologies, in: Proc. 17th IEEE VLSI Test Symposium, pp. 86–94 (1999).

8. S. Mitra, N. Seifert, M. Zhang, Q. Shi and K. S. Kim, Robust System Design with Built-In Soft-Error Resilience, *IEEE Computer* **38**(2), 43–52 (2005).

9. L. Anghel and M. Nicolaidis, Cost Reduction and Evaluation of a Temporary Faults Detecting Technique, in: Proc. DATE, pp. 591–598 (2000).

10. T. M. Austin, DIVA: A Dynamic Approach to Microprocessor Design, *Journal of Instruction-Level Parallelism* **2**, 1–6 (2000).

11. C. Weaver and T. Austin, A Fault Tolerant Approach to Microprocessor Design, in: Proc. Intl. Conf. Dependable Systems and Networks, pp. 411–420 (2001).

12. S. W. Wilson, Classifier Fitness Based on Accuracy, *Evolutionary Computation* **3**(2), 149–175 (1995).

13. LEON VHDL code is available at www.gaisler.com.

A Reconfigurable Ethernet Switch for Self-Optimizing Communication Systems

Björn Griese and Mario Porrmann
Heinz Nixdorf Institute and Institute of Electrical Engineering and
Information Technology
University of Paderborn, Germany
{bgriese, porrmann}@hni.upb.de

Abstract. Self-optimization is a promising approach to cope with the increasing complexity of today's automation networks. The high complexity is mainly caused by a rising amount of network nodes and increasing real-time requirements. Dynamic hardware reconfiguration is a key technology for self-optimizing systems, enabling, e.g., Real-Time Communication Systems (RCOS) that adapt to varying requirements at runtime. Concerning dynamic reconfiguration of an RCOS, an important requirement is to maintain connections and to support time-constrained communication during reconfiguration. We have developed a dynamically reconfigurable Ethernet switch, which is the main building block of a prototypic implementation of an RCOS network node. Three methods for reconfiguring the Ethernet switch without packet loss are presented. A prototypical implementation of one method is described and analyzed in respect to performance and resource efficiency.

1 Introduction

A prerequisite for the realization of self-optimizing systems is the availability of a hardware infrastructure that is able to adapt to changing application demands at runtime. Traditionally, embedded real-time systems have been designed in a static manner for pre-assigned hardware platforms [1]. The hardware in these systems is fixed and flexibility is only provided by software. In contrast to this we use dynamically reconfigurable hardware, which offers an additional degree of flexibility due to its ability to change the hardware structure at runtime [2]. In the context of dynamically reconfigurable real-time systems [3] new methods have to be developed to meet the real-time requirements in particular during the reconfiguration process.

This work was developed in the course of the Collaborative Research Center 614 – Self-optimizing Concepts and Structures in Mechanical Engineering – University of Paderborn, and was published on its behalf and funded by the Deutsche Forschungsgemeinschaft.

Please use the following format when citing this chapter:

Griese, B., Porrmann, M., 2006, in IFIP International Federation for Information Processing, Volume 216, Biologically Inspired Cooperative Computing, eds. Pan, Y., Rammig, F., Schmeck, H., Solar, M., (Boston: Springer), pp. 115–124.

In this paper we introduce reconfiguration methods for a Real-Time Communication System (RCOS). Our aim is to develop an RCOS for self-optimizing mechatronic systems that efficiently uses the available hardware resources. Self-optimizing systems are able to adapt automatically to dynamically changing environments and user requirements. For an efficient use of the resources, the tasks that control the actors and observe the sensors are distributed to appropriate computing nodes of the system. As a consequence, the real-time requirements and the communication requirements vary as the distribution of tasks changes in the considered mechatronic systems. In order to enable the adaptation to changing environments reconfiguration from the application level down to the hardware level is a required key technology.

The basis of our RCOS is formed by network nodes that allow setting up line and ring topologies. Each node consists of at least two network interfaces that connect the node to its neighbors and to an embedded processor. In order to be able to adapt the network nodes to changes in protocols and interface requirements, which can not be foreseen, we use an FPGA for the implementation of the network interfaces. The architecture of the reconfigurable RCOS network node is shown in Fig. 1.

The RCOS node handles two different types of data streams: data originated from or terminated at the processor and streams that are simply passed through. If network traffic is rather small or if real-time requirements are low or even nonexistent, comparatively simple network interfaces are sufficient, which occupy only a few resources. In this case, data packets are forwarded from one port to another by a software implementation on the embedded processor. This causes a high load for the processor, the internal bus and the memory while the FPGA resources can be utilized by other applications. If the software implementation is not able to deliver the required performance, e.g., due to increasing bandwidth or real-time requirements, the two separate interfaces are substituted by a single integrated hardware switch during runtime. This switch is able to forward data packets autonomously and, as a consequence, manages a much higher amount of traffic. However, the structure of this switch is more complex and requires additional FPGA resources, which are no longer available for other applications.

The idea to use reconfigurable logic for the integration of network applications into the network interface has been realized, e.g., by Underwood et al. [4]. Comparable network interfaces have been used for server and network applications, e.g., web servers, firewalls [5], and virus protection [6]. If the RCOS is implemented in an FPGA, packets that are stored in the active switch implementation may be lost if the switch is overwritten with a new one. Real-time requirements can only be supported if no packet loss is caused by the reconfiguration process. Therefore, three methods for the reconfiguration of RCOS network nodes without packet loss will be introduced in Section 2. Prerequisites for these methods are a packet based communication protocol and the possibility to implement both the software switch and the hardware switch simultaneously on the FPGA during reconfiguration. The RCOS network node is prototypically implemented by a dual-port Ethernet switch. Switched Ethernet technology is commonly used in real-time communication networks in the area of industrial automation, e. g., Industrial Ethernet [7] and PROFINET [8].

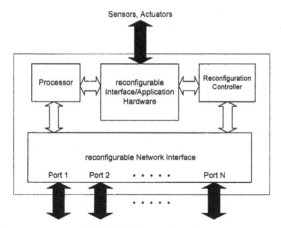

Fig. 1. RCOS network node

A prototypical implementation of our switch has been realized with our RAPTOR2000 System, a Rapid Prototyping System developed at the System and Circuit Technology research group at the University of Paderborn [9]. Xilinx Virtex-II Pro FPGAs are used, which comprise two embedded PowerPC processors in addition to fine-grained reconfigurable hardware resources. The Ethernet switch is implemented either in software or in hardware, as detailed in Section 3. For the prototypical implementation, the reconfiguration is triggered by the network load, which is continuously measured.

2 Strategies for Reconfiguration

The basic principles of dynamic reconfiguration of network interfaces without packet loss have been presented in [4]. Based on this theoretical approach, we present three reconfiguration methods and analyze their practical relevance. To avoid packet loss for all of the three alternatives, both the software switch and the hardware switch have to be active during reconfiguration in order to maintain connections to neighboring nodes. Furthermore, the transmit and receive processes have to be switched separately. As depicted in Fig. 2 the access to the shared Media Independent Interface (MII) is controlled by a hardware multiplexer. If currently no Ethernet packet is received the hardware switch is allowed to switch over the ports from one switch to the other switch. Hence, we use the Inter-Frame Gap (IFG) of the Ethernet protocol to hand over interface control.

In our first approach, the hardware multiplexer immediately switches the signals of the receive process to the "new" configuration if the reconfiguration is started within an IFG. Subsequently, received Ethernet packets are written into the receive buffers of the "new" configuration. Ethernet packets, which are still in the "old" configuration, must be copied to the transmit buffers in the "new" configuration to terminate the reconfiguration of the receive process.

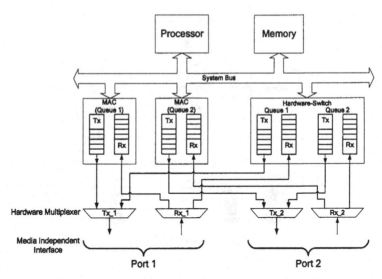

Fig. 2. Architecture of the reconfigurable switch

The transmit process of the "old" reconfiguration transmits all Ethernet packets residing in the send buffer before the hardware multiplexer can switch over the transmit signals. Due to the Ethernet standard, the transmit process has to keep a minimal IFG between two packets, even during the reconfiguration process. Therefore, the duration of a minimal IFG must elapse since the last transmission of a packet, before the signals are switched to the "new" configuration.

A rearrangement of the packet sequence can occur, if the hardware switch forwards a "new" packet before the copy operation from the software switch is finished. But the benefit of this method is a fast activation of packet forwarding by the hardware switch. Hence, no buffer overflow can occur during reconfiguration.

An alternative reconfiguration method is to forward the packets stored in the receive buffer of the "old" configuration to the transmit buffer of the "old" configuration by software. New arriving packets are directed to the hardware switch. The hardware multiplexer switches the transmit signals only when both the receive buffers and the transmit buffers become empty. Concerning the reconfiguration speed, this method is equal to the method described above, because only the write destination has changed. This method has a drawback if the processor is not able to forward all packets with the maximum data rate. The switching of the transmit signals to the "new" configuration is delayed by the copy operation. In this case, the hardware switch is not able to forward new arriving packets, because the transmit signals are still blocked. The risk of a buffer overflow in the hardware switch is present. Larger receive buffers can compensate for this risk. The advantage of this method is that no rearrangement of the packet sequence can occur. As a third alternative, the transmit signals can be switched immediately to the "new" configuration. Therefore, the processor move the content of the transmit buffer of the software switch to the transmit buffer of the hardware switch. This method allows a fast activation of the transmit process of the "new" configuration. The processor has to verify if receive and transmit buffers are empty. If necessary, the processor copies the packets to the corresponding transmit buffers, requiring additional processing time. The processor has to flush the transmit buffers first, to avoid a rearrangement of the packet sequence. In contrast to the second method that has been described, a rearrangement during the reconfiguration process is possible in this approach. Using this method, no status information must be given to the hardware multiplexer, e.g., no information about the receive and transmit buffer status is required. As described above, the reconfiguration process is finished when the reconfiguration of both receive and transmit processes is accomplished. Maintaining the original packet sequence cannot be guaranteed with the first and with the last presented reconfiguration method. This does not mean that the second method is the only possible solution, but the other methods require packet numbering and reordering functions. The first method allows for a fast activation of the hardware switch, but a rearrangement of the packet sequence is possible. The second method avoids a rearrangement of the packet sequence, but the reconfiguration process is delayed by the copy operations. The third method can be used if no status information of the MACs (Media Access Controller) is available. In this case, the processor is responsible for redirecting the remaining packets, thus decreasing the reconfiguration speed. In our prototypical implementation we used the first method to demonstrate a reconfiguration without packet loss. Due to performance issues of the embedded processor, and in order to achieve a minimum buffer size, our application requires a fast activation of the hardware switch.

3   Implementation of a dynamically reconfigurable Ethernet switch

The dynamically reconfigurable Ethernet switch consists of a software switch and a hardware switch. The software switch comprises two Ethernet Media Access Controllers that are connected to the system bus of the SoPC. For each port of the switch, one Ethernet MAC is required. The switching decision is made by the processor. I.e., the processor checks the destination address field of the Ethernet packets and copies the data from the receive buffer into the transmit buffer, if the packet has to be forwarded to another Ethernet port. The whole Ethernet traffic is transferred via the system bus. The hardware switch has the same capabilities as the Ethernet MACs. In contrast to the software switch, the switching decision is carried out in hardware. Therefore, the processor and the system bus are released from performing network infrastructure tasks.

For being able to implement the proposed RCOS we have developed an Ethernet MAC for Xilinx FPGA, which supports dynamic reconfiguration without packet loss. Therefore, the Ethernet MAC has to generate status information for the processor (e.g., network load and buffer state). In order to maintain the IFG between two Ethernet packets during the reconfiguration process, the transmit process has to be suspended. Additionally, packets already queued in the Ethernet MAC have to be prevented from being transmitted before the multiplexer has switched the transmit signals to the Ethernet port.

In addition to a software implementation of the Ethernet-switch, a hardware switch has been implemented, which relieves the processor of network infrastructure tasks. In order to avoid the transmission of corrupt packets, the hardware switch uses the store-and-forward switching method. It consists of two independent cross-connected sub-switches, which are connected to the system bus. One sub-switch component is able to forward packets in one direction. The sub-switch component is an extension of the Ethernet MACs presented before. It integrates an additional buffer for receiving and forwarding the packets that are not destined for the processor. Because of the hierarchical structure of our switch, the Ethernet software driver for both the software switch and the hardware switch are the same. For a reconfiguration of the switch no adaptation of application software is necessary.

Reconfiguration Options
To cope with the real-time requirements, the reconfigurable switch is able to collect information that is relevant for quality of service managment. Based on this information the Ethernet switch can be reconfigured. One of the measured parameters is the network load, which is determined by the MACs in our hardware implementation. The length of an Ethernet packet varies between 72 Bytes and 1526 Byte (8 Byte Preamble and Start-of-Frame-Delimiter included). But the measurement of the network load should not depend on the packet size, as far as possible. This can be achieved by measuring the time the data-valid signal (RX_DV) of the MII interface is active in a predefined interval, because RX_DV determines the beginning and the end of an Ethernet packet. Thus, the network load is calculated according to equation (1).

$$L = \frac{K \cdot IFG_{min} + RX_{active}}{T} \tag{1}$$

L is the network load in percent, where 100 % network load corresponds to the maximum data rate. The factor K represents the number of IFGs, occurring in the measurement interval T. IFG_{min} represents the minimal IFG (0,96 μs for 100 MBit/s) of the applied Ethernet protocol. $RXactive$ is the time, in which the RX_DV signal is set. This way of measuring the network load is independent on the packet size. In our prototypical implementation the reconfiguration from the software switch to the hardware switch is started if the network load exceeds 20 %.

Another possibility to maintain the real-time requirements is to reconfigure the Ethernet switch depending on the buffer state. Therefore, an impending buffer overflow is signaled to the processor by the MAC. In this case, the processor initiates a reconfiguration from the software to the hardware switch. Because the buffer is able to save further incoming packets during the reconfiguration process, packet loss is avoided if the reconfiguration is fast enough.

Fig. 3. Demand for low latency

A third alternative to optimize the efficiency of the communication system is to adapt the forwarding latency caused by the switch. Fig. 3 shows a typical situation in an RCOS. Node A, B and C are connected in a line topology. If Node A demands for a low latency to Node C, Node A sends a message to Node B. Node B initiates its reconfiguration and is now able to offer low forwarding latency. While the first two approaches that have been described above perform their optimizations based on local information, the third approach enables a self-optimization of distributed systems based on an interaction of the network nodes.

4   Performance evaluation

The latency of both switch configurations has been analyzed by means of a measurement circuit integrated in the switch implementation together with a network load generator. The network load generator has been configured to send packets with varying packet length to evaluate the correlation between packet size and latency. The values for the packet size given in this paper are related to the data field of the Ethernet protocol. The complete packet size can be calculated by adding 26 Bytes for the Ethernet header.

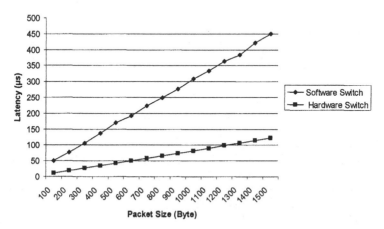

Fig. 4. Measured latency of the software switch and of the hardware switch

Because both the hardware switch and the software switch are store-and-forward implementations, the latency of both switches linearly depends on the packet size, as shown in Fig. 4. But the gradient of the latency of the software switch is 3.92 times higher than the gradient of the latency of the hardware switch. The main reason for the higher gradient is that the processor copies the Ethernet packets from one MAC to memory and from memory to the other MAC in the software implementation. The perturbation in the linearity of the latency graph is caused by processor operations that require a variable number of clock cycles, e.g., due to fetching instructions from external memory or from the instruction cache. Because of the high latencies, the software switch achieves in the worst case (i.e., for minimum packet size) a maximum data rate of 18 MBit/s, i.e., no packet is lost up to this data rate.

In contrast to the software switch the hardware switch supports the full data rate of Fast Ethernet (100 Mbit/s). In this implementation the perturbation in the latency graph is due to the integrated hardware monitor, which observes two buffers sequentially: one buffer for the processor queue and one for packet forwarding. If the hardware switch observes the buffer of the processor while a packet is "ready" to be forwarded, the latency increases by one clock cycle.

The easiest way to dynamically reconfigure from the software switch to the hardware switch is just to overwrite the first switch with the second one. Obviously, during reconfiguration no packets can be forwarded in this case. Reconfiguring the FPGA for exchanging the switches takes about 10 ms. During this reconfiguration period no communication via the switch is possible. In the worst case this results in a loss of more than 1400 packets. This problem can be solved by using both switches in parallel and by managing the reconfiguration with one of the three proposed methods.

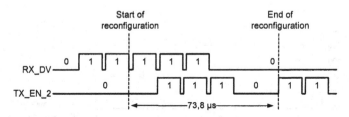

Fig. 5. Illustration of the packet flow during reconfiguration

For testing the proposed approach that uses both switches in parallel during reconfiguration, the reconfiguration has been initiated by forcing an impending buffer overflow in order to verify a lossless reconfiguration. In this scenario, the reconfiguration is initiated if two packets reside in the receive buffer. Five packets with a size of 100 Bytes were sent to the switch, as shown in Fig. 5. The RX_DV signal indicates incoming packets; the TX_EN_2 signal indicates the outgoing packets. The first marker Fig. 5 represents the start and the second marker the end of the reconfiguration process. We have measured a time of 73.8 μs for the reconfiguration process (i.e., the time between marker one and two). In this time 7 packets can reach the switch and have to be buffered or have to be forwarded.

Because at least one switch is always active, no packets are lost during reconfiguration.

Table 1 shows the resource utilization of the software switch, of the hardware switch and of both the hardware switch and the software switch during the reconfiguration process on the Virtex-II-Pro-20 FPGA in terms of required Slices and BlockRAMs. The results have been obtained by synthesizing the design with Xilinx ISE 6.1. The packet forwarding of the software switch is executed by one of the two embedded PowerPC processors. The software switch comprises 24 kByte of Block RAM while the hardware switch occupies 36 kByte due to an additional buffer, which is required for communication with the processor. Therefore, the switch requires 60 kByte for buffering during reconfiguration (when both switches are active).

Table 1.: Resource requirements of the switch implementations

Parameter	Software switch		Hardware switch		Switch during reconfiguration	
Resources	Used/Total	%	Used/Total	%	Used/Total	%
Slices	*2523/9280*	*27*	*6640/9280*	*71*	*9167/9280*	*98*
RAM16	*44/88*	*50*	*52/88*	*59*	*64/88*	*72*

As expected, the high performance of the hardware switch (in terms of low latency and high bandwidth) comes with the cost of large area requirements on the FPGA. If this high performance is required, there is no alternative to a hardware implementation. But if low bandwidth requirements come together with low or no real-time requirements, a small software based network interface is sufficient. In this case the hardware resources of the switch can be used, e.g., to speed up other applications. In order to support a lossless reconfiguration, it is a must that both switch implementations (hardware and software) are able to run concurrently. Therefore, the required FPGA resources for our system are at least given by the sum of the resources of both switches. During reconfiguration nearly 100 % of the Virtex-II-Pro-20 FPGA Slices are occupied (cf. Table 1). After reconfiguration, 30 % of the FPGA resources are available if the hardware switch is active and about 70 % of the reconfigurable logic is available if the software implementation is executed by the processor.

5 Conclusion

In this paper we have introduced methods to use the dynamic reconfiguration capability of FPGAs in real-time communication without violating real-time requirements. A dynamically reconfigurable dual-port Ethernet switch has been used as an example for a prototypical implementation of our approach. The Ethernet switch is able to adapt to changing requirements of an application during runtime. A software switch has been developed for minimum resource consumption and a hardware switch has been realized for maximum performance. The Ethernet switch detects increasing communication requirements by continuously measuring the network load. These mechanisms enable a self-optimization of the communication infrastructure in distributed systems. The implemented reconfiguration methods described in this paper support loss-less packet processing even throughout the reconfiguration, which is necessary to guarantee real-time behavior in communication systems.

6 References

1. Rammig, F.J.: Autonomic Distributed Real-Time Systems: Challenges and Solutions. In: *7th International Symposium on Object-oriented Real-time Distributed Computing (ISORC 2004)*, May 12-14, 2004.
2. Torresen, J.: Reconfigurable Logic Applied for Designing Adaptive Hardware Systems. In: *Proc. of Int. Conference on Advances in Infrastructure for Electronic Business, Education, Science, and Medicine on the Internet (SSGRR 2002W)*, 2002.
3. Carter, A.: Using Dynamically Reconfigurable Hardware in Real-Time Communications Systems, University of York, November 2001
4. Underwood, K.D.; Sass, R.R.; Ligeon, W.B.: A Reconfigurable Extension to the Network Interface of Beowulf Clusters. In: *Proceedings of the IEEE Conference on Cluster Computing (Cluster 2001)*, 2001.
5. Friedman, D.; Nagle, D.: Building Firewalls with Intelligent Network Interface Cards. Technical Report CMU–CS–00–173. CMU, May 2001.
6. Lockwood, J.W.; Moscola, J.; Reddick, D.; Kulig, M.; Brooks, T.: Application of Hardware Accelerated Extensible Network Nodes for Internet Worm and Virus Protection. In: *Proceedings of the International Working Conference on Active Networks (IWAN)*, 2003.
7. Furrer, F.: Ethernet TCP/IP for industrial automation. Huethig, 1998.
8. PROFIBUS Working Group: PROFInet: Architecture Description and Specification Version 2.01, August 2003.
9. Kalte, H., Porrmann, M., Rückert, U.: A Prototyping Platform for Dynamically Reconfigurable System on Chip Designs. In: *Proc. of the IEEE Workshop Heterogeneous reconfigurable Systems on Chip*. Hamburg, Germany, 2002.
10. Vonnahme, E., Griese, B., Porrmann, M., Rückert, U.: Dynamic reconfiguration of real-time network interfaces. In: *Proceedings of the 4th International Conference on Parallel Computing in Electrical Engineering (PARELEC 2004)*. Dresden, Germany, 7 - 10 September 2004.

Learning Useful Communication Structures for Groups of Agents

Andreas Goebels

International Graduate School of Dynamic Intelligent Systems
Knowledge Based Systems, University of Paderborn, Germany
swarmgroup@upb.de

Abstract. Coordination of altruistic agents to solve optimization problems can be significantly enhanced when inter-agent communication is allowed. In this paper we present an evolutionary approach to learn optimal communication structures for groups of agents. The agents learn to solve the *Online Partitioning Problem*, but our ideas can easily be adapted to other problem fields. With our approach we can find the optimal communication partners for each agent in a static environment. In a dynamic environment we figure out a simple relation between each position of agents in space and the optimal number of communication partners. A concept for the establishment of relevant communication connections between certain agents will be shown whereby the space the agents are located in will be divided into several regions. These regions will be described mathematically. After a learning process the algorithm assigns an appropriate number of communication partners for every agent in an - arbitrary located - group.

1 Introduction

Multi Agent Systems (MAS) and Swarm Intelligence (SI) are two quite recent but very promising topics in current computer science research. SI deals with large sets of individuals or agents that can be seen as a self organizing system showing emergent behaviour[1][2]. Ideas from biology are used often and successfully to solve (optimization) problems in the computer science area. In both fields, communication between the single agents or particles plays an important role. In nature this communication is, for instance, realized with the environment as communication partner, the so called stigmergy concept, first introduced by the biologist Grassé [3], or with special dance moves that can be found at several bee colonies[4]. In both examples the concept of *locality* and *self organization* plays an important role. In most swarms, flocks or schools in nature we can hardly observe global communication.

If we have to solve an optimization problem and need inter-agent communication to enhance or even enable solutions, we could make use of a complete communication structure that allows direct communication between all pairs of agents. But if we are in settings that deal with a huge number of agents, such complete structures might produce high communication costs and/or are

Please use the following format when citing this chapter:

Goebels, A., 2006, in IFIP International Federation for Information Processing, Volume 216, Biologically Inspired Cooperative Computing, eds. Pan, Y., Rammig, F., Schmeck, H., Solar, M., (Boston: Springer), pp. 125–135.

not manageable because of information inferences or other real world problems. Therefore, it would be nice if we would have a concept that can produce a very small and cheap communication structure without significantly reducing the quality of the solution.

In this paper, we consider the *Online Partitioning Problem (OPP)* introduced in [5]. This problem, which is located in the area of Multi Agent Systems and Swarm Intelligence, deals with the association of agents with very limited and mostly local knowledge with different tasks represented as targets. The agents distribute themselves in an Euclidean space according to the following three objectives:

(1) The agents have to be distributed uniformly.
(2) Minimize the overall distance toward the targets.
(3) The abilities of the agents should be very simple.

Each of these goals is oppositional to any other, so we look for the best possible solution fitting in all objectives in quite an acceptable way. The knowledge of each agent is limited to a (preferable small) communication radius. They are able to communicate with their direct neighbours and know the distance to all targets according to their position. A more detailed description of the abilities of the agents can be found in [5]. There, several basic strategies have been presented to distribute a small number of agents onto two targets, coping with the three objectives mentioned before. It turns out that the communicative strategies perform better than the non-communicative ones. In general, Matarić discusses in [6] some advantages of using communication in multi agent systems to reduce locality by addressing two key problems, the hidden state and credit assignment problem.

In this paper we present an algorithm that is able to construct a successful communication structure to solve the *OPP* by defining useful communication connections between agents. This is done by dividing the space into regions depending on the position of each agent in relation to the targets and by learning an ideal number of communication partners for agents in these regions.

This paper is organized as follows. In the next section some terms will be defined. As an introduction, we roughly present an idea that deals with static settings. In the main section 4 we present our approach for dynamic groups of agents and do some mathematical considerations of the single regions we divided the space into. To show the quality of our approach we present in section 5 several simulation runs.

2 Definitions

In this paper, we denote the set of all agents with $\mathcal{A} = \{a_1, ..., a_n\}$ and the set of targets with $\mathcal{T} = \{t_1, ..., t_m\}$ $(n, m \in \mathbb{N})$. $\delta(p_1, p_2)$ defines the geometric distance between two points in the Euclidean space. This function works in the same way if we consider two arbitrary agents a and a' or an agent a and a target t, then $\delta(a, a')$ and $\delta(a, t)$ calculate the distance between the positions of two agents or between an agent and a target, accordingly.

3 The static approach

In this section we consider a static setting, i.e. a set of agents on fixed positions in a two-dimensional, Euclidean space dealing with the OPP. They have to decide for one target regarding the objectives we mentioned in the introduction. For given parameters dictating communication costs and parametrizing the objective function for the OPP we try to find an optimal communication structure among the agents. Because of the unknown structure and the size of the solution space we make use of a genetic algorithm to search for good solutions. With this approach, a solution that optimally fulfils an evaluation function can be found very fast. We will give only a rough idea of this algorithm, more details and the results can be found in a master thesis [7] that was done under our supervision.

3.1 Evaluate the Quality of a Communication Structure

The quality or fitness f of a communication structure can be calculated at any time by the following formula. The notation is related to the notation in [7]. We sum up the single optimization criteria, i.e. the partitioning quality, the distance quality and the communication costs, and weight the single parts.

$$f = \alpha \cdot \left(\frac{\prod\limits_{i=1}^{m} b_i}{\prod\limits_{i=1}^{m} o_i} \right) + \beta \cdot \left(\frac{\sum\limits_{i=1}^{n} \min\limits_{j=1..m}(\delta(a_i, t_j))}{\sum\limits_{i=1}^{n} \delta(a_i, target(a_i))} \right) + \gamma \cdot \left(1 - \frac{\sum\limits_{i=1}^{n} \sum\limits_{j=1}^{n} c_{(i,j)} \cdot \delta(a_i, a_j)}{\sum\limits_{i=1}^{n} \sum\limits_{j=1}^{n} \delta(a_i, a_j)} \right)$$

with $\alpha + \beta + \gamma = 1; \alpha, \beta, \gamma \geq 0$

In this formula, b_i denotes the number of agents that have chosen the target t_i in the current partitioning decision and o_i the number of agents that would have chosen target t_i in an optimal partitioning. $target(a_i)$ defines the target currently chosen by agent a_i and $c(i, j)$ is either 1 or 0 depending on the existence of a directed communication link from agent a_i to a_j. The highest possible fitness is $f = 1.0$.

3.2 The genetic algorithm

We implemented a standard genetic algorithm and guide the search among all possible communication structures by the mentioned fitness function that consist of three summands representing the different objectives. Therefore, we consider a multi-objective optimization problem and its single objective representation.

One individual in our GA is a $n \times n$-matrix $\mathcal{C}$ describing the connectivity of the agents among each other. A '1' on position (i, j) allows agent a_i to communicate with agent a_j (directed communication). In other words, $\mathcal{C}$ is the adjacency matrix of the communication graph of the agents.

As a selection operator we use the *Best* selection and for mutation we simply swap bits in $\mathcal{C}$ with a low probability. The crossover method is a modification of the *Single-Point Crossover*. We apply this operator to two communication matrices $\mathcal{C}_1$ and $\mathcal{C}_2$ by choosing a random field (i, j) with $i, j \in [1; n]$ in the communication matrix. The two new individuals will exchange a corresponding rectangular part of the matrix defined by (i, j) as the upper left and (n, n) as the lower right corner.

4 The Dynamic Approach

In the former section we introduced a static approach to learn optimal communication structures for a given set of fixed agents. But this structure strongly depends on the special setting it was trained on and cannot be used for other groups of agents or other positions of the same agents, especially if we consider communication costs that are constrained by the distance between two communication partners. In this section, we will present an idea to learn a useful communication structure that is independent from the distribution of the agents in space.

Therefore, we construct a communication network for a dynamic setting in a totally different way. The agents do not learn what the best communication partners are, but they try to find out how many communication partners are useful for the position they are located at (depending on the position of the targets). That means, the agents learn a function that connects a region that can be computed locally with an ideal number of communication partners. Since the agents do not know the extension of the simulation area, the agents have to calculate the area they are in only with regard to the distances to the targets. Therefore, we calculate a q-value for each agent position (x, y) by

$$q_{x,y} = \frac{min(\delta((x, y), t_1), ..., \delta((x, y), t_n))}{max(\delta((x, y), t_1), ..., \delta((x, y), t_n))} \in \mathbb{R}$$

Or, to put it in a more informal description, we calculate the quotient for each agent position by dividing the distance to the closest target by the distance to the farthest target[1]. With this procedure we can calculate values that represent the area an agent is in without paying attention to its real distance. In the further text we will call this value the q-value. Because we are in a continuous space, there is an infinite number of different q-values. Therefore we combine the different q-values in intervals of the same size. For l categories, we obtain the following intervals $I_1, ..., I_l$ with

---

[1] In this paper we focus on settings with two targets. If we would consider a higher number, we maybe will have to make the calculation of the q-value more complicated. This will be focus of an upcoming paper.

$$I_k = \begin{cases} \left[\frac{k-1}{l}; \frac{k}{l}\right] & \text{for } k \neq l \\ \left[\frac{k-1}{l}; 1\right] & \text{for } k = l \end{cases}$$

4.1 Our Approach

We solved the *Online Partitioning Problem (OPP)* for huge agent sets and enhanced the knowledge base of a selection of agents by enabling communication with its neighbours.

Table 1. The number of communication partners based on the q-interval. For each interval, an appropriate number of communication partners can be defined.

q-interval	I_1	I_2	...	I_l
number of communication partners	n_1	n_2	...	n_l

Therefore, the agents have to learn the number of communication partners depending on the q-interval they are located in. Or, in other words, they learned an appropriate assignment for each n_i in table 1. We call such a table q-table.

4.2 Size and Properties of the q-Intervals in Space

In this section we will give a short mathematical insight into the regions we created with our intervals. We consider an arbitrary q-value, denoted by q'. All positions in space that produce exactly the value q' are located on two circles with the same radius r around two centre points. The targets are somewhere inside this circles. The distance between the two targets is fixed and denoted by D.

Theorem

All points in space that have one specific q-value according to two targets t_1 and t_2 on positions (t_{1_x}, t_{1_y}) and (t_{2_x}, t_{2_y}) lie on the circles C_1 and C_2 with centre points

$$M_1 = \left(\left(\frac{t_{2_x} - q^2 \cdot t_{1_x}}{1 - q^2}\right), \left(\frac{t_{2_y} - q^2 \cdot t_{1_y}}{1 - q^2}\right)\right), M_2 = \left(\left(\frac{t_{1_x} - q^2 \cdot t_{2_x}}{1 - q^2}\right), \left(\frac{t_{1_y} - q^2 \cdot t_{2_y}}{1 - q^2}\right)\right)$$

and radius $r = \frac{q \cdot D}{(1 - q^2)}$.

Proof

q is calculated for an arbitrary point $p = (x, y)$ by the formula

$$\frac{\text{dist. to nearest target}}{\text{dist. to farthest target}}.$$

Without loss of generality we assume that target t_2 is the nearest one and t_1 the farthest one. Therefore, q can be expressed by:

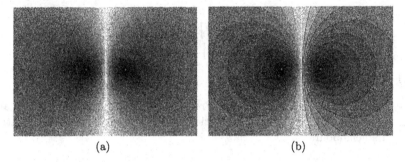

(a)   (b)

Fig. 1. Figure (a) shows the distribution of the q-values when calculated for arbitrary positions in space. Each grey tone represents one specific q-interval. In this example there are 30 different q-intervals. In (b), the circles for the interval borders (here we have 12 intervals), obtained by our mathematical examination, are visualized. They perfectly cover the regions.

$$q = \frac{\sqrt{(x - t_{2_x})^2 + (y - t_{2_y})^2}}{\sqrt{(x - t_{1_x})^2 + (y - t_{1_y})^2}}$$

This can be transformed to:

$$\left(\sqrt{\frac{q^2 \cdot t_{1_x}^2 + q^2 \cdot t_{1_y}^2 - t_{2_x}^2 - t_{2_y}^2}{1 - q^2} + \left(\frac{t_{2_x} - q^2 \cdot t_{1_x}}{1 - q^2} \right)^2 + \left(\frac{t_{2_y} - q^2 \cdot t_{1_y}}{1 - q^2} \right)^2} \right)^2$$

$$= \left(x - \left(\frac{t_{2_x} - q^2 \cdot t_{1_x}}{1 - q^2} \right) \right)^2 + \left(y - \left(\frac{t_{2_y} - q^2 \cdot t_{1_y}}{1 - q^2} \right) \right)^2$$

and this can be simplified to a standard circle equation:

$$\left(\frac{q \cdot D}{(1 - q^2)} \right)^2 = \left(x - \left(\frac{t_{2_x} - q^2 \cdot t_{1_x}}{1 - q^2} \right) \right)^2 + \left(y - \left(\frac{t_{2_y} - q^2 \cdot t_{1_y}}{1 - q^2} \right) \right)^2$$

These are centre point M_1 and radius r in our Theorem. If target t_1 is the nearest one, we obtain the other centre point M_2 by using the same transformations. $\square$

4.3 The Genetic Algorithm

There is a huge number of possible assignments for such a structure as presented in table 1, especially when dealing with large numbers of agents. Each n_i can be assigned to a value from $\{0, ..., (n - 1)\}$ with $n = |\mathcal{A}|$ representing the number of agents. Therefore, we have $(n - 1)^l$ possible assignments. We use a genetic algorithm to search for good ones because we have no prior information about the structure of the solution space. The fitness of a solution obtained with a table assignment is the quality of the solution of the *OPP*. It is set in relation to the optimal solution, regarding communication costs, and is calculated by the formula:

$$fitness(tableAssignment) = \alpha \cdot fitness_{OPP} + (1 - \alpha) \cdot fitness_{Communication}$$

The fitness of a OPP solution is calculated as in [8] by

$$fitness_{OPP} = \beta \cdot \left(\frac{\prod_{i=1}^{m} b_i}{\prod_{i=1}^{m} o_i} \right) + (1 - \beta) \cdot \left(\frac{\sum_{i=1}^{n} \min_{j=1..m} (\delta(a_i, t_j))}{\sum_{i=1}^{n} \delta(a_i, target(a_i))} \right)$$

We use the same notation as we did in section 3.

The **Communication Costs** in the fitness function will be calculated by regarding the communication distances between two agents that are allowed to communicate. The number of communication partners is defined in the q-table. When establishing n_k connections for an agent located in the interval I_k, this agent will create communication lines to its n_k nearest agents. The sum of these costs will then be set in relation to the maximum costs for communication that could appear if it holds for each entry in the q-table that n_i is equal to $(n - 1)$. Hence, we can define a partial fitness function for the communication costs:

$$fitness_{Communication} = \frac{q - table\ defined\ communication\ graph\ costs}{complete\ communication\ graph\ costs}$$

We assume that a subset of agents that own communication connections among each other will be able to calculate an optimal partial solution for the *OPP*.

The **crossover** operator is simple, we use *One-Point Crossover*. Therefore, a random point p from $\{1, ..., l\}$ is chosen. Then we create two new q-tables by recombining the tables from two parental individuals split at this particular point (or column) p. We think that we can maintain coherences between the table entries with this operator if they exist.

For the **selection** of individuals for the next generation we implemented the *Roulette Wheel* and the *Best* selection. In comparison runs the *Best* selection shows slightly better results, therefore we made our final experiments with this method. For both algorithms, we use a (μ, λ)-scheme and chose 50% of the individuals for the new generation out of the old generation.

For the **mutation** of a q-table we make use of two mutation parameters, p_I defines the probability for mutating one individual. The second parameter p_t determines the probability of mutating one table entry. When an entry I_k has been selected to become mutated, we adjust the n_k value in the table by adding a random value $r \in \{-(n - 1), ..., (n - 1)\}$ to the entry and check if the value is out of range with the formula $mutation(n_k) = max(min(n - 1, n_k + r), 0)$.

4.4 Our Algorithm

We use a genetic algorithm to find the appropriate number of communication partners for each interval in the q-table. The most interesting part of the algorithm is the calculation of the fitness of an individual in the population, i.e. the fitness of a q-table. To rate such a q-table $\mathcal{Q}$, we test the quality of a set of agents working on the *Online Partitioning Problem* that use a communication structure developed from Q. The fitness of each Q can be calculated by the following algorithm:

```
001:  FUNCTION double calculateFitness(qTable Q)
002:  {
003:      agentSet = new random set of agents;
004:      place targets on random positions in space;
005:      agentSet.createCommunicationGraph(Q);
006:
007:      commFitness = calculateCommunicationFitness(agentSet);
008:      oppFitness = calculateOPPSolutionFitness(agentSet);
009:
010:      RETURN α · oppFitness + (1 − α) · commFitness;
011:  }
```

The function *calculateCommunicationFitness(agentSet)* simply applies the communication fitness function as described in 4.3. The higher this value is the less communication is used.[2] The more interesting function is the one calculating the *OPP* solution fitness, this is shown here in more details:

```
001:  FUNCTION double calculateCommunicationFitness(agentSet)
002:  {
003:      // create reference solution
003:      d = minimal overall distance to targets in optimal partitioning;
004:      s = optimal number of agents on each target in optimal partitioning;
005:
006:      FOR EACH agent a in agentSet DO
007:      {
008:        IF (#outgoingConnections(a) > 0) //derived from q-table
009:          calculateLocalOptimalSolution(a, communicationPartners);
010:        ELSE
011:          choose nearest target;
012:      }
013:      d' = calculateDistanceFitness(agentSet, d);
014:      s' = calculateDistributionFitness(agentSet, s);
015:
016:      RETURN β · d' + (1 − β) · s';
017:  }
```

The function *calculateLocalOptimalSolution(a, communicationPartners)* in line 9 assumes that an agent can calculate the optimal partitioning for the agents it communicates with. This is quite an idealistic picture because we still have a hard problem, but we can take this calculation power into account by increasing the influence of the communication costs for the fitness function. Anyway, if this function can calculate only an approximation, our algorithm will still work.

The pseudocode algorithms show only the most important steps of our algorithm, for a more detailed insight you can have a look at the original Java sources that are available for download and further experiments via our webpage[3].

---

[2] In our simulations we repeated lines 3-8 several (five) times to obtain more meaningful fitness values.

[3] http://www.upb.de/cs/ag-klbue/de/staff/agoebels/index.html

5 Results

In this paper, we concentrate on the results for the dynamic approach presented in section 4, the results for the static approach (section 3) can be found in [7]. There, a good communication matrix could be found fast for every given fixed set of agents.

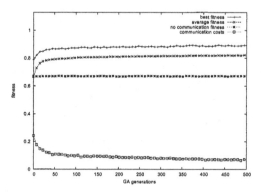

Fig. 2. This figure presents the development of the fitness over 500 generations. We show the average fitness of the whole generation and the fitness development of the best individual in population. This graph illustrates the average result over 25 runs. The parameters we made use of can be found in the source code package. The fitness rises while the communication cost could be reduced. The single graphs are smoothed with a Bezier curve for better visibility.

5.1 Fitness Development

First of all, we examined how the fitness of the GA develops. Figure 2 shows a typical fitness development. Both the best and the average fitness rise very fast to a high level and remain there. As a reference we present the fitness value of a non communicative algorithm choosing always the nearest target for each agent. This reference fitness is significantly lower than the fitness value achieved with our approach. By adjusting the weights for the communication costs we can obtain any fitness value between 1.0 (no communication cost, $\alpha = 1$) and the reference function ($\alpha = 0$). Hence, we can conclude that inter-agent communication enhances the solution quality of the whole group and our approach finds good *OPP* solutions for given communication costs or restrictions.

5.2 Development of q-Table values

Once we could see that our idea works, we wanted to get more insight into the communication structure the agents learn. Therefore, we observed the changes of the q-table entries during the learning process. Figure 3 shows a typical picture representing the value development.

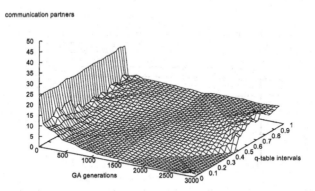

Fig. 3. The development of the q-table entries during the learning process.

After several hundred generations the q-tables look similar for all settings. In this figure the average over all q-tables in 25 runs is presented. In the early generations the number of communication partners is high and nearly identical for all intervals. But the communication structure becomes fastly sparser and in the last generations we can see that the q-table can be divided into 2 parts. For intervals containing small q-values the agents learned to have nearly no communication partners[4]. For q-values greater than 0.5 it seems to make sense to communicate with a small number of neighbours to increase the fitness to a near optimum value. One other key result is that the overall number of communication connections between agents is very low compared to the maximum possible value. This shows that a communication structure does not necessarily have to be very complex or massive if we generate it in an intelligent way.

6 Conclusion & Future Work

In this paper we presented a genetically guided approach to learn qualified communication structures for sets of agents to solve an optimization problem. For a

---

[4] The intervals I_1 and I_2 contain all q-values below 0.1. As we saw in 4.2, the area in space representing all possible values in these intervals is very small compared to the remaining space, hence the probability for an agent to be placed in one of these areas is very low and it does not influence the fitness significantly.

static environment we presented a rough idea how the optimal communication structure can be found by an algorithm adjusting a communication matrix. For dynamic and random settings we presented a new approach which offers guidelines to create a small set of communication connections. Therefore, only the position in space in relation to some targets is necessary, the optimal or near optimum number of communication partners can be found by our approach. In our future research we will restrict the values in the q-table and will try to learn or cope with restricted communication distances. This will enlarge the possible number of real-world applications. We also will examine the influence of the different probabilities for each q-interval on the fitness development and the overall solution quality.

References

1. Eric Bonabeau, Marco Dorigo, and Guy Theraulaz, *Swarm Intelligence - From natural to artificial Systems*, Oxford University Press, 1999
2. James Kennedy and Russel C. Eberhart, *Swarm Intelligence*, Morgan Kaufmann, 2001
3. P.-P. Grassé, *La Reconstruction du nid et les Coordinations Inter-Individuelles chez Bellicositermes Natalensis et Cubitermes sp. La théorie de la stigmergie: essai d'interprétation du comportement des termites constructeurs*, Insectes Sociaux, 1959.
4. K. von Frisch, *The Dance Language and Orientation of Bees*, Harvard University Press, Cambridge, 1967
5. Andreas Goebels, Hans Kleine Büning, Steffen Priesterjahn, Alexander Weimer, *Towards Online Partitioning of Agent Sets based on Local Information*, Proceedings of the International Conference on Parallel and Distributed Computing and Networks (PDCN), 2005
6. Maja J. Matarić, *Using Communication to Reduce Locality in Distributed Multi-Agent Learning*, Journal of Experimental and Theoretical Artificial Intelligence, special issue on Learning in DAI Systems, Gerhard Weiss, ed., 10(3), 1998, 357-369.
7. Lars Beckmann, *Evolutionäre Entwicklung und Optimierung von Kommunikationsstrukturen zur Koordination von Agenten [Evolutionary Development and Optimization of Communication Structures for Agent Coordination]*, Master Thesis, Univ. of Paderborn, 2005
8. A. Goebels, A. Weimer, S. Priesterjahn, *Using Cellular Automata with Evolutionary Learned Rules to Solve the Online Partitioning Problem*, in Proceedings of the IEEE Congress on Evolutionary Computation (CEC'05), Edinburgh, 2005, pp. 837-843

Maintaining Communication Between an Explorer and a Base Station[*]

Miroslaw Dynia[1], Jarosław Kutyłowski[2], Paweł Lorek[3],
and Friedhelm Meyer auf der Heide[4]

[1] DFG Graduate College "Automatic Configuration in Open Systems",
Heinz Nixdorf Institute, University of Paderborn
[2] International Graduate School, Heinz Nixdorf Institute, University of Paderborn
[3] Mathematical Institute, Wrocław University
[4] Heinz Nixdorf Institute, University of Paderborn

Abstract. Consider a (robotic) explorer starting an exploration of an unknown terrain from its base station. As the explorer has only limited communication radius, it is necessary to maintain a line of robotic relay stations following the explorer, so that consecutive stations are within the communication radius of each other. This line has to start in the base station and to end at the explorer.

In the simple scenario considered here we assume an obstacle-free terrain, so that the shortest connection (the one which needs the smallest number of relay stations) is a straight line. We consider an explorer who goes an arbitrary, typically winding way, and define a very simple, intuitive, fully local, distributed strategy for the relay stations – our GO-TO-THE-MIDDLE strategy – to maintain a line from the base station to the robot as short as possible.

Besides the definition of this strategy, we present an analysis of its performance under different assumptions. For the static case we prove a bound on the convergence speed, for the dynamic case we present experimental evaluations that show the quality of our strategy under different types of routes the explorer could use.

1 Introduction

In our research we investigate the exploration of a planar terrain without obstacles. To achieve this goal, an explorer is used who starts its work at a base station and progresses to gather information about the whole terrain. In order to construct a communication path between this explorer and the base station, we employ mobile relay stations. These relay stations are small, mobile robots

[*] Partially supported by the EU within the 6th Framework Programme under contract 001907 (DELIS) and by the DFG-Sonderforschungsbereich SPP 1183: "Organic Computing. Smart Teams: Local, Distributed Strategies for Self-Organizing Robotic Exploration Teams".

Please use the following format when citing this chapter:

Dynia, M., Kutylowski, J., Lorek, P., auf der Heide, F.M., 2006, in IFIP International Federation for Information Processing, Volume 216, Biologically Inspired Cooperative Computing, eds. Pan, Y., Rammig, F., Schmeck, H., Solar, M., (Boston: Springer), pp. 137–146.

which are responsible for routing messages between the explorer and the base station.

In order to minimize the number of necessary relay stations, they should be organized on a line close to the straight line connecting the explorer and the base station. Furthermore it is necessary that the relay stations can communicate with each other, so consecutive stations must be placed in a limited distance on this line.

Since we allow the explorer to walk along an arbitrary route, its position updates frequently. Arranging all relay stations on the straight line would thus require to communicate its position updates to the whole path, resulting in a globally controlled strategy incuring a substantial communication load. Thus we are looking for simple distributed, local strategies which allow the relay stations to arrange near to their optimal positions based on very local information. We introduce a strategy, our GO-TO-THE-MIDDLE, which does not use any communication – relay stations perform their movement basing only on sensed positions of their communication partners. This approach is called "interaction via sensing" as defined in [1].

In Section 2 we introduce a local and distributed strategy which keeps the relay stations close to their optimal positions on the line. This strategy is very intuitive and could also be used by human explorers. A similar behavior can be observed in bird flocks maintaining formation (see [2]).

We analyze our strategy both in a static and in a dynamic setting. In Section 3 we describe the static setting, where the explorer does not move, and the relay stations are initially placed on an arbitrarily winding route taken by the explorer until now. We give a worst-case theoretical analysis which describes the time needed for the relay stations to converge to positions near the straight line between the base station and the explorer. In Section 4 we let the explorer move and let the relay stations continuously apply our strategy. We experimentally evaluate the performance of the strategy, using three different types of routes taken by the explorer. The proofs of several technical lemmas can be found in the full version of this paper.

1.1 Related work

From a general point of view, our work can be positioned in the area of swarm intelligence [3], particularly in the field of robotic intelligent swarms [4, 5, 1].

Our work has much in common with the prior research in the areas of pattern formation and formation maintenance. The work described in [6, 7, 8, 9, 10] considers swarms of robots which should self-organize to form a pattern (a line, circle, ...) on a plane or to maintain a formation while marching.

The most similar work to ours is [6]. Among others it presents an algorithm CONTRACTION which is very similar to our strategy. Nevertheless, although the topic of forming a geometric pattern on a plane has been considered very often, we are not aware of any analysis giving strong theoretical bounds on the worst-case performance of a strategy. Up to our knowledge the topic of mobile robots self-organizing to form a line has not been evaluated experimentally under the performance aspect yet.

1.2 Model

We construct a graph modeling the base station, the explorer and the relay stations with vertices. The vertices are always logically organized in a path $(v_1, v_2, \ldots, v_{n-1}, v_n)$, where v_1 corresponds to the base station, v_n to the explorer and $v_2, \ldots, v_{n-1}$ to the relay stations. To represent the path we introduce undirected edges (v_i, v_{i+1}) for every $i \in \{1, \ldots, n-1\}$. The communication is routed along this path from v_1 to v_n or in the other direction. The graph is embedded on a plane, thus we will use the notion of a position $p(v)$ of a vertex v. Distances between vertices are given by the L_2 norm and described by $|(v_i, v_{i+1})|$.

The goal of a strategy minimizing the distance between the relay stations is to arrange the relay stations on the line between v_1 and v_n in equal distances from each other, or, in other words, to bring the relay stations as near to this optimal positions as possible.

We require every edge on the path $v_1, \ldots, v_n$ to have at most length d, so that the maximum transmission distance of d is not exceed and communication links between partners on the communication path can be hold up. A communication path fulfilling this property is called valid.

2 The Go-To-The-Middle Strategy

The following GO-TO-THE-MIDDLE strategy is executed repeatedly by every relay station. Relay station i observes the positions $p(v_{i-1})$ and $p(v_{i+1})$ of its communication partners and moves itself into the middle of the interval from v_{i-1} to v_{i+1}.

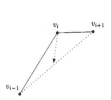

Fig. 1. Node v_i executes GO-TO-THE-MIDDLE strategy by moving into the middle of the interval between v_{i-1} and v_{i+1}.

For simplification of the analysis we will assume that the GO-TO-THE-MIDDLE strategy is invoked in discrete time steps. Each time step is subdivided into two shorter substeps. In the first one, all relay stations check the positions of their neighbors. In the second substep all relay stations move to the middle of the observed positions of its neighbors as described above.

Since the explorer moves, it may be necessary to extend the path of relay stations. We perform this at the end of the path, between the last relay station and the explorer. This happens every time the distance between v_{n-1} and v_n increases to more than d. We rename the vector v appropriately, so that v_{n+1} describes the explorer and v_n the new relay station. The new relay station is inserted in the middle of the interval connecting the last relay station and the explorer.

If the explorer can carry a sufficiently large pool of relay stations then this strategy is easily executed, since new relay stations are available at the explorer's position.

If this is not the case, the base station has to make sure that enough relay stations are on the path. As it does not know about the position and movement of the explorer, we modify the strategy slightly. We add to each relay station v_i a second one, its partner, at the same position as v_i. During each GO-TO-THE-MIDDLE step, a relay station and its partner perform the same movement. Afterward, one of them goes the next relay station and becomes its partner. At the base station, a new relay station is introduced as the partner of v_2. At the explorer there are two possibilities. If the explorer has not moved far away from v_n, the partner of v_n starts going back to the base station and is reused there. If a new relay station is needed to hold up the communication with the explorer, the partner of v_n is used. Limiting the maximal speed of the explorer to $d/2$ it will be necessary to insert a new relay station to the communication path at most every two rounds. Thus the new relay station in the communication path will obtain its partner in the next round after it has been inserted.

This modified strategy uses at most $2n$ relay station in addition to those needed by GO-TO-THE-MIDDLE, half of them being the partners of all relay stations and half of them being on their way back to the base station.

We may also consider removing relay stations when they are close enough to each other. Formally, a relay station v_i can be removed from the path if the distance $|(v_{i-1}, v_{i+1})| \leq d$. The vector v is then re indexed appropriately and the released station goes back along the communication path to the base station.

We show that both strategies preserve the validity property of the communication path in the following theorem.

Theorem 1. *If a communication path is valid then, after applying the* GO-TO-THE-MIDDLE *strategy, it remains valid.*

3 Static setting

We analyze the convergence rate of GO-TO-THE-MIDDLE and assume a static scenario – the explorer does not move. We measure the time which is required so that every relay station is within some given distance from the straight line connecting the base station and the explorer.

For the purpose of this analysis we assume that the number of nodes on the path is n. We do not remove any nodes from the path, even if they are very close to each other. The positions of nodes v_1 and v_n are fixed – they do not move during the execution of GO-TO-THE-MIDDLE, while all other nodes can move. This corresponds to an explorer standing at its position, and all relay stations executing the GO-TO-THE-MIDDLE strategy.

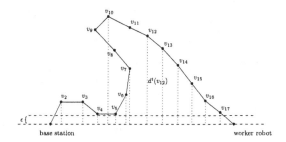

Fig. 2. Relay stations and the area of diameter ε around the straight line

For a node v_i we define $d^t(v_i)$ to be the distance of node v_i to the straight line crossing nodes v_1 and v_n before step t of the execution GO-TO-THE-MIDDLE. Distance of a point to a line is defined in the usual geometrical way, as depicted in Fig. 2. We assume that at the beginning all nodes (relay stations) are on one side of the line connecting the explorer and the base station. If not, the nodes can be divided into distinct segments, and the analysis can be applied in each segment separately. The case, when all nodes are on one side yields the worst case.

Theorem 2 (Main Theorem). *Consider a valid communication path with $n - 2$ relay stations. Then after at most $9n^2 \log \frac{1}{\varepsilon} n$ steps for every i it holds $d(v_i) \leq \varepsilon$ for any $\varepsilon > 0$.*

Proof. Obviously it holds $d^t(v_1) = d^t(v_n) = 0$ for all $t \geq 1$. We define $A^t := [d^t(v_2) \ldots, d^t(v_{n-1})]$ to be the vector of distances of relay stations to the straight line. A^0 describes the start configuration.

Then after one step of GO-TO-THE-MIDDLE the distance

$$d^t(v_i) = \frac{d^{t-1}(v_{i-1}) + d^{t-1}(v_{i+1})}{2},$$

for all $1 < i < n$, which effectively means that $d^t(v_2) = d^{t-1}(v_3)/2$ and $d^t(v_{n-1}) = d^t(v_{n-2})/2$ since $d^t(v_1) = d^t(v_n) = 0$.

We can describe the changes of the vector A^t by multiplying it with an appropriate transition matrix L so that $A^t = A^{t-1}L = A^0L^t$. This $n \times n$ matrix is defined as follows: $L(i,j) = \frac{1}{2}$ for all i,j such that $|i - j| = 1$. For all other i,j we have $L(i,j) = 0$.

$$
L = \begin{pmatrix}
1/2 & & & & & & \\
1/2 & 1/2 & & & & & \\
& 1/2 & \ddots & & & & \\
& & 1/2 & 1/2 & & & \\
& & & \ddots & 1/2 & & \\
& & & & 1/2 & 1/2 & \\
& & & & & 1/2 &
\end{pmatrix}
$$

Matrix L is symmetric, substochastic and irreducible. By Lemma 1 all eigenvalues of L are different and thus L is diagonalizable. The rest of the proof of the Main Theorem goes in the following way. We will compute the eigenvalues and eigenvectors of L. A lemma about the convergence rate of L^t will allow us to give an upper bound on the largest value of L^t after t steps. From this we will conclude a bound on the largest value of A^t and the Main Theorem easily.

Lemma 1. *The eigenvalues of the matrix L are*

$$
\lambda_j = \cos\left(\frac{j\pi}{n+1}\right), \quad j = 1,\ldots n .
$$

The corresponding eigenvectors are

$$
x_j(i) = \sin\left(\frac{\pi ji}{n+1}\right), \quad i = 1,\ldots,n, \quad j = 1,\ldots,n .
$$

Lemma 2. *For a diagonalizable, irreducible, symmetric, substochastic $n \times n$ matrix P and any i,j we have*

$$
P^k(i,j) \le n\alpha\beta^k ,
$$

where β is the largest absolute value of eigenvalues of the matrix P and $\alpha = \max_{i,j,i',j'} |x_j(i) \cdot x_{j'}(i')|$ with x_j denoting the j-th eigenvector of matrix P.

The proofs of both lemmas can be found in the full version of the paper. After t steps, we have $L^t(i,j) \le n\alpha\beta^t$ for any i,j, sticking to the definitions of α and β from Lemma 2. As all entries of all eigenvectors of L are not larger than 1, we have $\alpha \le 1$. The value of $|\cos\frac{j\pi}{n+1}|$ is the largest for $j/(n+1)$ approaching 0 or 1. Without loss of generality we set $j = 1$. Then we have $\beta = \cos\frac{\pi}{n+1}$.

Now assuming that the communication distance between nodes is d, we know that A^0 can contain an entry as big as dn. On the other hand we know that entries of L^t are always non-negative. Recall that $A^t = A^0 L^t$. Then to have $d^t(v_i) \le \varepsilon$ we must have each element of L^t smaller than $\frac{\varepsilon}{dn^2}$ since $d^0(v_i) \le dn$.

We thus have to find a t such that $L^t(i,j) \le \frac{\varepsilon}{dn^2}$ for all i,j. Using Lemma 2 we should then have $n\alpha\beta^t \le \frac{\varepsilon}{dn^2}$ and accordingly $\beta^t \le \frac{\varepsilon}{dn^3}$. We still have to find an upper bound on β. As argued before, β is largest, when $\pi/(n+1)$ approaches 0. Thus let us expand $\cos x$ around $x = 0$ from the Taylor series. We obtain $\cos x \le 1 - \frac{x^2}{2} + \frac{x^4}{24}$, and set $x = \pi/(n+1)$. Since $\pi^2/2 \ge 1$ and $\pi^4/24 \le 5$ we obtain

$$\cos \frac{\pi}{n+1} \le 1 - \frac{\pi^2}{2(n+1)^2} + \frac{\pi^4}{24(n+1)^4}$$

$$\le 1 - \frac{1}{(n+1)^2} + 5\frac{1}{(n+1)^4}.$$

Since $\frac{5}{(n+1)^4} \le \frac{1}{2(n+1)^2}$ for a sufficiently large n we have $\cos \frac{\pi}{n+1} \le 1 - \frac{1}{2(n+1)^2}$. This lets us conclude that for $t = 2(n+1)^2$ we obtain $\beta^t \le 1/e$ and for $t = 2(n+1)^2 \cdot \ln \frac{1}{\varepsilon} dn^3$ we get $\beta^t \le \frac{\varepsilon}{dn^3}$. Assuming that d is constant and upper bounding $2(n+1)$ with $3n$ we have that $\beta^t \le \frac{\varepsilon}{dn^3}$ for $t = 9n^2 \ln \frac{1}{\varepsilon} n$. This proves that after $t = 9n^2 \ln \frac{1}{\varepsilon} n$ steps we have $d^t(v_i) \le \varepsilon$. $\square$

4 Dynamic setting

In this section we investigate the performance of the GO-TO-THE-MIDDLE strategy in a dynamic scenario. We first present a route for the explorer which apparently is a hard instance for our strategy. In the second part we investigate our strategy on a very regularly winding route, and on a random walk.

4.1 A hard case

We set the maximum transmission distance of stations to 5 units. The experiment starts with the explorer in distance r from the base station. Relay stations are aligned on a straight line between the base station and the explorer, each of them in distance 5 from its neighbors.

Then the explorer starts to walk on a circle with radius r around the base station. The relay station path has to keep up with the motion of the explorer. We let the explorer move always with the same constant speed of 1 unit per time step.

We have discovered that direction changes are profitable for the GO-TO-THE-MIDDLE strategy – see for example the experiments in the next subsection. According to this observation a cyclic scenario is very hard for the GO-TO-THE-MIDDLE – since the explorer steadily moves on the circle, it does not meaningfully change its movement direction and has a high angular speed.

We can alter the speed of the relay stations by allowing them to execute a variable number of GO-TO-THE-MIDDLE rounds per time unit. We denote the number of GO-TO-THE-MIDDLE rounds per time unit as the speed of the relay stations.

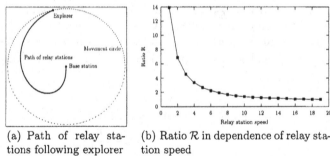

(a) Path of relay sta-   (b) Ratio $\mathcal{R}$ in dependence of relay stations following explorer   tion speed

Fig. 3. GO-TO-THE-MIDDLE for the hard movement model

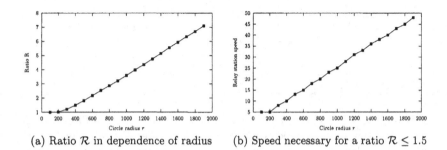

(a) Ratio $\mathcal{R}$ in dependence of radius   (b) Speed necessary for a ratio $\mathcal{R} \leq 1.5$

Fig. 4. Performance of GO-TO-THE-MIDDLE in the hard movement model

The performance of the GO-TO-THE-MIDDLE strategy is measured in terms of the length of the communication path between the explorer and the base station. In an optimal solution, this length would be always equal to r. Since the relay stations may not keep up with the explorer, the length of the line may increase to more than r (obviously new relay stations are introduced then).

We observe that for each radius r and each speed s there is some length l_{max} of the communication line which is stable, i.e. the communication line length won't exceed this value no matter how long the experiment runs. Figure 3(a) shows the typical curve of the communication line after it reached its stability point. This curve will now only rotate with the movement of the explorer on the circle.

To visualize the performance of the strategy we introduce the ratio $\mathcal{R}$ between the length of the communication line l_{max} and the length of the optimal interval connecting the explorer and base station. This ratio is investigated in Fig. 3(b) for different speeds of relay stations. Fig. 4(b) shows the ratio $\mathcal{R}$ in dependence of the radius r with the speed fixed to 10 for all radii.

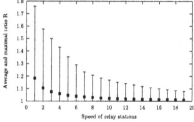

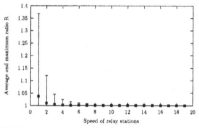

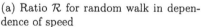

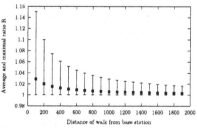

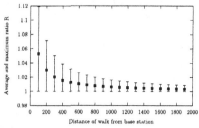

(a) Ratio $\mathcal{R}$ for random walk in dependence of speed

(b) Ratio $\mathcal{R}$ for snake-like exploration in dependence of speed

(c) Ratio $\mathcal{R}$ for random walk in dependence of distance

(d) Ratio $\mathcal{R}$ for snake-like exploration in dependence of distance

Fig. 5. Performance of GO-TO-THE-MIDDLE for average-case movement models

The maximum length of the communication path $l_{\max}$ (and thus the ratio $\mathcal{R}$) grows with the radius r, since with the radius r the number of employed relay stations grows and the propagation of the explorer's position updates takes longer time. The growth of $\mathcal{R}$ is linear with the radius.

Fig. 4(b) shows the speed necessary for the ratio $\mathcal{R}$ to be not greater than 1.5. This calculated speed is thus necessary to have a communication path which is a fairly well approximation of the optimal one. We also see a linear increase here.

4.2 Average cases

Within this section we investigate two movement models for the explorer. One of them is a random walk on the plane, performed with a constant speed, with a direction randomly chosen in each time step. The direction is chosen uniformly at random from the angle $(-30, +30)$ degrees from the current direction of the explorer. The movement patterns are depicted in the full version of the paper.

For both movement models the ratio between the optimal communication path length and the actual communication path length $\mathcal{R}$ has been computed in each time step. Figures 5(a) and (b) show the average and maximum values of this ratio for both movement models and for different speeds. The same movement pattern can be executed in various distances from the base station.

Figure 5(c) and (d) shows the results. Interestingly, when the movements are performed in a large distance from the base station, the ratio between the optimal communication path length and the actual path length is low – this comes from the fact that a small movement of the explorer in a large distance from the base stations does not cause large changes in the position of the optimal path and the angular speed of the explorer is low.

5 Conclusion

The experiments and theoretical considerations regarding the performance of GO-TO-THE-MIDDLE allow to compute a relay station speed which will give a good approximation factor of the optimal communication path by the relay stations.

The experimental analysis has been performed to obtain information on the behavior of our strategy in various situation. This analysis gives several hints on how to choose the speed of relay stations when the movement pattern of the explorer is not known beforehand. The experimental average-case analysis proves that our strategy can effectively maintain the communication path within an approximation factor of 1.5 with a relay station speed as low as 3, when certain assumptions about the movement of the explorer are known.

References

1. Y. U. Cao, A. S. Fukunaga, and A. B. Kahng. Cooperative mobile robotics: Antecedents and directions. In *Autonomous Robots*, volume 4, pages 1–23, 1997.
2. C. W. Reynolds. Flocks, herds, and schools: A distributed behavioral model. In *Computer Graphics*, pages 25–34, 1987.
3. Y. Liu and K. M. Passino. Swarm intelligence: Literature overview.
4. R. Arkin. Behavior-based robotics. Cambridge, MA: MIT Press, 1998.
5. G. Dudek, M. Jenkin, E. Milios, and D. Wilkes. A taxonomy for swarm robotics. In *IEEE/TSJ International Conference on Intelligent Robots and Systems*, pages 441–447, 1993.
6. K. Sugihara and I. Suzuki. Distributed motion coordination of multiple mobile robots. In *5th IEEE International Symposium on Intelligent Control*, volume 1, pages 138–143, 1990.
7. Ichiro Suzuki and Masafumi Yamashita. Distributed anonymous mobile robots: Formation of geometric patterns. *SIAM J. Comput.*, 28(4):1347–1363, 1999.
8. I. Chatzigiannakis, M. Markou, and S. Nikoletseas. Distributed circle formation for anonymous oblivious robots. In *LNCS*, volume 3059, pages 159–174, 2004.
9. Q. Chen and J. Y. S. Luh. Coordination and control of a group of small mobile robots. In *IEEE International Conference on Robotics and Automation*, volume 3, pages 2315–2320, 1994.
10. H. Ando, Y. Oasa, I. Suzuki, and M. Yamashita. Distributed memoryless point convergence algorithm for mobile robots with limited visibility. In *IEEE Transactions on Robotics and Automation*, volume 15, 1999.

Active Patterns for Self-Optimization
Schemes for the Design of Intelligent Mechatronic Systems

Andreas Schmidt

UNITY AG, Lindberghring 1, D-33142 Büren, Germany,
Andreas.Schmidt@unity.de, http://www.unity.de

Abstract. Self-optimizing mechatronic systems react autonomously and flexibly to changing conditions. They are capable of learning and optimize their behavior throughout their life cycle. The paradigm of self-optimization is originally inspired by the behavior of biological systems. The key to the successful development of self-optimizing systems is a conceptual design process that precisely describes the desired system behavior. In the area of mechanical engineering, active principles based on physical effects such as friction or lever are widely used to concretize the construction structure and the behavior. The same approach can be found in the domain of software-engineering with software patterns such as the broker-pattern or the strategy pattern. However there is no appropriate design schema for the development of intelligent mechatronic systems covering the needs to fulfill the paradigm of self-optimization. This article proposes such a schema called Active Patterns for Self-Optimization. It is shown how a catalogue of active patterns can be derived from a set of four basic active patterns. This design approach is validated for a networked mechatronic system in a multiagent setting where the behavior is implemented according to a biologically inspired technique – the neuro-fuzzy learning method.

1 Introduction – Self-Optimization in Mechatronic Systems

Future systems in the area of mechanical engineering will comprise configurations of intelligent system elements, where the communication and cooperation between these elements shape the behavior of the overall system. In terms of software engineering these are distributed systems of interacting agents. Agents are autonomous and adaptive function modules which can themselves initiate actions. These function modules are heterogeneous subsystems with mechanical,

Please use the following format when citing this chapter:

Schmidt, A., 2006, in IFIP International Federation for Information Processing, Volume 216, Biologically Inspired Cooperative Computing, eds. Pan, Y., Rammig, F., Schmeck, H., Solar, M., (Boston: Springer), pp. 147–156.

electronic and information technology components. The agents' behavior can be modified while the system is in operation – this is expressed by the term "adaptive".

A self-optimizing system is characterized by four fundamental aspects (Fig. 1): the target system, in the sense of a hierarchy of a number of targets; the structure, e. g. the topology of mechanical components, sensors and actuators; the behavior, which is the system's reaction to influences from its environment; and the parameters that characterize the system components [1].

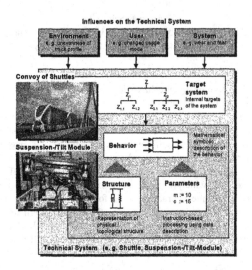

Fig. 1. Aspects of Self-Optimizing Systems

According to [2], intelligent mechatronic systems can be divided up into three layers: the *Multifunction-Module* layer (MFM) that is close to the sensor-/actuator, e. g. suspension-/tilt-modules. The *Autonomous Mechatronic System* (AMS) layer covers system elements that act autonomously in its environment such as single shuttles. The *Networked Mechatronic System* (NMS) layer represents unions of AMS, e. g. convoys that pursue common goals such as crossing a switch[1].

The aim is to carry out self-optimization on the basis of mathematical models, e. g. using a realistic physical model of the controlled system supplemented by excitation and evaluation models. Frequently, it will not be practicable to use models for reasons of cost, so model-based self-optimization is combined with what is called "behavior-based self-optimization" which acts quasi-nondeterministic. This means that changes occurring during operation are sensed and analyzed, and then, depending on the results of this analysis, either another appropriate mathematical optimization model is loaded, or, if the limitations of available models are exceeded, the system reverts to using past experience in the form of learned structures or

---

[1] The sample mechatronic system originates from the New Railway Technology project Paderborn (NBP) [3]. NBP has set-up a test-track where railway shuttles autonomously drive on an innovative magnetic track system.

parameter settings from its knowledge base. The self-optimization process proceeds continuously and repeatedly according to the subsequent three actions:

1. **Analysis of current situation:** The system records its own state and the state of its environment. The necessary information may be obtained by communicating directly with other systems or by accessing previously recorded observations.
2. **Determination of targets:** The system determines its current target system in view of the current situation, and, if necessary, also adapts it.
3. **Adaptation of the system behavior:** The adaptation itself is carried out by modifying the parameters, the structure, and/or the behavior of individual system elements.

2   Current Situation – Design of Intelligent Mechatronic Systems

The design of self-optimizing systems is based on systems engineering [4], design methods of conventional mechanical engineering [5] and the design methodology of mechatronics [6] and extends those methods with essential aspects of the self-optimization paradigm. The conception phase constitutes one of the most decisive stages within the design of self-optimizing systems (Fig. 2). This is when fundamental functionalities (Function Hierarchy) and the structure (Construction Structure and Component Structure) of the system are determined.

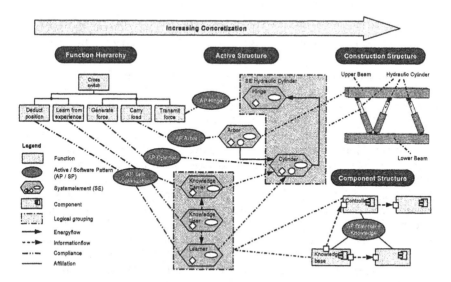

Fig. 2. Core steps of the early stages of system conception

In order to reuse successfully proven previous system engineering knowledge, active patterns are utilized. Active patterns contain template system elements and behavior to realize functions that are concretized in an active structure. Fig. 3 depicts a categorization of domain-specific patterns [1], e. g. active principles AP of mechanical engineering according to [5] such as *AP Cylinder* in Fig. 2 or software patterns SP such as the *broker pattern* according to [7] or *SP Distributed Knowledge* in Fig. 2. However, those patterns do not address the specific needs for the superior paradigm of self-optimization, namely specifying intelligent and autonomous behavior in an unknown or partially known environment by analysis of the current situation, determination of targets and adaptation of the system behavior. This is where the demand for active patterns for self-optimization comes into play shown as AP Self-Optimization (Fig. 2) and categorized as a pattern of information processing (Fig. 3).

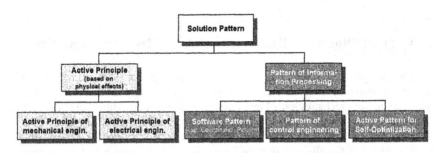

Fig. 3. Category of Patterns for the Design of Intelligent Mechatronic Systems

3 Approach – Design with Active Patterns for Self-Optimization

Active patterns for self-optimization (AP_{SO}) realize functions for self-optimizing systems such as autonomous planning, cooperation, and learning. AP_{SO} constitute templates which specify generally accepted, autonomous and intelligent behavior by using principle-models, application-scenarios, structure-models, behavior-models and method-models (Fig. 4). The principle-concept characterizes the basic idea of the AP_{SO}. It is used to allow the designer an intuitive access to the AP_{SO}. Application-scenarios depict situations in which the AP_{SO} have already been applied successfully in the past. Those scenarios shall help the designer to select an appropriate AP_{SO} for the task at hand. The structure-model specifies necessary participating system-elements and their relations among each other. One or more behavior-models describe adaptation-processes as a kind of state changes. The focus is on the modeling of autonomous intelligent behavior, which activates, supports and/or executes these state changes. This way a system is transformed from a given initial state to a desired target-state by the use of specific methods. Method-models specify those methods in detail.

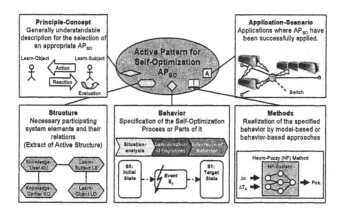

Fig. 4. Components of Active Patterns for Self-Optimization

We structure active patterns according to the *House of Active Pattern for Self-Optimization* (Fig. 5).

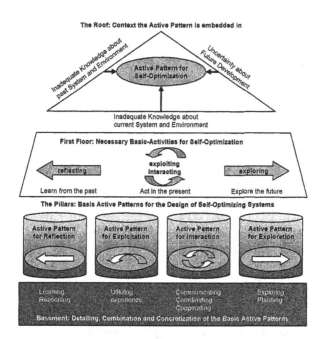

Fig. 5. The House of Active Patterns for Self-Optimization

Four basic active patterns can be differentiated which are derived from the pattern context and necessary activities for fulfilling the self-optimization process. The context may involve problem areas such as inadequate knowledge about past system and environment behavior, inadequate knowledge about the current system and environment behavior or uncertainty about the future behavior. The context specifies demands for necessary basic-activities, such as learning from the past which we call *reflecting*, acting in the present which we denominate *exploiting* knowledge as well as *interacting* with other system elements and finally *exploring* the future. This approach leads to the four basic *Active Patterns for Reflection, Exploitation, Interaction* and *Exploration*.

The basic active patterns can be detailed, combined and concretized (Fig. 6). Detailing an active pattern means to specialize the pattern structure and pattern behavior according to the method which shall execute the system behavior, e. g. detail *Reflection* towards *Reinforcing Reflection* in order to use the method reinforcement learning [8] where successful past behavior is rewarded. Basic patterns can be combined to form typical compound behavior, e. g. the combination of *Exploitation* and *Reflection* leads to a typical compound behavior in a multiagent setting of exploiting the knowledge of distributed system elements to direct the learning behavior of the whole system [9]. Eventually, the pattern structure and pattern behavior needs to be concretized towards the active structure and finally to the construction and component structure of the system.

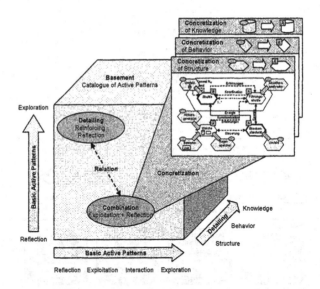

Fig. 6. Catalogue of Active Patterns

The catalogue of active patterns has been applied to several application scenarios of intelligent mechatronic systems, e. g. to shuttles driving on tracks by implementing the active patterns of *Exploration* and *Interaction* [10] or to the suspension-/tilt-module of a shuttle using the active patterns of *Interaction* and *Exploitation* [11]. The following chapter depicts the application of active patterns on the Networked Mechatronic System layer to design collaborative behavior of shuttles crossing a switch.

4   Validation – Collaborative Behavior of Shuttles Crossing a Switch

The application scenario of crossing a switch is as follows (Fig. 7): A Networked Mechatronic System of two convoys C_A and C_B, each consisting of several autonomous shuttles A_i und B_j, approach a switch. The passage of a single shuttle shall be designed such that the approaching convoys C_A and C_B are merged to a virtual convoy C_V. The shuttles shall optimize themselves autonomously and under restricted or no prior knowledge about an optimum behavior according to their own targets after each successfully completed crossing procedure. The whole scenario is split up into three zones – a decision, an execution and a learning zone.

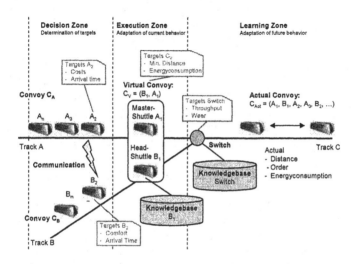

Fig. 7. The application-scenario of crossing a switch

In the course of the early conception stage, a function hierarchy is built up (Fig. 8). Let us illustrate the increasing concretization at the function of *Determination of Sequence* which shall define the passage sequence of shuttles. Based on prior design experience [11] this function can be realized by implementing the AP_{SO} *Exploitation*. The pattern structure of the AP_{SO} consists of two system-elements – the Knowledge-Carrier and the Knowledge-User. The pattern behavior can be specified by a statechart which specifies the adaptation process by a neuro-fuzzy method [12]. The AP_{SO} is concretized towards the active structure as follows. Every shuttle can be a Knowledge-Carrier because of its implicit experience about the determination of sequence generation with the help of neuro-fuzzy methods. The master-shuttle represents the Knowledge-User because it determines the passage-sequence for the remaining shuttles. Eventually, the adaptation of the behavior is detailed by a statechart which specifies possible adaptation processes for the generation of a virtual convoy C_v – here the adaptation process from an initial state S_0 – head-shuttles A_1 and B_1 right ahead of the switch – to the target-states $S_1 := C_v = (A_1, B_1)$

that is A_1 drives first, afterwards B_1 – as well as $S_2 := C_v=(B_1,A_1)$ that is B_1 drives first, then A_1.

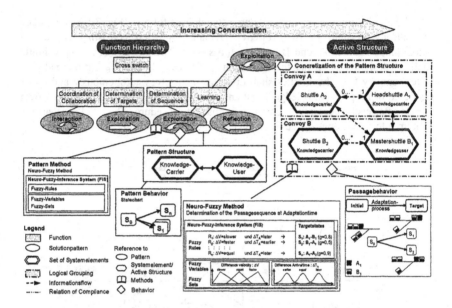

Fig. 8. Concretization in Design - Application Scenario of Crossing a Switch

In particular, the AP_{SO} *Interaction* specifies how the shuttles communicate with each other and determines the master-shuttle (Fig. 9). The AP_{SO} *Exploration* designs how target states such as S_1 or S_2 can be determined or newly created. A neuro-fuzzy system takes input-variables such as the velocity of shuttles $\Delta v = (v_{A1} - v_{B1})$ and arrival-time $\Delta T_A = (t_{A1} - t_{B1})$ at the switch to assign passage-classes such as $C_1 := (A1\text{-}B1) = $ *Master-Shuttle drives first* and class $C_2 := (B1\text{-}A1) = $ *Master-Shuttle drives second.* Because of the inherent uncertain and vague knowledge about environment- and system-states, fuzzy-variables are introduced, e. g. $\Delta v = $ (slower, equal, faster) and $\Delta T_A = $ (earlier, equal, later). Fuzzy-rules realize the assignment of passage-classes, e. g. *If (Δv = slower and ΔT_A = later) Then (A1 – B1).* The AP_{SO} *Exploitation* allows the system to start from initial knowledge and initial rules in system-state S_0 for setting up the neuro-fuzzy system. Once a target state such as S_1 is reached, AP_{SO} *Reflection* specifies, how the experience that was accumulated during the adaptation process can lead to adapted fuzzy-sets and new rules. This is done by evaluating the degree of fulfillment of committed targets such as minimum distance between shuttle Δd_{min} and maximum energy consumption E_{max} and consequently adapting the weights of the neural network of the neuro-fuzzy system leading to adapted fuzzy-sets and possibly to new fuzzy-rules.

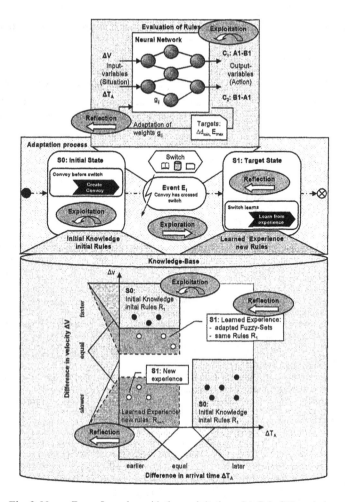

Fig. 9. Neuro-Fuzzy Learning with the exploitation of A-Priori Knowledge

5 Conclusion and future work

This article has proposed a schema called *Active Patterns for Self-Optimization* in order to design self-optimizing mechatronic systems in the early design stage. A set of four active patterns established the basis for the specification of a catalogue of patterns along the dimensions of detailing, combining and concretizing. The design approach was validated for a networked mechatronic system namely the crossing of a switch by convoys which consist of individually and autonomously acting shuttles. The pattern behavior was implemented according to the biologically inspired technique of neuro-fuzzy learning. Altogether it was shown, that active patterns for self-optimization constitute an applicable approach for the design of intelligent mechatronic systems in the early design stages.

In order to cope with functional demands that arise from endogenous needs of agents as opposed to given external targets, future research will deal with the extension of active pattern schema towards cognitive behavior. Also, the pattern catalogue will be extended as new application scenarios of intelligent mechatronic systems demand a detailing and concretization of pattern structures and behavior.

6 References

1. Frank, U.; Giese, H.; Klein, F.; Oberschelp, O.; Schmidt, A.; Schulz, B.; Vöcking, H.; Witting, K.; Gausemeier, J. (Hrsg.): Selbstoptimierende Systeme des Maschinenbaus - Definitionen und Konzepte. HNI-Verlagsschriftenreihe Band 155, Paderborn, 2004
2. Lückel, J.; Hestermeyer, T.; Liu-Henke, X.: Generalization of the Cascade Principle in View of a Structured Form of Mechatronic Systems. IEEE/ASME International Conference on Advanced Intelligent Mechatronics (AIM 2001), Villa Olmo ; Como, Italy, 2001
3. New Railway Technology Paderborn (NBP) – A Research Initiative for the Improvement of the Attraction of the Railway-System. http://nbp-www.upb.de, 2005
4. Daenzer, W. F.; Huber, F.: Systems Engineering – Methoden und Praxis. 8. verbesserte Auflage; Verlag Industrielle Organisation; Zürich, 1994
5. Pahl G.; Beitz W.; Feldhusen, J.: Engineering Design – A Systematic Approach. 3. ed., Springer-Verlag, Berlin 2006
6. Verein Deutscher Ingenieure (VDI): Design Methodology for Mechatronic Systems. VDI Guideline 2206, Beuth Verlag, Berlin, 2004
7. Gamma, E.; Helm, R.; Johnson, R.; Vlissides, J.: Design Patterns – Elements of Reusable Object-Oriented Software. Addison-Wesley, München, 1996
8. Berenji, N.R., Khedar, P.: Learning and Tuning Fuzzy Logic Controllers through Reinforcements. In: IEEE Trans. Neural Networks, No. 3, IEEE Press, Piscataway, NJ, USA 1992, pp. 724-740
9. Santamaría, J. C.: Learning Adaptive Reactive Agents. Doctoral Thesis, College of Computing, Georgia Institute of Technology, Atlanta, Georgia, 1997
10. Gausemeier, J.; Frank, U.; Giese, H.; Klein, F.; Schmidt, A.; Steffen, D.; Tichy, M.: A Design Methodology for Self-Optimizing Systems. In: Contributions to the 6th Braunschweig Conference of Automation, Assistance and Embedded Real Time Platforms for Transportation (AAET2005), Feb. 16th and 17th 2005, Technical University of Braunschweig, GZVB, 2005, Vol. II, pp. 456-479
11. Gausemeier, J.; Frank, U.; Schmidt, A.; Steffen, D.: Towards a Design Methodology for Self-Optimizing Systems. In: ElMaraghy, H.; ElMaraghy, W. (Hrsg.): Advances in Design, Springer Verlag, 2006, pp. 61-71
12. Koch, M; Kleinjohann, B.; Schmidt, A.; Scheideler, P.; Saskevic, A.; Gambuzza, A.; Oberschelp, O.; Hestermeyer, T.; Münch, E.: A Neuro-Fuzzy Approach for Self-Optimizing Concepts and Structures of Mechatronic Systems. In: Chu, H.-W.; Savoie, M.; Sanchez, B.: Proc. of the International Conference on Computing, Communications and Control Technologies (CCCT2004), Austin, USA, 14.- 17.08.2004, pp. 263-268

Acute Stress Response for Self-optimizing Mechatronic Systems

Holger Giese[1], Norma Montealegre[2], Thomas Müller[2], Simon Oberthür[2], and Bernd Schulz[3]

[1] Software Engineering Group, University of Paderborn, Germany
[2] Heinz Nixdorf Institute, University of Paderborn, Germany
[3] Power Electronics and Electrical Drives, University of Paderborn, Germany

Abstract. Self-optimizing mechatronic systems have the ability to adjust their goals and behavior according to changes of the environment or system by means of complex real-time coordination and reconfiguration in the underlying software and hardware. In this paper we sketch a generic software architecture for mechatronic systems with self-optimization and outline which analogies between this architecture and the information processing in natural organisms exist. The architecture at first exploits the ability of its subsystems to adapt their resource requirements to optimize its performance with respect to the usage of available computational resources. Secondly, the architecture achieves, inspired by the acute stress response of a natural being, that in the case of an emergency it makes all recources available to address a given threat in a self-coordinated manner.

1 Introduction

The next generation of advanced mechatronic systems is expected to behave more intelligently than today's systems. They adjust their goals and behavior according to changes of the environment or system and build communities of autonomous agents. The agents exploit local and global networking to enhance their functionality (cf. [17]). Such mechatronic systems will thus include complex real-time reconfiguration of the underlying software and hardware as well as complex real-time coordination to adjust their behavior to the changing system goals leading to self-adaptation (or self-optimization) [15, 10, 12, 5].

As advanced mechatronic systems usually consist of a complex network of concurrently running components which are also called (software) agents, we have developed a general architectural model of its components the so-called Operator-Controller Module (OCM) [9]. Within a single autonomous mechatronic system, a hierarchy of OCMs is employed to define the strictly hierarchical architecture. In contrast, at the top level the OCMs are free to connect to their peers to establish the required coordination. In this paper, we will outline which analogies between our architectural approach and related phenomena in nature exists but also where are the limits of these analogies.

Please use the following format when citing this chapter:

Giese, H., Montealegre, N., Müller, T., Oberthür, S., Schulz, B., 2006, in IFIP International Federation for Information Processing, Volume 216, Biologically Inspired Cooperative Computing, eds. Pan, Y., Rammig, F., Schmeck, H., Solar, M., (Boston: Springer), pp. 157–167.

While the proposed OCM architecture is mainly driven by the requirements for self-optimizing mechatronic behavior, it also shows some similarities with several proposed layered architectures. [8] suggests that a two level architecture with a low-level execution and a higher-level control layer represents a general pattern present in natural as well as artificial organic systems. A related practical approach explained in [14] is the Observer/Controller architecture for Organic Computing systems. Similar to the OCM it is inspired in the *brain stem* as low level structures which reacts to sensory inputs and the *limbic system* as a high-level structure which observes and manipulates the first one. In contrast to this work, the OCM also supports higher cognitive behavior which matches the planning layer of the Touring Machines [4] (autonomous agents with attitudes) and tries to reach the goal of a general model for autonomous cognitive agents as stated in [16], which explains the action selection paradigm of mind for conscious software agents and how the most relevant behavior/action is selected and executed, supporting approach concerning to the method for emergency situations described below.

Following support for the OCM architecture exist: The model-driven development with MECHATRONIC UML [2] and block diagrams is provided by the CASE tool Fujaba and CAE tool CAMeL. Additionally, methods for verification of the real-time behavior, excluding adverse effects due to complex reconfiguration in hierarchical OCM architectures, [7, 6] exists. The MECHATRONIC UML approach also permits to specify resource-aware OCMs which can adapt their resource consumption in form of different operational profiles [1]. These resource-aware OCMs are further supported by a specific extension of the real-time operating system DREAMS [11]. It optimize the system usage of the computational resources at run-time. This is similar to the conscious mind which devotes its attention and efforts for different control behavior so that the result is optimized.

Concerning dependability, the existing techniques [7, 6] require that hazards or detected faults are explicitly handled within the OCM hierarchy. Such an explicit handling has to abstract drastically from the different failure configurations of its subsystems, otherwise the resulting combinatoric explosion would render the development prohibitively expensive. To overcome this limitation and better handle unanticipated faults, we developed a generic self-organizing scheme how an self-optimizing mechatronic system can exploit the ability of its parts to adapt their resource requirements. The scheme is inspired by the "acute stress response" of a natural being (cf. [3]). It enables that in the case of an emergency all available resources are assigned in such a manner that the threat can be addressed with priority.

The structure of the paper is as follows: We start with an example of a self-optimizing mechatronic system in Section 2 and then introduce our general architectural model for self-optimizing mechatronic systems, its modeling, and their ability to adapt their resource consumption using this example. Then, the safety-driven self-organizing resource management is outlined in Section 3 before we conclude the paper.

2 Example and Modeling

As a concrete example, we use the Paderborn-based RailCab research project[1]. The modular railway system combines sophisticated undercarriages with the advantage of new actuation techniques as employed in the Transrapid[2] to increase passenger comfort, enabling efficient transportation at a high average speed, and (re)using of the existing railway tracks. We will use in the following a specific element of the motion control as a running example.

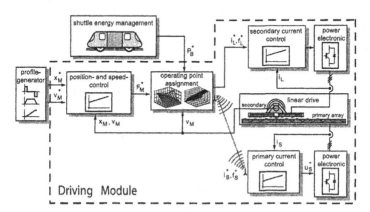

Fig. 1. Structure of the Driving Module with operating point assignment

Fig. 1 shows the structure of driving module of the linear motor of the railway system. The driving module consists of doubly fed linear drive with magnetic active coils at the track and at the vehicle. The magnetic fields of the coils are supported by the electrical currents, which are predetermined with their frequency by the operating point assignment. The product of the current defines the thrust 1 and with its frequency it also gives the transferred power to the vehicle 2. Thence, the operating point assignment of the linear drive is pivotal for the proper work of the whole vehicle. Without a suitable operating point assignment, a safe and dependable work of the railway system is not possible.

$$F_M = K_M I_{1d} I_{2q} \quad (1) \qquad P_B = 3(\pi f_L \frac{L_h N_2}{N_1} I_{2q} I_{1d} - R_2 I_{2q}^2) \quad (2)$$

A simple operating point assignment can be handled by a full powered primary at the track. This fix operation point leads to an inefficient operation of the system. To improve this efficiency the operating point assignment can be done by a simple efficiency-optimal algorithm outlined in [13]. The concept of

[1] http://www-nbp.upb.de/en
[2] http://www.transrapid.de/en

self-optimizing in mechatronic systems allows a more powerful operating point assignment [18]. This self-optimizing operating point assignment enables the system self-adapting to the system objectives as a response to changes in the surrounding of the system.

In case of a low charge state at energy storage system in the vehicle, the losses in the vehicle became more important than the efficiency of the whole system. Otherwise, the efficiency of the whole system can be maximized while the power transfer is not in the focus of the operating point assignment. Moreover, the importance of the power transfer to the vehicle depends on the expected consumption and distance profile of the track.

2.1 Architecture

As illustrated by the example, even the control software of the Driving Module results in a complex network of concurrently running components. Therefore we suggest to structure the software architecture using Operator-Controller Modules (OCM) as depicted in Fig. 2 (cf. [9]) as basic building blocks of a hierarchy.

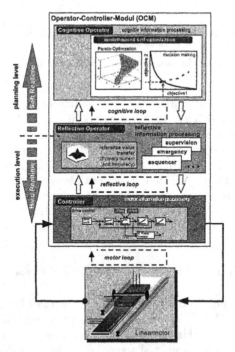

Fig. 2. Structure of the Operator-Controller-Module for operating point assigment

The OCM suggests the following internal structuring: (1) On the lowest level of the OCM, there is the *controller* which realizes the currently active control strategy, processes measurements, and produces the control signals. This part consists in the example of the drive control for the linear drive. (2) The *reflective operator*, in which monitoring and controlling routines are executed, monitors the controller. In the example, at this level the transfer of the reference value for the operating point assignment as well as fault detection and management is done. (3) The *cognitive operator* is trying to improve the behavior of the OCM in soft real-time. The calculation and optimization of new reference values in the example OCM are located here.

The OCM defines the so called micro architecture of the system somehow inspired by the organization of the information processing as found in more advanced animals. The behavior located in the cognitive operator relates to the conscious decisions and planning. The reflective operator more or less fits to the non conscious behavior which ensures that for a specific situation appropriate reflexes and control strategies are activated. However, in contrast to natural organisms the proposed architecture suggest to separate these levels in each OCM of the hierarchy while in information processing of an organism this separation only exists for the whole organism. Another distinction is that in nature evolution ensures that unsafe behavior is eliminated while in our systems even the loss of a single individual due to such an "experiment of life" could not be justified. Therefore, guarantees must be provided using, for example, formal verification techniques (cf. [7, 6]).

2.2 Modeling

During the implementation of the software for a Hardware-in-Loop test bed, we modeled the operating point assignment module as an OCM. We peresent in Fig. 3 a simplified state chart, which depicts the parallel processing of the different layers in the cognitive- and reflective operator as well as the controller.

The controller has to support the motion Control of the vehicle at all circumstances. The reflective operator at first has to support the critical tasks of Analyzing the advisability of the optimized set values for the controller. In the parallel Adjust state, the reflective operator remains in the Normal state and provides optimized set values to the controller as long as suitable operating points set values where available. Otherwise, in case of inappropriate operating point set values, which can be the result of an unexpected thrust demand or quick changing parameters of the motor, the Adjust state of the reflective operator will switch over to the Emergency state. In parallel, the Parameter Estimation state is required for parameter estimation of the motor parameters to enable the cognitive operator to make a suitable optimization. In the cognitive operator of the OCM suitable objectives for the next optimization cycle are elected in the Pre-Adjust state. At the Optimization state, the multi objective optimization is done and afterwards the pareto point selection follows in the Decision Making state. The selected operating point for a discrete time is then employed in the

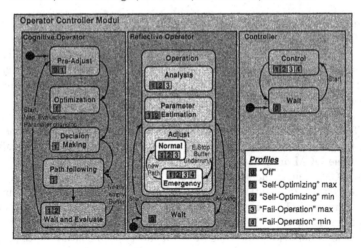

Fig. 3. States and profiles of the Operating Point Assigment OCM

Path Following state to calculate the selected operating point for the next few seconds. This calculated path will be send the reflective operator and a review of the calculated optimization results in the Wait and Evaluate state is used to decide whether a new optimization cycle is required or whether it is sufficient to continue the path jumping to the Path Following state.

2.3 Resource Management

The resource-aware OCM becomes possible due to our RTOS named DREAMS (Distributed Real-time Extensible Application Management System) which provides a special resource manager [11] (Flexible Resource Manager - FRM). DREAMS is tailored to the special demands of the dynamic class of self-optimizing applications. The manager tries to optimize the resource utilization at run-time. The optimization includes a safe overallocation of resources, by putting resources that are held back for worst-case szenarios by OCMs at other OCMs disposal. The interface to the FRM is called Profile Framework. By means of the Profile Framework the developer can define a set of profiles per application. Profiles describe different *service levels* of the application, including different quality and different resource requirements.

All states belonging to one profile build the state space that can be reached when the profile is active. In Fig. 3 the inclusion of the states in profiles is depicted by assigning the related profile numbers. The required resources of the controller are always the same if the system is in operation. Therefore, the Control state must be in all profiles. The resource requirements of the reflective operator in contrast vary depending on the current profile. In the "Self-Optimizing min/max" profiles all three parallel states are active while in "Fail-Operation min/max" they are subsequently disabled. The cognitive operator can be switched off if required. Therefore, the states Pre-Adjust, Optimizing, and Decision Making, which require high calculation-resources are only supported in the "Self-Optimizing max" profile. On the other hand the Path Following and Wait and Evalute state, which needs just less resources, are also in the "Self-Optimizing min" profile. None of this states are present in any of the "Fail-Operation min/max" profiles. This reflects the fact that the decoupling of the OCM concept permits to suspend the complete cognitive operator at any time. A recovering of the cognitive features will leads to possible restart of the optimization cycle.

The mentioned profile information can be generated out of the state chart as described in detail in [1].

3 Safety driven resource management

The different profiles can be assigned to specific *emergency categories* using a generic monitoring concept for self-optimizing systems. We developed this concept originally in order to protect OCMs systematically against hazards or faults. These hazards or faults might result from their cognitive self-optimizing behavior themselves, but self-optimizing behavior can also support the reallocation of resource to handle threats as outlined in the following.

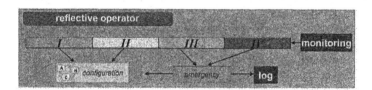

Fig. 4. Monitoring Concept for self-optimizing Systems

We have integrated the monitoring in the reflectoring operator of the OCM. The monitoring concept is a guideline, when and how self-optimization is reasonable to use. Furthermore it describes which emergency categories should be supported and when a switching between them should be initiated to avoid major consequences (cf. Fig. 4) and which characteristics a profile should fulfill in order to be included in each category. The monitoring concept distinguishes four different emergency categories:

I The system operates regularly and uses the self-optimization for the major system objectives; e.g. comfort and energy efficiency if useful. All regular profiles fall into this category, in our example "Self-Optimizing max/min".

II A possible threat has been detected and the self-optimization is not only used to optimize the behavior but also reach system states, which are considered to be safer than the current one. We describe in the next section our nature inspired method which ensures that the system can in this case provide more resources to enable more efficient countermeasures. In our example the Analysis substate of the reflective operator will detect this problem and only the profiles "Self-Optimizing max/min" and "Fail-Operation max" fit to this category.

IIIA hazard has been detected that endangers the system. Fast and robust countermeasures, like a reflex, are performed in the reflective operator in hard real-time in order to reach a safer state (I or II). Depending on the specific OCM, profiles where the cognitive reactions runs in the background may still be employed, profiles with additional functionality may be employed, or only robust profiles without self-optimization are used. The "Fail-Operation min/max" profiles fit into this category, which use robust standard parameter settings to get back to a safe operational behavior.

IVThe system is no longer under control; the system must be immediately stopped or a minimal safe-operational mode must be warranted, to minimize damage. In rare cases, cognitive reactions in the OCM may be employed in order to rescue the system if no fail-safe or minimal fail-operational behavior is possible. In our example the "Fail-Operation min" profile may be employed during the emergency brake of the system.

3.1 Emergency categories and the acute stress response

The American physiologist Walter Cannon published the "Fight-or-flight"-Theory in 1929 [3], also known as *acute stress response*. It describes the reaction of humans and animals to threats. In such "stress" situations specific physiological actions are taking place by the sympathetic nervous system of the organism as an automatic regulation system without the intervention of conscious thought. For example, epinephrine a hormone is released which causes the organism to release energy to react on the threat (fight or flight).

We imitate this behavior inside our OCMs with support of our resource management of the RTOS. The idea is, when an OCM of the system detects a threat for the system the agent releases virtual epinephrine. This distributed epinephrine force non-critical OCMs in a profile with lower resource consumptions to free resources and thus permits the agent to hanlde the threat more appropriatley by switching in a profile of the emergency category II.

Concrete the epinephrine carries the information how much additional resources the OCM, which released the epinephrine, requires to activate his optimal profile to handle the threat (eg. figure 3). All OCMs are sorted according their safety critical nature. As the blood system in an organism, our resource manager distributed the epinephrine to the OCMs. Starting with the OCMs with the lowest safety level, the epinephrine is injected to this OCMs and it can react on the epinephrine by switching into a special profile with lower resource requirements. If the OCM is only responsible for comfort it could for example switch to a "Off" profile with no or minimal resource requirements. The OCM "consumes" the epinephrine, this means the information inside the epinephrine how much resources are still required is updated. Then the resources manager distributes the updated epinephrine to the next OCM, even if no resources are required anymore, so every OCM has information about the threat and can react accordingly. This procedure has the advantage that we achieve a faster self-organized reallocation than in the case of the regular resource optimization of the RTOS.

In practice the switching to lower proviles of none or low critical OCMs is done, after collecting the information from all OCMs. This is done to ensure that all profile switches can be realized. The complexity of this process is linear to the number of OCMs. The reaction of the OCMs to the epinephrine (consuming it) is specified to be done in a short, constant time. The methodology to derive the profiles ensures that the basic safety countermeasures of the OCM to react to threats are always included in a current profile. So the countermeasures can be initiated without any delay, as no additional resources are required, while more advanced responses, which require additional resources can only be employed if the required additional resources are made available due to the stress response. If higher emergency categories such as II or IV are present, the outlined mechanism will propagate the resource demands in a similar manner considering the emergency category into account.

4 Conclusion

The presented generic OCM software architecture borrows the distinction between different levels of information processing present in natural organisms to handle better the complexity of mechatronic systems with self-optimization. In addition, a generic monitoring concept for each OCM and its self-coordination via the RTOS have been presented which emulate the acute stress response of a natural beings in the case of an emergency such that available resources are best allocated to address a given threat. The outlined self-coordinated adaptation of the system promises to enhance the dependability of systems as resources are employed more focused. It promizes to be also helpful for unanticipated problems as the investment of more resources to the control of misbehaving mechatronic subsystems is in many cases sufficient to compensate smaller systematic failures.

References

1. S. Burmester, M. Gehrke, H. Giese, and S. Oberthür. Making Mechatronic Agents Resource-aware in order to Enable Safe Dynamic Resource Allocation. In B. Georgio, editor, *Proc. of Fourth ACM International Conference on Embedded Software 2004 (EMSOFT 2004), Pisa, Italy*, pages 175–183. ACM Press, September 2004.
2. S. Burmester, H. Giese, and M. Tichy. Model-Driven Development of Reconfigurable Mechatronic Systems with Mechatronic UML. In U. Assmann, A. Rensink, and M. Aksit, editors, *Model Driven Architecture: Foundations and Applications,*

volume 3599 of *Lecture Notes in Computer Science*, pages 47–61. Springer Verlag, Aug. 2005.

3. W. B. Cannon. *Bodily Changes in Pain, Hunger, Fear and Rage: An Account of Recent Research Into the Function of Emotional Excitement.* Appleton-Century-Crofts, 1929.

4. I. A. Ferguson. Touringmachines: Autonomous agents with attitudes. *IEEE Computer*, 25(5):51–55, 1992.

5. U. Frank, H. Giese, F. Klein, O. Oberschelp, A. Schmidt, B. Schulz, H. Vöcking, and K. Witting. *Selbstoptimierende Systeme des Maschinenbaus - Definitionen und Konzepte.* Number Band 155 in HNI-Verlagsschriftenreihe. Bonifatius GmbH, Paderborn, Germany, first edition, Nov. 2004.

6. H. Giese, S. Burmester, W. Schäfer, and O. Oberschelp. Modular Design and Verification of Component-Based Mechatronic Systems with Online-Reconfiguration. In *Proc. of 12th ACM SIGSOFT Foundations of Software Engineering 2004 (FSE 2004), Newport Beach, USA*, pages 179–188. ACM Press, November 2004.

7. H. Giese, M. Tichy, S. Burmester, W. Schäfer, and S. Flake. Towards the Compositional Verification of Real-Time UML Designs. In *Proc. of the 9th European software engineering conference held jointly with 11th ACM SIGSOFT international symposium on Foundations of software engineering (ESEC/FSE-11)*, pages 38–47. ACM Press, September 2003.

8. A. Herkersdorf. Towards a framework and a design methodology for autonomic integrated systems. In M. Reichert, editor, *Proceedings of the Workshop on Organic Computing*, 2004.

9. T. Hestermeyer, O. Oberschelp, and H. Giese. Structured Information Processing For Self-optimizing Mechatronic Systems. In H. Araujo, A. Vieira, J. Braz, B. Encarnacao, and M. Carvalho, editors, *Proc. of 1st International Conference on Informatics in Control, Automation and Robotics (ICINCO 2004), Setubal, Portugal*, pages 230–237. INSTICC Press, Aug. 2004.

10. D. J. Musliner, R. P. Goldman, M. J. Pelican, and K. D. Krebsbach. Self-Adaptive Software for Hard Real-Time Environments. *IEEE Inteligent Systems*, 14(4), July/Aug. 1999.

11. S. Oberthür and C. Böke. Flexible resource management - a framework for self-optimizing real-time systems. In B. Kleinjohann, G. R. Gao, H. Kopetz, L. Kleinjohann, and A. Rettberg, editors, *Proceedings of IFIP Working Conference on Distributed and Parallel Embedded Systems (DIPES'04)*, pages 177–186. Kluwer Academic Publishers, 23 - 26 Aug. 2004.

12. P. Oreizy, M. M. Gorlick, R. N. Taylor, D. Heimbigner, G. Johnson, N. Medvidovic, A. Quilici, D. S. Rosenblum, and A. L. Wolf. An Architecture-Based Approach to Self-Adaptive Software. *IEEE Intelligent Systems*, 14(3):54–62, May/June 1999.

13. A. Pottharst. *Energieversorgung und Leittechnik einer Anlage mit Linearmotor getriebenen Bahnfahrzeugen.* Dissertation, University of Paderborn, Powerelectronic and Electrical Drives, Dec. 2005.

14. T. Schöler and C. Müller-Schloer. An observer/controller architecture for adaptive reconfigurable stacks. In M. Beigl and P. Lukowicz, editors, *ARCS*, volume 3432 of *Lecture Notes in Computer Science*, pages 139–153. Springer, 2005.

15. J. Sztipanovits, G. Karsai, and T. Bapty. Self-adaptive software for signal processing. *Commun. ACM*, 41(5):66–73, 1998.

16. J. F. Vincent Decugis. Action selection in an autonomous agent with a hierarchical distributed reactive planning architecture. In *Proceedings of the second international conference on Autonomous agents*, pages 354–361. ACM Press, 1998.
17. M. Wirsing, editor. *Report on the EU/NSF Strategic Workshop on Engineering Software-Intensive Systems*, Edinburgh, GB, May 2004.
18. K. Witting, B. Schulz, A. Pottharst, M. Dellnitz, J. Böcker, and N. Fröhleke. A new approach for online multiobjective optimization of mechatronical systems. Accepted for Int. J. on Software Tools for Technology Transfer STTT (Special Issue on Self-Optimizing Mechatronic Systems), 2006.

The Self Distributing Virtual Machine (SDVM): Making Computer Clusters Adaptive

Jan Haase, Andreas Hofmann, and Klaus Waldschmidt

Technische Informatik
J. W. Goethe Universität
Post Box 11 19 32, 60054 Frankfurt a. M., Germany
{haase|ahofmann|waldsch}@ti.informatik.uni-frankfurt.de**

Abstract. The Self Distributing Virtual Machine (SDVM) is a middleware concept to form a parallel computing machine consisting of a any set of processing units, such as functional units in a processor or FPGA, processing units in a multiprocessor chip, or computers in a computer cluster. Its structure and functionality is biologically inspired aiming towards forming a combined workforce of independent units ("sites"), each acting on the same set of simple rules.

The SDVM supports growing and shrinking the cluster at runtime as well as heterogeneous clusters. It uses the work-stealing principle to dynamically distribute the workload among all sites. The SDVM's energy management targets the health of all sites by adjusting their power states according to workload and temperature. Dynamic reassignment of the current workload facilitates a new energy policy which focuses on increasing the reliability of each site.

This paper presents the structure and the functionality of the SDVM.

1 Introduction

In the past, the user's increasing demand for capacity and speed was usually satisfied by faster single processors. Nowadays the increase in clock rates seems to have slowed down. The exploitation of parallelism is one way to enhance performance in spite of stagnating clock speeds. Its use isn't limited to the field of supercomputers; nowadays even Systems-on-Chip(SoC) with a lot of processors, so called MPSoCs, are in production.

Task scheduling and data migration for parallel computers, especially if embodied as a cluster of processing units, are complex problems if solved centralized. The use of biologically-inspired mechanisms can reduce complexity without sacrificing performance. The properties of biological systems like self-organization, self-optimization and self-configuration can be used to ease programming and administration of parallel computing clusters. These properties can be implemented efficiently using a paradigm common in complex biological systems: the collaboration of autonomous agents.

** Parts of this work have been supported by the Deutsche Forschungsgemeinschaft (DFG).

Please use the following format when citing this chapter:

Haase, J., Hofmann, A., Waldschmidt, K., 2006, in IFIP International Federation for Information Processing, Volume 216, Biologically Inspired Cooperative Computing, eds. Pan, Y., Rammig, F., Schmeck, H., Solar, M., (Boston: Springer), pp. 169–178.

Using biologically inspired techniques to implement a parallel computing system is only the means to the end in meeting user requirements. With the introduction of parallel computing, speed is not the only property which users are interested in; others too have come to the fore. In the following, several of those properties are presented. These properties focus on MIMD computer clusters. Such a cluster consists of an arbitrary number of independent processing units called *sites* which are connected using any kind of network.

Despite the performance of parallel computers the computations may take serveral days to finish. For large scale machines like the ASCI-Q machine, the mean time between failures (MTBF) for the whole system is estimated to be mere hours [1]. Thus *system stability* even in the face of failure of single components is an important goal. Parallel systems must therefore detect failures and intercept them transparently and unnoticed by the user. Presently, a system won't be able to repair itself physically, but the other sites should adapt to the changed environment and take over the work from the faulty site. This could be termed "self healing" of a system.

A main cause for the limited use of parallel computers lies in the challenging programmability: For single processors, scheduling in time is sufficient, but for multiprocessor systems, the spatial dimension has to be considered, too. Spatially and timely scheduling of the chunks of a program is a non-trivial optimization problem for the programmer, especially as the parallelism of an application can vary greatly over execution time and depends on the input data. Therefore a possible solution would be to relieve the programmer of the spatial scheduling at all, and let the system decide it at runtime using convenient heuristics automatically. The resulting *transparent parallelization* is similar to the goal of self-optimization, known from the subject of organic computing [2].

Experience shows that the performance demands increase over time. To be cost-effective, it suggests itself to prolong the life-span of a system instead of replacing it with a new system every few years. In the case of a parallel system this can be done by adding new processors or computers to increase its processing power. A parallel computing middleware should therefore support *scalability*. The benefit even increases if the growing and shrinking of the system is possible at runtime to cope with short-time processing power demand peeks.

In the beginning parallel systems were implemented as dedicated clusters. These days they more and more consist of clusters of workstations, multiprocessor embedded systems, or even multicore FPGA-based devices. Thus environmental parameters change frequently and sometimes fast. Configuration by hand of such a dynamically changing system is hard or even impossible. Thus it should *configure itself autonomously*. Concerning parallel systems, for well-founded configuration decisions the sites must be informed about the other sites' load, speed, etc., automatically. This can be denominated as the goal of self-configuration.

In section 2, the concept of the SDVM and its underlying mechanisms are described. After a list of some speedup results in section 3, this paper closes with a conclusion in section 4. The SDVM prototype is implemented in C++ and its complete source code is freely downloadable [3].

2 The SDVM

The Self Distributing Virtual Machine (SDVM) is a middleware to form an adaptive parallel system which is applicable to different granularities like functional units on an FPGA, processors in a multiprocessor SoC, or a cluster of customary computers(see Figure 1). The SDVM is currently implemented as a prototype in software running as Linux daemons on a workstation cluster.

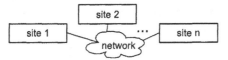

Fig. 1. The SDVM connects processing units (sites) to form a cluster, regardless of the topology of the connection network.

The SDVM actually implements several of the concepts inspired by biological systems, namely the cooperation of somewhat autonomous systems, self-controlled adaptivity to changing environments (as the size of the cluster or its heterogeneity) and decentralization of task scheduling. The sites that build the cluster are basically equal with no master or fixed division of functions. Furthermore, the SDVM supports self-healing by the use of checkpoints, to ensure proper program execution irrespective of failing cluster members.

2.1 The concept

The SDVM can be seen as a dataflow machine augmented with a distributed shared memory: An application to be executed by the SDVM is cut into several chunks of code, the *microthreads*. Each microthread needs certain parameters when run, therefore these parameters have to be collected prior to execution of the microthread. The data container collecting the parameters is called the *microframe* (see Figure 2).

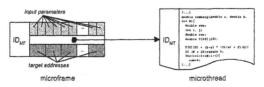

Fig. 2. Microframe and Microthread

A microframe is filled over time with the parameters it awaits. When all parameters have been received, the corresponding microthread is executed using these parameters and in the process calculates results needed by other microframes as parameters. Microframes can travel throughout the cluster while being filled. As the corresponding microthread is only needed when they are actually executed, the microthread is not included in the microframe to lessen bandwidth consumption when moving from one site to another.

While a microframe is being filled, the SDVM has not yet decided which site will execute this microframe with its corresponding microthread. When a site autonomously decides to execute a microframe locally, it finally needs the corresponding microthread which is then read from the local code cache or copied over the network. In this way the application itself (in terms of its microthreads) spreads automatically throughout the cluster over time—the sites will request just what they need and when they need it.

Microframes are not the only way to exchange data between parts of a program. The entirety of the SDVM provides a distributed shared memory (DSM) like SCI [4] and FLASH [5]. SDVM-programs can allocate and use this memory just like heap memory is used in C/C++. The memory addresses pointing to allocated memory regions can be passed as microframe parameters between microthreads. This global memory consists of the sum of all sites' memories. If a site is shut down (shrinking the cluster) the data stored in its local part of the global memory is pushed out to other sites before.

Any site which has nothing to do will ask other sites for work and will in return get a microframe which is ready for execution, if available. Any new site joining the cluster will just notice that its work queue is empty and act like any site which is out of work. In this way a site autonomously provides itself with work. This is called the *work stealing principle* (also referred as "receiver-initiated load balancing"), as opposed to the *work sharing principle* ("sender-initiated load balancing") where overloaded sites try to push away work to less loaded sites. Nearly all load balancing mechanisms base on work sharing, work stealing, or a combination of both [6]. On heavy loaded clusters work sharing leads to an even higher burden due to unsuccessful load balancing attempts.

As the SDVM provides a way of virtualization, it can connect heterogeneous machines to form a cluster: Several underlying architectures, platform types and operating systems are supported. If a site wants to execute a microthread which doesn't exist in its needed binary format yet, it must be generated somehow. If the SDVM is used as a middleware for computer clusters, it will request the source code and compile it on-the-fly and at runtime using the locally installed compiler (like gcc). The results show that the compilation time is fast enough, because the microthreads are small chunks of code and don't have to be linked (this is done automatically by the SDVM when receiving a microthread anyway). When the SDVM is used as a firmware for MPSoCs, techniques like code morphing can be used to translate the binary of the microthreads.

As a middleware the SDVM connects several machines. In contrast to client/server concepts like CORBA [7], the machines are treated equally, though. The SDVM cluster consists of the entirety of all sites, which are SDVM daemons running on participating machines. The number of sites, their computing power, and the network topology between them is irrelevant, as the SDVM automatically adapts to any cluster it is run on, even when the cluster grows or shrinks at runtime by adding or removing sites [8].

The SDVM daemon consists of several managers with different fields of responsibility. Some deal with the execution of code fragments, some attend to communications with other sites, some are concerned with the actual decision-making (see Figure 3). The latter implement the self-x features of the SDVM. They are described in the next sections.

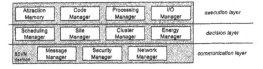

Fig. 3. An SDVM daemon consists of several managers.

2.2 The execution layer

The execution layer is responsible for the handling and execution of the code and data. Furthermore it provides I/O virtualization.

Microframes waiting for more parameters as well as global memory objects are kept in the *attraction memory*. If a data object is requested, it is first sought locally. In case of a miss the site it actually resides on is determined and then the data object is moved or copied to the local site.

The microthreads are only requested when they are to be executed locally. The local caching of microthreads and the compilation of microthreads, if needed, is done by the *code manager*.

The *processing manager* executes the microthread/microframe pair. To accomplish this, it provides an interface for the microthread to read the parameters of its microframe. When the execution has finished the processing manager deletes the no longer needed microframe. To hide network latencies when e.g. an access to a remote part of the global memory is needed, the processing manager may execute several microthread/microframe pairs concurrently. Test runs suggest that a number of 5 parallel processing manager threads are a good value for applications having much communication between the microframes.

The *input/output manager* manages user interaction and accesses local resources like hard disks or printers.

2.3 The communication layer

The communication layer manages sending and receiving of messages between sites. The *message manager* is the central communication hub for all other managers. It generates serialized data packets to be sent to other sites, adds information about the local site and determines its address before optionally passing them to the *security manager*. This manager may then encrypt and sign the data packets to avoid e.g. eavesdropping and spoofing. On the receiving site it will validate the signature and decrypt the message, if necessary, before passing it to the message manager.

The *network manager* is the part of the SDVM which is responsible for the actual transportation of the data packets. For the currently existing cluster realization it uses TCP/IP to send data to other sites. For an implementation of the SDVM on SoCs or multiprocessor chips it would have to use the on-chip network to pass data to the receiving site.

2.4 The decision layer

While the responsibilities of the managers in the execution and communication layers are more or less usual in computer systems, the decision layer implements the more sophisticated parts and the self-x-properties of the SDVM.

The SDVM features distributed scheduling which is done by the *scheduling manager*. Most scheduling methods assume a central calculation of the execution order, combined with a centrally managed load balancing. They take advantage of the accord that all information is collected on one site and thus good scheduling decisions can be made. However, in big clusters this central machine may become a bottleneck or even a single point of failure.

The SDVM works without client-server concepts as far as possible. Therefore the scheduling is done autonomously by each site. The sites therefore don't have knowledge about the current global execution status of the application, but only about the locally available executable microframes. Some information can be extracted in advance, though: The dataflow graph of the application contains all microthreads and therefore the critical path of an application and regions of high data dependencies can be detected. These parts will then be executed with higher priority resp. executed preferably on the same site.

The *site manager* collects data about the local site, e.g. processing speed, current load, number of applications the site works on, etc. This information is then passed (piggyback on other messages) to other sites' *cluster managers*, measuring the current network latency between these sites on the way. The cluster manager then possesses performance data about any site it directly works together with. Thus it can provide hints on which microframes to pass to which site. For example, a slow site with long network latencies will not be given a microframe which lies in the critical path of the application—another microframe which will be needed a bit later and therefore can afford to be calculated slower would be a better choice.

Another job of the cluster manager is the crash management. If a site does not respond to messages anymore, it is (after a while) regarded as crashed. The cluster is informed about the crash, then the applications which were executed on this site are determined by the other sites, as these applications have to be restarted. To avoid a whole restart of an application the SDVM features a checkpointing mechanism: Any microthread may not only apply its calculation results to the microframe awaiting them but also to a special microframe, the checkpoint frame (see Figure 4(a)). When a crash occurs, the site holding the youngest complete checkpoint frame is determined. This site then creates a recovery frame which recreates the not-yet executed microframes and reapplies

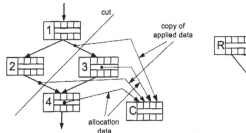
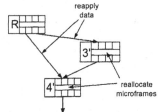
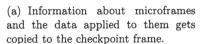

(a) Information about microframes and the data applied to them gets copied to the checkpoint frame.

(b) After a crash occured, the recovery frame is generated and executed. It recreates the stored microframes and reapplies the stored data.

Fig. 4. The checkpointing mechanism works on the CDAG (controlflow dataflow allocationflow graph) [9] of an application

the parameters to them (see Figure 4(b)). The application then runs on from that point undisturbed.

2.5 Freedom of adaptivity

The optimization success of an application's execution depends on how the current environment properties can be dealt with. Therefore an application which doesn't make too many restricting assumptions before runtime is more easily optimized at runtime. Typical assumptions are e.g. the platform type the application will be run on, the performance needed, the size of the cluster, the degree of parallelism, etc. The later those degrees of freedom are exploited and actual information taken into consideration, the more this information will be accurate with regard to the execution environment—and thus the system be made adaptive and the optimization improved.

In order to cope with the mentioned degrees of freedom, the SDVM acts as a virtualization layer which hides most properties of the underlying hardware from the applications. Therefore the SDVM may decide single-handedly where and when to execute specific microframes. In the area of reconfigurable hardware, the SDVM may even decide to resize the cluster by configuring additional processors and thus react to performance demand peeks. Based on available space and application requirements microthreads themselves can be configured as hardware at runtime and thus executed much faster.

The support for heterogeneous hardware architectures and varying cluster sizes makes it possible to upgrade hardware while the software runs on: Add new hardware and shut down the old.

2.6 Reliability and dynamic power management

The SDVM features another interesting concept which can be useful to enhance the reliability of a cluster or better yet of a multiprocessor chip it runs on.

The *energy manager* monitors the current load of the whole cluster and decides whether more processing power than needed is available. In this case it will send some sites a signal to work in a slower mode or even shut down completely. This reduces energy consumption and avoids overheating of processors. In case the load increases sites will get a signal to recur from sleep or shutdown mode.

Since energy management has an impact on the reliability of a system [10], the reliability can be further enhanced by introducing a new energy management policy. Unlike usual strategies which try to minimize energy consumption or reduce it without sacrificing performance, the new policy aims towards a minimal number of temperature changes. Thermal cycles induce mechanical stress which is a major contributor to chip failure [11]. Thus reducing thermal cycles reduces mechanical stress and therefore prolongs lifetime.

The SDVM is well suited for this kind of energy management policy, because the workload distribution adapts automatically to the changing performance of each site. Sites which fail to request work are not slowed down immediately in order to reduce thermal cycling. Similarly, sites having high load levels are not put to a higher performance level immediately if there are still underworked sites present in the cluster.

A method where any site may freely decide for itself its energy status may result in a situation where all sites simultaneously decide to shut down; therefore, as a mitigation of the distributed paradigm, the energy managers use an election algorithm to define a master which then is the only one to decide. The master may even decide to shut down its own site or to quit being the master; then the election is simply started again among the remaining sites.

3 Results

In this section some results are shown for a simple application, namely the Romberg numerical integration algorithm [12]. This algorithm partitions the area to be measured into several portions of constant width. Those can be measured independently and the results added eventually. The first microthread will generate a target microframe where the results are finally added and then, in our example, 100 or 150 other microframes containing the Romberg algorithm, which can be run in parallel.

The SDVM needs a lot of calculations and communication to distribute code and data. Therefore a question is whether the additional overhead is small enough to maintain the concept.

First, it shall be demonstrated how much overhead is generated by using the SDVM. To show this, run times on a stand-alone SDVM site are compared with the run times of a corresponding sequential program (see Figure 5). This overhead appears to be about 2%, even if the microthreads have to be compiled before execution.

In the next step, it has to be shown that the speedup is in expected regions. On a cluster of identical machines (Pentium IV, 1.7 GHz), a value for the

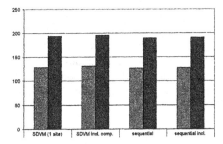

Fig. 5. Romberg algorithm: Comparison of the run times (in seconds) of a sequential program and the SDVM with one site. Values are given with and without compilation time, respectively, for width 100 and 150.

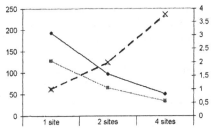

Fig. 6. Romberg algorithm: Run times and speedup depending on the number of sites

	1 site	2 sites	4 sites
width 100	128	65	34
width 150	193	97	51
speedup width 100	1	1.97	3.76
speedup width 150	1	1.99	3.78

speedup is shown in Figure 6. It reaches roughly the number of participating sites, which is a good result.

4 Conclusion

The Self Distributing Virtual Machine is a middleware which connects any functional units to form an adaptive parallel computing system. Both structure and functionality are biologically inspired as it is built from autonomous interacting units, features decentralized decision making and supports self-healing from cluster member faults. The SDVM detects failed members, removes them from the cluster and enables applications to efficiently recover from failure by the use of checkpointing.

The SDVM is self-organizing as a new SDVM-enabled unit which wants to join only needs a communication channel to a site which is already part of the cluster. As sites may join or leave at runtime without disturbing the execution of running applications, the cluster may grow or shrink to any convenient size, moreover regardless of the sites' operating systems, hardware or even the network topology between them. The cluster scales automatically.

It is self-optimizing as it automatically distributes data and program code to sites where it is needed, thereby dynamically balancing the workload of the whole system. Furthermore, this vastly facilitates a hardware upgrade while the system is running by shutting down old hardware and signing on new hardware—the applications will be relocated automatically and continue to run nonetheless. Similarly, resources can be added temporarily to cope with short term peeks in computing power demand.

The distributed scheduling of the SDVM provides the foundation for a new energy management policy which can improve the reliability of the participating systems. It differs from usually applied policies in its focus to reduce the number of thermal cycles of the system while minimizing the negative impact on performance. The tradeoffs between performance and reliability, and number of thermal cycles and mean temperature levels are currently investigated.

A prototypical implementation of the SDVM has been created and evaluated for the area of cluster computing. The prototype and its full source code is freely downloadable [3]. The SDVM is currently being adapted to multi-core processor systems.

References

1. George Bosilca, Aurelien Bouteiller, Franck Cappello, Samir Djilali, Gilles Fedak, Cecile Germain, Thomas Herault, Pierre Lemarinier, Oleg Lodygensky, Frederic Magniette, Vincent Neri, and Anton Selikhov. Mpich-v: toward a scalable fault tolerant mpi for volatile nodes. In *Proceedings of the 2002 ACM/IEEE conference on Supercomputing*, pages 1–18. IEEE Computer Society Press, 2002.
2. VDE/ITG/GI-Arbeitsgruppe Organic Computing. Organic Computing, Computer- und Systemarchitektur im Jahr 2010. Technical report, VDE/ITG/GI, 2003.
3. The SDVM homepage, 2006.
4. *SCI: Scalable Coherent Interface, Architecture and Software for High-Performance Compute Clusters.* Springer-Verlag, 1999.
5. Jeffrey Kuskin, David Ofelt, Mark Heinrich, John Heinlein, Richard Simoni, K. Gharachorloo, J. Chapin, D. Nakahira, J. Baxter, M. Horowitz, A. Gupta, M. Rosenblum, and J. Hennessy. The stanford flash multiprocessor. In *25 years of the international symposia on Computer architecture (selected papers)*, pages 485–496. ACM Press, 1998.
6. Mukesh Singhal and Niranjan G. Shivaratri. *Advanced Concepts in Operating Systems.* McGraw-Hill, New York, 1994.
7. Object Management Group. *The Common Object Request Broker: Architecture and Specification.* Object Management Group, 2.5 edition, September 2001.
8. Jan Haase, Frank Eschmann, Bernd Klauer, and Klaus Waldschmidt. The SDVM: A Self Distributing Virtual Machine. In *Organic and Pervasive Computing – ARCS 2004: International Conference on Architecture of Computing Systems*, volume 2981 of *Lecture Notes in Computer Science*, Heidelberg, 2004. Springer Verlag.
9. Bernd Klauer, Frank Eschmann, Ronald Moore, and Klaus Waldschmidt. The CDAG: A Data Structure for Automatic Parallelization for a Multithreaded Architecture. In *Proceedings of the 10th Euromicro Workshop on Parallel, Distributed and Network-based Processing (PDP 2002)*, Canary Islands, Spain, January 2002. IEEE.
10. K. Mihic, T. Simunic, and G. De Micheli. Reliability and power management of integrated systems. In *DSD - Euromicro Symposium on Digital System Design*, pages 5–11, 2004.
11. Jayanth Srinivasan, Sarita V. Adve, Pradip Bose, Jude Rivers, and Chao-Kun Hu. Ramp: A model for reliability aware microprocessor design. In *IBM Research Report, RC23048 (W0312-122)*, December 2003.
12. G. Dahlquist and A. Bjorck. *Numerical Methods.* Prentice Hall, Englewood Cliffs, NJ, 1974.

Teleworkbench: An Analysis Tool for Multi-Robotic Experiments

Andry Tanoto[1], Jia Lei Du[1], Ulf Witkowski[1], and Ulrich Rückert[1]

Heinz Nixdorf Institute
System and Circuit Technology
University of Paderborn, Germany
{tanoto, jialdu, witkowski, rueckert}@hni.upb.de

Abstract. This paper presents a tool, one component of the Telework-bench system, for analyzing experiments in multi-robotics. The proposed tool combines the video taken by a web cam monitoring the field where the experiment runs and some computer generated visual objects representing important events and information as well as robots' behavior into one interactive video based on MPEG-4 standard. Visualization and data summarization enables the developer to quickly grasp a situation, whereas the possibility of scrolling through the video and selectively activating information helps him analyzing interesting events in depth. Because of the MPEG-4 standard used for the output video, the analysis process can be done in a wide range of platforms. This trait is beneficial for education and research cooperation purposes. [1]

1 Introduction

One way to design and develop multi-robot systems is the use of bio-inspired swarm principles. Swarm systems usually consist of many homogeneous agents that follow a small set of simple rules. Communication, either explicitly or implicitly via the environment, is strictly locally constrained. There is no central coordination, and cooperation among the agents and global effects result from the individual behavioral rules. When developing such robot swarm systems, the setup, observation and analysis of experiments can be tedious and challenging for the roboticist. Numerous robots need to be charged and the programs downloaded onto the robots. When executing the experiment, it is difficult to concurrently observe all robots, which run in real-time and possibly over a long period. It is our intention to provide an analysis tool for experiments in multi-robotics. This analysis tool is meant to help roboticists in assessing their robot programs or algorithms for any application when being tested in real experiments. Through this tool the observable as well as the unseen behavior of robots

[1] This work was developed in the course of the Collaborative Research Center 614 Self-optimizing Concepts and Structures in Mechanical Engineering University of Paderborn, and was published on its behalf and funded by the Deutsche Forschungsgemeinschaft.

Please use the following format when citing this chapter:

Tanoto, A., Du, J.L., Witkowski, U., Rückert, U., 2006, in IFIP International Federation for Information Processing, Volume 216, Biologically Inspired Cooperative Computing, eds. Pan, Y., Rammig, F., Schmeck, H., Solar, M., (Boston: Springer), pp. 179–188.

during experiments will become more transparent to the roboticists, which is an invaluable factor in debugging the robot programs.

For analysis purposes, robots are usually programmed to send or to record a lot of information. The question now is how to effectively summarize all information produced in a way that the actual situation of robots at any particular time can be conveyed to and easily comprehended by robot programmers. One way to do this is through visualization. Visualization can be used to show the behavior and especially to make complex states of behavior comprehensible to human.

The tool we propose works by processing information acquired from the Teleworkbench system [1] during an experiment and outputs one multimedia file visualizing acquired information. The visualization is built based on MPEG-4 standard. There are some reasons for using MPEG-4: its interoperability, flexibility, reusability, and interactivity. With MPEG-4, we can easily combine several multimedia sources, whether it is video or audio, into one file playable in a wide range of hardware and operating systems. This trait is advantageous for exchanging and storing the result of the experiment. Moreover, we can have a "'run once, analyze many"' analysis tool that requires us to run the analysis process only once but enables us to have many perspectives of the problems we are trying to solve at later time. Furthermore, with MPEG-4 we can also embed computer-generated objects into the video data, which is essential for providing a sense of reality for users. In the case of our analysis tool, we use one video taken by an overhead web cam monitoring a field where the experiment is executed and embed computer-generated objects on top of it. These video objects represent information important for analysis, e.g. robots' path, communication message, internal state, sensor values, or even images. To provide interactivity, there is a menu area with which users can select the most relevant information for a certain situation.

To date, there are some tools for analyzing robot experiments, ranging from general-purpose software such as MATLAB [2] and SysQuake [3] as well as application- and robot-specific software such as KITE [4], beTee [5], and PyKhep [6]. However, none of them offers all the features we mentioned above.

In this paper, we present the proposed tool for analyzing experiments using minirobot Khepera. However, it does not necessarily mean that this analysis tool can be used only for this type of robot. The idea of this tool is extensible to any robotic platform.

The paper is structured as follow. After shortly stating the problem and our proposed solution in Chapter 1, we will give a short overview of our Teleworkbench system in Chapter 2. Next, the description of the analysis tool will be presented in Chapter 3. Afterward, Chapter 4 will describe how our proposed tool can help us in analyzing an experiment in bio-inspired robotics. This paper will be concluded in a short summary in Chapter 5.

2 Teleworkbench - A Short Overview

We have presented the Teleworkbench System in [1]. Teleworkbench is a tele-operated platform or testbed for managing experiments involving one or many mini-robots Khepera. The idea behind the Teleworkbench is to provide remote setup and execution of experiments in multi-robotics and also to facilitate an easy analysis on the resulted data. To enable long-time experiments, the Teleworkbench is equipped with recharging stations to enable robots recharging their batteries during runtime. The Teleworkbench is connected to the Internet to allow easy access for remote users located in any part of the world.

2.1 Teleworkbench Features

- **Internet connectivity.** The Teleworkbench is connected to the Internet, which allows easy access for remote users located on every part of the world.
- **Remote experiment setup and execution.** Remote users can setup and execute experiments involving many mini-robots Khepera with various extension modules. The Teleworkbench has one field, measuring 2m x 2m, which is partitionable into four fields of size 1m x 1m.[2]
- **Robot positioning system.** The robot positioning system will track every robot captured by a web cam and extract robots' position relative to the field. At the current version, 36 robots can be identified and localized.
- **Wireless robot communication.** The Teleworkbench system uses Bluetooth technology as the medium for robot communication. With our Bluetooth module [7], the communication among robots is more reliable and faster (up to 57600 bps) than the normal Khepera Radio Turret.
- **Remote program-download to robot.** Remote users are allowed to directly control the behavior of the robots by downloading their own programs to robots.
- **Live-video of the experiment.** During experiments, users can in real-time watch how the experiments proceed through the live-streamed-video of the experiment taken by web cams monitoring the fields.
- **Events and messages logger.** Every occurred events and exchanged messages are recorded and retrievable.
- **Post-experiment analysis tool.** Immediately after the experiment completion, an interactive MPEG4-video is generated showing some important information recorded during the experiment. With this, we can have a *"run once, analyze many"* analysis tool. Thus, analysis of the experiment is easy and convenient. Moreover, since all information is stored in one file, the MPEG4-based video file, it is very comfortable for exchanging and presenting research result.

---

[2] The main field is more or less equal to a field of size 11.6m x 11.6m for robot Pioneer3-DX (44cm x 38cm x 22cm).

- **Interoperability**. The Teleworkbench system was designed to allow communication with other programs, which can be implemented simply by using socket communication. Result in [8] shows how one program acting as a gateway passes an XML-based messages from a remote user to the robot through the Teleworkbench system.

2.2 Teleworkbench Components

The Teleworkbench system (see Figure 1) comprises one field with several cameras monitoring it, a wireless communication system, and some computers connected to a local area network with tasks such as image processing, databasing, message redirecting, and web-hosting.

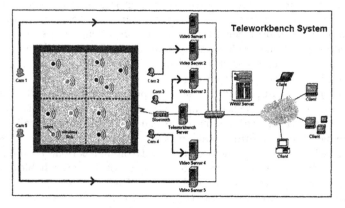

Fig. 1. The diagram of the Teleworkbench system showing the system architecture.

The experiments will be executed on the field which has the resources required as defined by the users during the experiment setup. During the experiment, the web cam above the field will become active and send the video information to the Video Server. This server will process the captured video data to extract any robot on the field and calculate the position and orientation of the robots. To allow the extraction of robot position, every robot has a color mark on top. The detected robots along with their position will be recorded in a log file called *"Position Log File"*. Concurrently, this server will also encode the video and stream it to the Video Streaming Server, to provide live video of the experiment.

During experiment, robots can communicate wirelessly with each other or ask the Teleworkbench Server through the Bluetooth module. In some experiments, robots might need to send some internal information for analysis process. Every messages sent by the robot will be recorded in a log file called *"Communication Log File"*.

If required by the users, it is also possible to involve some intelligent agents running on separate computers (For security reason, we allow only computers inside our LAN) connected to the Teleworkbench Server. These agents then can communicate or even control the robots during the experiment.

After the experiment is over, the Teleworkbench Server will call the Post-Experiment Tool module to generate the visualization of the experiment. This tool will generate an MPEG-4-based video with some computer generated objects superposed on it. These objects represent some important information needed by the roboticists for analysis purpose. Further detail on this analysis tool will be presented in the following chapter.

3 The Teleworkbench Post-Experiment Analysis Tool

The proposed tool consists of two main parts, which are MPEG-4-based video serving as a user interface and visualization generator. The former is actually the output of the latter.

3.1 The Analysis Tool

Video as User Interface A snapshot of the video is shown in Fig. 3(a). The part in the middle is the video taken by a web cam located above the field where experiments run. In the same area, some computer-generated objects will be superimposed onto the video near the corresponding robot. These objects representing information such as robots' body, communication messages, robots' path, battery level, internal states, and linear camera data.

In the area on the right side, there are two sub-areas, the first sub-area above is the menu area at which users can select the information they want to see at any particular of time. The second one below is the detail-information area in which users can have a more detailed visualization of selected information.

Visualization Generator The block diagram of the visualization generator is shown in Fig. 2. The input for the visualization is the position and communication log file as well as the video monitoring the platform where the experiment is running. The video and position log file are generated by the Robot Positioning system mentioned at the previous section, while the communication log file is provided by the Data Logger. At the other end, the process will produce a video serving as the user interface and the visualizer.

The visualization generator is basically composed of data extractor, scene generator and MPEG-4 scene encoder. In the following paragraphs, a more detailed description of each component will be presented.

Data Extractor Data extractor is responsible to extract information needed by the scene generator. The input data are position and communication log file. The position log file is generated by the robot positioning system, which calculates the position of all robots taken by the overhead web-cam. Hence, it contains only robot external information. Meanwhile, communication log file captures all exchanged messages among the robots or between the server and the robots. Thus, it preserves robots' internal information.

Position log file provides two important information for the data extractor. The first one is the frame information in the form of frame number and time stamp. This information is required to synchronize the computer generated objects with the input video data. The second information is the position and orientation information in pixel unit. This information is required for drawing some objects at the right position and orientation.

In the case of communication log file, we can basically program the robot to send as various information as possible to provide robot programmers with their desiring information. But for the time being, we support only several information to be visualized, which are infra-red sensors, linear camera, robots' states, and other communicated messages. The last one means all messages which do not belong to any of the first three types of information. To differentiate the messages, we use a specific character as a header for each type of information.

Scene Generator Scene generator is responsible to generate scene description which is required by the MPEG-4 scene encoder for creating a computer-generated animation overlaying the input video data. The scene description is based on XMT-A, which is one of the Extensible Markup Language (XML)-based formats supported by the MPEG-4 standard.

The scene description contains the information describing how the robots move, how the visualization of the sensors' values, the communication messages, and the robot's internal state are varying over time, as well as how users interact with the visualization content.

MPEG-4 Scene Encoder MPEG-4 scene encoder has a function to generate an MPEG-4 file based on the scenery information written in XMT-A format. The heart of this component is the open source software called MP4BOX, a command-line MPEG-4 scene encoder. The output from MP4Box is a video file in MP4 format. There are two reasons that we are using this software. First, it supports many types of multimedia file, e.g. MPEG-4 video and audio, JPEG

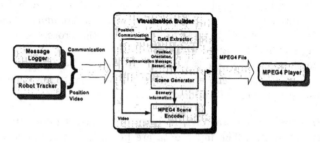

Fig. 2. The process flow of the visualization generator.

and PNG images, AVI, etc, which means we can easily combine many kinds of multimedia file into one file. Second, it is an open source software, which means it is free of charge. For more detail on the GPAC project in general and the MP4BOX in particular, interested readers are referred to the aforementioned reference.

3.2 The Implementation

At present, the data extractor and scene generator are built using C language and run under Linux. However, it will be easy to port these modules to other operating systems. In the case of MPEG-4 scene encoder, we downloaded and installed the GPAC project. From this package we get two important programs, which are MP4BOX and OSMO4. The former is an MPEG-4 scene encoder and the latter is an MPEG-4 player which we use for playing back the output produced by the former.

4 Experiment

In research, models have been developed to simulate the behavior of human crowds in panic and escape situations [9]. The findings gained from such simulations help engineers design escape routes of areas where mass panic situations may occur. When performing such simulations, researchers usually have a global view and are interested in total system behavior. In these simulations people are often modeled as particles. The resulting speed of a particle is calculated in dependence of the desired direction as well as attractive and repulsive forces of other particles and static obstacles like walls. The particles often have global knowledge to make their decisions and are able to sense and move omnidirectionally.

Inspired by the idea of escape simulations for large crowds, we aimed to develop evacuation strategies for multi-robot-systems. Evacuation strategies for robot systems may become necessary when an area must be vacated quickly through a limited number of exits or when a large number of robots have to board a transport robot. However, in difference to the particle-based simulation models above, the individual robots generally do not have global knowledge and cannot sense and move omni-directionally. Our objective was to develop an evacuation strategy for multi-robot-systems based on simple, robust policies relying only on local sensing and information.

For our implementation and experiments we used the Khepera II robot equipped with our Bluetooth communication module, and the Teleworkbench. Using the Teleworkbench, the setup and execution of an experiment is significantly simplified. Several experiments can be pre-planned and are then automatically executed consecutively by the Teleworkbench. For example, if the effects of different program parameters need to be tested, it is possible to pre-compile the robot software with the different parameters, transfer those programs to the Teleworkbench and let the Teleworkbench automatically run the tests.

The setup of our experiment is shown in Fig. 3(a). The objective of the robots is to leave the left side of the operational area through the exit in the middle. One major challenge is to avoid mutual blockage and deadlock situations. For perception, the robots only use their integrated infra-red proximity sensors with a range of vision of about 4 cm. In our experiments the approximate direction of the exit is known to the robots. They use the integrated odometry system to keep track of their direction. We implemented a simple, distributed strategy in which robots first try to rush towards the exit individually. When the robots detect an obstacle or another robot, they try to circumnavigate it.

The analysis tool presented in this paper helps the developer in debugging multi-robot systems as it automatically matches and merges internal information from the robots with external information extracted from the recorded film. The result is presented in a single, interactive interface where the developer can fast forward or backward to situations and selectively activate information. Visualization and data summarization enables the developer to quickly grasp a situation, whereas the possibility of selectively activating information helps him analyzing interesting events in depth. The integration in a single user-friendly interface helps the developer concentrating on the analysis of relevant incidents and software debugging.

One concrete example for a useful feature in this particular case is the display of the superposed robot trajectories which allows us to analyze the global effects of our evacuation algorithm (see Fig. 3(b)). Furthermore, the presentation of the individual robot paths together with the respective sensor values and internal states in a single analysis window, and the possibility to fast forward and backward to important situations helps us to verify and debug the code as the analysis and explanation of the robot behaviors is significantly simplified.

5 Conclusion

We have described an analysis tool which is part of our Teleworkbench system. This tool can be very beneficial for robot programmers due to its ability to provide a video of the experiment embedded with computer-generated visual objects representing important events and information as well as the robots' behavior during an experiment. The use of MPEG-4 standard is very helpful because it eases the visualization process and gives us flexibility in providing interactivity between users and the content. We have demonstrated the functionality of the analysis tool in a bio-inspired robotic experiment. From the demonstration, we can see how the proposed tool can give us insight on the actual internal and external behavior of robot(s), which is invaluable for debugging.

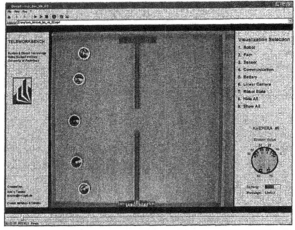

(a) Setup of the experiment. The robots try to evacuate the left side of the area through the middle gate as quickly as possible.

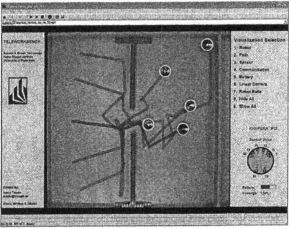

(b) Analysis of the experiment. Visualization of the superposed robot paths. All robots passed through the gate efficiently except robot number 12.

Fig. 3. Snapshots of the output video of the proposed analysis tool in a bio-inspired experiment involving five mini-robots Khepera II.

References

1. A. Tanoto, U. Witkowski, and U. Rückert, "Teleworkbench: A teleoperated platform for multi-robot experiments," in *Proceedings of the 3rd International Symposium on Autonomous Minirobots for Research and Edutainment (AMiRE 2005)*, Awara-Spa, Fukui, JAPAN, 20 - 22 Sept. 2005.
2. I. The MathWorks, "Matlab user's guide," 24 Prime Park Way, Natick, MA 01760, Jan. 1990.
3. SysQuake, "SysQuake." [Online]. Available: http://www.k-team.com/software/ sysquake.html
4. E. Sahin and P. Gaudiano, "KITE: The Khepera integrated testing environment," in *Proceedings of the First International Khepera Workshop, Paderborn, Germany*, 1999, pp. 199–208.
5. A. Bredenfeld, "Behavior engineering for robot teams," in *Proceedings of Autonomous Minirobots for Reseach and Edutainment (AMiRE 2001), Paderborn*, 2001.
6. P. Stöhr, "PYKHEP: A python based visualisation toolkit for the khepera robot," in *Proceedings of the First International Khepera Workshop, Paderborn, Germany*, 1999, pp. 209–218.
7. M. Grosseschallau, U. Witkowski, and U. Rückert, "Low-cost bluetooth communication for the autonomous mobile minirobot khepera," in *IEEE International Conference on Robotics and Automation - ICRA05*, Barcelona, Spain, 18 - 22 Apr. 2005, pp. 4205–4210.
8. J. L. Du, U. Witkowski, and U. Rückert, "Teleoperation of a mobile autonomous robot using web services," in *Proceedings of the 3rd International Symposium on Autonomous Minirobots for Research and Edutainment (AMiRE 2005)*, Fukui, Japan, 20 - 22 Sept. 2005.
9. D. Helbing, I. Farkas, and T. Vicsek, "Simulating dynamical features of escape panic," *Nature*, vol. 407, no. 6803, pp. 487–490, Sept. 2000.

Trading off Impact and Mutation of Knowledge by Cooperatively Learning Robots

Willi Richert, Bernd Kleinjohann, Lisa Kleinjohann

Intelligent Mobile Systems, University of Paderborn / C-LAB, Germany,
richert@c-lab.de

Abstract. We present a socially inspired approach that allows agents in Multi-Agent Systems to speed up their own learning process through communication. Thereby, they are able to trade off impact of knowledge by mutation dependent on the recent performance of the interacting agents. This is inspired by social interaction of humans, where the opinions of experts have greater impact on the overall opinion and are incorporated more exactly than those of newbies. The approach is successfully evaluated in a simulation in which mobile robots have to accomplish a task while taking care of timely recharging their resources.

1 Introduction

A lot of useful techniques exist for groups of agents that learn to behave optimally to reach a given task while adapting to their environment. Especially reinforcement learning (RL) [1, 2], where the agent does not need a predefined environment model and learns through reward and punishment that it receives from its environment, has been shown to be a viable solution for groups of behavior-based learning agents [3]. This approach has also been successfully used to learn in groups of agents to connect the individual agent's innate states to the proper behaviors it has to execute when being in the according state [4]. The success of such reinforcement learning systems depends in general on the careful design of the state and action space and the reward function. In many situations these have to be found out by careful analysis of the domain followed by a trial and error period — often leading to suboptimal solutions. In Multi-Agent Systems (MAS) the problem is on the one hand amplified since the interferences of the agents cannot be anticipated by the designer. This is especially true for environments, in which no central intelligence is available for coordination and optimization. On the other hand it can be relieved if proper learning methods are combined with robust mechanisms for spreading the learned knowledge between the agents.

In this case, however, the problem arises, how to integrate the received information into its own knowledge base if only sporadic communication possibilities exist. Our socially inspired approach that we describe in this paper contributes to this problem with the following properties:

Please use the following format when citing this chapter:

Richert, W., Kleinjohann, B., Kleinjohann, L., 2006, in IFIP International Federation for Information Processing, Volume 216, Biologically Inspired Cooperative Computing, eds. Pan, Y., Rammig, F., Schmeck, H., Solar, M., (Boston: Springer), pp. 189–198.

- The impact of knowledge learned by individuals is weighted in the communication process based on the recent performance of the participants, called "expert state". The more "expert" an agent is regarded the more influence it has on the final knowledge arbitration of the other participant.
- Mutation fosters new solutions based on the expert level of the participants. The less "expert" an agent is regarded the more mutated his information are transmitted.
- The number of expert agents is allowed to vary.
- In unknown or changing environments the performance of agents will decline resulting in more mutation until the first agent finds a way to perform better, that in turn increases his expert state and impact on the subsequent knowledge exchange. Thereby, this approach is robust to environmental change.

In our previous work we have shown how the knowledge transfer in societies of autonomous systems leads to the propagation of the most valuable information units that offer the biggest performance advantage [5, 6]. In that experiment we modeled the knowledge as a discrete sequence of actions which have influence on the agent's intrinsic performance evaluation. Based on the outcome of the imitated action sequences these were distributed in the agent society. Encouraged by these results, we use the imitation process in form of group learning to deal with continuous information units: the information, how the continuous state space is best to be discretized. The discretization in the current work is inspired by learning in human societies, where humans exchange their knowledge from time to time. Typically in this group learning process firstly the opinion of experts counts more than the opinion of less experienced group members. Furthermore, expert opinions tend to be more exactly integrated into the learning result. A good measure for experience are the age or lifetime of an agent and its accumulated performance. In this way, the propagation of useful knowledge in form of information units is not only dependent on the current state of the imitated agent, but also on its lifetime achievement. In this vein, we are approaching the optimization of the state space from the memetic point of view according to Dawkins [7, 8].

We evaluate the approach in a mobile robot application that simulates three of our soccer robots *Paderkicker* [9]. They have to learn how to optimally perform a given task under strict resource constraints.

2 Related Work

Many existing approaches have shown, that communication can and should be used in MAS to improve the group performance [10, 11]. Riley and Veloso [12] demonstrate how coaching between the individual agents can improve the performance for Q-learning agents. Tan [4] investigated the issue of exchanging information between multiple Q-learning agents. He found that the exchange of learned policies among agents "speeds up learning at the cost of communication". Dahl et al. [13] show how inter-agent communication in conjunction with

RL can improve the capability of agent groups to organize themselves spatio-temporally. In his work the agents communicate the reward to speed up the learning process — the state space itself is predefined and kept fixed for the whole learning process. In contrast to Dahl our approach deals with the adaptation of the state space based on the experience level of the communicating agents.

In this work we are not concerned with the optimization of joint actions in cooperative MAS, as it is investigated e.g. by Kapetanakis et al. [14] who demonstrate how agents employing their FMQ algorithm have the ability to converge towards the optimal joint action when teamed-up with one or more simple Q-learners which are in touch all the time. A more general investigation on cooperation in MAS is done by Claus et al. [15]. Instead, we are interested in mechanisms that allow for robust spreading of learned efforts between agents where the experience and the number and the visible agents may vary. The work on expert balancing algorithms, e.g. [16], typically relies on a fixed set of experts that issue recommendation at fixed time interval and the agent in question only has to choose one every time step. However, situations of this kind are very seldom in real-world application. Often we are happy if there is someone within reach to communicate with and we have to make ad-hoc decisions about how much value his information provides and how we integrate it into our own knowledge. For this situation we present our approach.

3 The Problem Domain

We consider an environment where mobile robots have to maximize their performance performing an abstracted task while keeping track of their limited resources. A robot collects a so-called task point in every time step when it executes the proper task action in the task area. The agent has to pay attention to resources of m types which are consumed at an individual rate. For each resource type the actual resource level is measured by a continuous value between 0 (resource of this type exhausted) and 1 (resource of this type is filled). The agent's main goal is to collect as many task points per lifespan as possible. For this it has to interrupt the main task in order to timely arrive at the filling station of the correct type that satisfies the agent's resource needs. In the environment there are multiple energy bases for every resource type. If one resource level is zero the agent dies and is restarted with zero task points. This way they have to trade off task accomplishment and lifetime extension through timely taking care of resources.

4 Architecture

The agents learn on two levels (Fig. 1): 1) the individual learning level, where the best mapping from the state space to the action space is learned using standard Q-learning, and 2) the knowledge exchange level, where the agents exchange their knowledge when encountering each other.

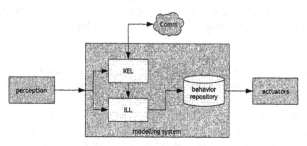

Fig. 1. Agent architecture: The interplay between the knowledge exchange level (KEL) and the individual learning level (ILL).

4.1 Individual Learning Level (ILL)

An agent is provided with hand-coded reactive behaviors [17] that move toward one of the two resource type areas or to the task area, respectively. The behaviors are constructed out of low level basic actions that move the agent toward the desired goal and avoid obstacles on the basis of potential fields [18]. The agents have to learn the best mapping of their intrinsic resource level state to the predefined behaviors using reinforcement learning. For every resource the following states are possible: 0 for "drive immediately to the proper energy filling station", 1 for "resource OK", and 2 for "resource maximum". State 2 is used to denote that the agent can stop the refuel process. States 1 and 2 say that it is save to perform the actual task to collect performance points. The threshold that the agent will have to adapt at runtime through cooperative learning divides states 0 and 1 and thus discretizes the continuous resource fill level into discrete states usable for RL. The reinforcement-learning agents use the one-step Q-learning algorithm [19] to learn the correct mapping of the resource input state vector to the proper behavior.

Since the actions take some time to be accomplished, the Q-values are not updated at every time step, but only after the chosen action has been finished. The Q-values for the state-action pairs are calculated with the standard Q-learning approach:

$$Q(s,a) \leftarrow Q(s,a) + \alpha \left(r + \gamma \max_x Q(s',x) - Q(s,a) \right) \qquad (1)$$

Here, s denotes the state combining the state of two resource types, in this example called "R" for red and "B" for blue. The variable a denotes one of the three approaching abstract behaviors. The learning factor α was set to

$\alpha = \frac{1}{n(s,a)}$ with $n(s,a)$ being the counter for executing action a in state s. The probability $p(a|s)$ for choosing the best action a in state s is calculated as

$$p(\arg \max_a Q(s,a)|s) = 0.999^u \cdot 0.3,$$

with u being the global update counter that is increased at every Q-value update. The reward was given after $r = 0.01(c_w - c_b) + 5c_t$, with c_w counting the time steps the agent has been performing its task and c_b counting the time steps the agents resources were below the threshold. c_t was set to 1 if the agent managed to turn around one of its resources meaning a successful refuel since the last update, and 0 otherwise. The discount factor γ is set to 0.1. These values were empirically determined to run reasonably well even for a pure RL approach without the expert learning level for later comparison.

4.2 Knowledge Exchange Level (KEL)

In parallel to the learning process at the ILL the agents where enabled with communication means to optimize the segmentation of their continuous state space through group learning. The knowledge to exchange in our problem domain are the threshold values of each resource type in $R = \{1, \ldots, m\}$. These values determine when an agent will stop his task performing actions and drive immediately to the proper energy filling station. The adjustment of the thresholds is done at run-time, thereby adjusting to a moving target, since it might for instance become easier to reach a particular refilling station.

If an agent has a found a better segmentation this will be acknowledged at the next communication process, because it will most likely lead to a better performance. The knowledge weighting in combination with mutation is done as follows: The knowledge of agents that have a better recent performance will also have a greater impact on the final adapted knowledge of both agents. Furthermore, also the agents' knowledge accuracy should be dependent on the agents' experience. I.e. the less experienced an agent is the more noisy it's knowledge will enter the final outcome. This is done by trading off the impact and the mutation rate at the exchange of knowledge when communicating, leading to the computation of the adapted knowledge: The new thresholds of agent $i \in D$, where $D \subseteq A$ with $A = \{1, \ldots, n\}$ denoting the entire group of n agents depending on m different resources $r \in R$ is described by equation (2):

$$t_i^r = \sum_{a \in D} \frac{w_a}{\sum_{a \in D} w_a} \cdot \hat{t}_a^r \tag{2}$$

$\hat{t}_a^r$ is drawn randomly from the Gaussian distribution $N\left(t_a^r, \sigma_a^2\right)$ with the standard deviation $\sigma_a \sim e(a)^{-1}$, thereby modeling the mutation that is introduced at every communication process. The impact w_a is proportionally dependent on the expert state $e(a)$ of that agent. $e(a)$ can be modeled to denote the moving average of the agent's lifetime or task achievement. The greater $e(a)$ is the more impact on the estimation of threshold t_i^r it has.

Thus, the "expert impact" $e(a)$ affects the overall threshold adjustment in two ways: On the one hand directly through the weight w_a, and on the other hand through the accuracy modeled by the normal distribution $N\left(t_a^r, \sigma_a^2\right)$. This has the counterpart in real life where usually more attention is paid to the experts than to newbies. In practice, the expert impact $e(a)$ of agent a defined as $e(a) = lifetime(a) + performance(a)$ has shown to yield a reasonably good expert measurement in our domain. The performance is calculated as one point per time step when performing the task. The thresholds are adjusted in two ways:

1. At a fixed time frame the agents get the chance to communicate with other agents staying close enough defined by a radius. Given, that agent i comes close enough to communicate with j, they both exchange their own estimation of the thresholds t^r, $r \in R$, as shown by Formula (2) from the i's point of view. In this case, $D = \{i, j\}$. The thresholds are computed separately for every agent which leads to different thresholds for both and encourages them to explore the state space. It showed that letting the agents communicate too often will prevent the convergence to sound threshold values since the agents have no time to see the effect of the new thresholds.
2. If an agent dies, because one of its resources is exhausted, it is restarted with full resources and its thresholds are calculated from the thresholds of all agents $(D = A)$ randomized and weighted dependent on their experience $e(a)$.

In this experiment, we restricted the agents to apply the group learning to only the thresholds segmenting the state space. However, it could be easily applied to other areas like, e.g. the Q-values.

5 Experimental Setting

The approach has been evaluated in simulation with three Pioneer2DX robots [20] having sonar (90°) for obstacle avoidance, laser range-finders for detection of the individual markers, and differential gear. The experiments were performed on the *Player/Stage* [21] simulation environment. Usually, controllers written for the Stage simulator can be used on real Pioneers [13]. The agents were equipped with 360° fiducial finders, so that we could turn off foraging and map building control and concentrate on the learning task at hand.

The agents were anonymous in that they could not detect each others identity. When communicating they only were allowed to transmit their evaluation function, i.e. the resource thresholds for the two energy types "R" and "B", and their expert state, i.e. their current age. The distribution of the energy bases in the environment can be seen in Fig. 2. At the upper and lower left corners of the 8x6m area there are located two resources of type "R". In the middle of the left wall there is the task area: agents staying near this marker were said to execute the desired abstract task and thus gathering a point for every predefined

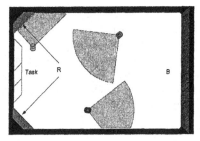

Fig. 2. Environment containing the task area and the energy bases of type "R" and "B".

timer interval. At the right side there is the resource of type "B" located. The setting thus has the property that resource "R" is located right beside the task area, whereas the agents have to travel across the entire field width to arrive at resource "B" to fuel their resource tank.

The environment shows the wanted realistic properties without distracting from the experiment under investigation: 1) It differs from the blocks-world examples, in that the individual actions take time that cannot be foreseen and perception being noisy. Although the distance between the different marker areas are approximately known and could be computed, the time to travel from one to another cannot be calculated in advance with adequate accuracy, because the interference of agents that have not managed to dodge each other introduces the time needed to perform a relieve maneuver. 2) Resources can be blocked by another agent so that an agent that also wants to reach the resource has to wait for an unknown time.

The parameters were set as follows: In formula (2) β was set to 0.2, $\sigma_i^2 = 0.2 \cdot e^{-\frac{e(i)}{100}}$, setting the variance to 0.2 for unexperienced agents and decreasing with the agent's experience. Although this also had to be empirically determined, it usually has to be done only once — changes in the environment do not render the once chosen value for σ useless, as opposed to the thresholds which have to be measured empirically every time anew without this form of social adaption.

6 Experimental Results

The experiment was run for 120 minutes per trial. We performed 10 trials for the random version, and 30 trials for the pure RL experiment (only ILL) and the hybrid version (ILL + KEL).

One would normally think that setting the threshold of "R" to something like 0.2 and that of "B" to approximately 0.8 would yield the best performance and lifetime of the agents, since "R" is much nearer to the task area and thus the behavior to drive to the "R" refuel station could be triggered much more later. However, as the experiments showed, the agents' thresholds converged to approx. 0.54 for "R" and 0.66 for the "B" thresholds as shown by Fig. 3. A close look to the experiment showed that it is not much more difficult for the agents to reach the "B" energy base as it is for the "R" base, although "B" is further away. This is the case because the area in front of "R" is most of the time occupied by another agent and thus unreachable for the agent, whereas "B" is farer away but most of the time clear of other agents since there are more "B" bases available.

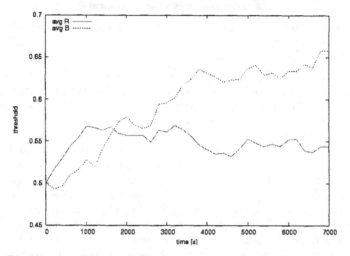

Fig. 3. Development of the threshold adjustment through group learning. The upper curve shows the threshold development for resource "R", the lower for "B"

The average lifetime development of the MAS is displayed in Fig. 4. We included the random policy for additional comparison. The significant data starts at $50s$ – the point when the first resource is exhausted. After approximately 100 seconds the agents start to die because they have not yet learned which action to take when the individual resources are going to be exhausted. As the agents learn more and more at the ILL the pure RL method departs from the random method, but as the graph suggests the parameters for the thresholds seem not to be optimal since it performs not that much better than the random method. The hybrid method, having RL at the policy level and group learning as described in section 4.2 at the KEL, outperforms the pure RL version. And this not only by the average lifetime measure, but also in the performance plot, as can be seen in Fig. 4. It takes, however, $3000s$ until the hybrid version performs better than the pure RL version. After $5000s$ the difference is significant and amounts to approx. 200 performance points at the end of the run.

One might ask why the hybrid solution does not reach a point where the agents live eternally, since they must have found the optimum thresholds. This

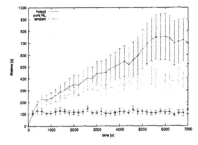 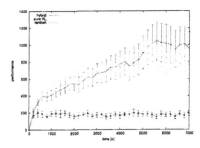

Fig. 4. The average lifetime (left) and performance (right) of the agents. Shown are the means and error bars using 95% confidence interval.

is because of the agent's interferences in front of the resource filling stations, which is not predictable, so that the death is always possible. The agents are thus trading off life time with performance points. Even with both resource thresholds set to 1.0 they would not be immune to death.

As can be seen in Fig. 4 the confidence intervals are very big. This is consistent with real human societies where the transmitted knowledge does not immediately result into a sudden and clearly defined benefit. Here, a much longer simulation interval would be needed to see the development over several days to months. This is planned in our future work.

7 Conclusion

For Multi-Agent environments without a central intelligence and with only sporadic communication possibilities for the individual participating agents we have presented a method to combine the individual learning process with a new way to integrate the learned knowledge of other participants. Based on the previous success of the agents (their "expert state") their knowledge is weighted and mutated. This results in a greater impact and accuracy of the knowledge of the better performing agents. Thus we trade off the accuracy of considered to be correct knowledge with the utility of introducing mutation for exploring knowledge for better performance. As shown in the experiment, it is interesting that this can lead to solutions that are clearly not intuitive to the engineer, instead lead to better behavior when seen with the agent's eyes.

We plan to apply this approach to our real world soccer robots: In addition to the adaptation of the state space this also includes e.g. the individual behaviors, the reward function and the learning rate α. Furthermore, we plan to choose the optimal level of aggressiveness in a soccer play as seen from their perspective: Being as aggressive as it is possible while avoiding to receive the red card would be a nice experiment to investigate with our soccer robots *Paderkicker* [9].

198   Willi Richert, Bernd Kleinjohann, Lisa Kleinjohann

References

1. M. L. Littman L. P. Kaelbling and A. W. Moore. Reinforcement learning: A survey. *Journal of Artificial Intelligence Research*, 4:237–285, 1996.
2. R. S. Sutton and A. G. Barto. *Reinforcement Learning: An Introduction.* MIT Press, Cambridge, 1998.
3. M. J. Matarić. Reinforcement learning in the multi-robot domain. *Autonomous Robots*, 4(1):73–83, 1997.
4. M. Tan. Multi-agent reinforcement learning: Independent vs. cooperative learning. In M. N. Huhns and M. P. Singh, editors, *Readings in Agents*, pages 487–494. Morgan Kaufmann, San Francisco, CA, USA, 1997.
5. L. Kleinjohann W. Richert, B. Kleinjohann. Learning action sequences through imitation in behavior based architectures. In *Systems Aspects in Organic and Pervasive Computing - ARCS 2005*, number 3432 in LNCS, pages 93–107. Springer-Verlag Berlin, 14 - 17 March 2005.
6. A. Saskevic M. Koch, W. Richert. A self-optimization approach for hybrid planning and socially inspired agents. In *Second NASA GSFC/IEEE Workshop on Radical Agent Concepts*, NASA Goddard Space Flight Center Visitor's Center Greenbelt, MD, USA, 2005.
7. R. Dawkins. *The Selfish Gene.* Oxford University Press, Oxford, 1976.
8. S. Blackmore. *The Meme Machine.* Oxford University Press, 1999.
9. M. Koch B. Kleinjohann, W. Richert, P. Adelt, and S. Rose. Paderkicker. http://paderkicker.upb.de, 2006.
10. T. Balch and R. C.. Arkin. Communication in reactive multiagent robotic systems. *Autonomous Robots*, 1(1):27–52, 1994.
11. M. Matarić. Learning to behave socially. In *SAB94: Proceedings of the third international conference on Simulation of adaptive behavior : from animals to animats 3*, pages 453–462, Cambridge, MA, USA, 1994. MIT Press.
12. P. Riley and M. Veloso. Coaching advice and adaptation. In B. Browning D. Polani, A. Bonarini and K. Yoshida, editors, *RoboCup-2003: The Sixth RoboCup Competitions and Conferences.* Springer Verlag, Berlin, 2004.
13. T. S. Dahl, M. J. Matarić, and G. S. Sukhatme. Adaptive spatio-temporal organization in groups of robots. In *IEEE/RSJ International Conference on Robotics and Intelligent Systems*, pages 1044 – 1049, Lausanne, Switzerland, Oct 2002.
14. S. Kapetanakis and D. Kudenko. Reinforcement learning of coordination in heterogeneous cooperative multi-agent systems. In *AAMAS '04: Proceedings of the Third International Joint Conference on Autonomous Agents and Multiagent Systems*, pages 1258–1259, Washington, DC, USA, 2004. IEEE Computer Society.
15. C. Claus and C. Boutilier. The dynamics of reinforcement learning in cooperative multiagent systems. In *AAAI/IAAI*, pages 746–752, 1998.
16. N. Cesa-Bianchi, Y. Freund, D. Haussler, D. P. Helmbold, R. E. Schapire, and M. K. Warmuth. How to use expert advice. *J. ACM*, 44(3):427–485, 1997.
17. R. A. Brooks. A robust layered control system for a mobile robot. *IEEE Journal of Robotics and Automation RA-2*, pages 14–23, 1986.
18. R. C. Arkin. *Behaviour-Based Robotics.* MIT Press, 1998.
19. C. J. C. H. Watkins and Dayan. *Q-learning.* 1992.
20. ActivMedia. URL for the Pioneer robot: http://www.activrobots.com, 2003.
21. B. P. Gerkey, R. T. Vaughan, and A. Howard. The player/stage project: Tools for multi-robot and distributed sensor systems. In *Proceedings of the International Conference on Advanced Robotics*, pages 317–323, Coimbra, Portugal, Jul 2003.

Emergent Distribution of Operating System Services in Wireless Ad Hoc Networks

Peter Janacik and Tales Heimfarth

Heinz Nixdorf Institute, University of Paderborn
Fuerstenallee 11, 33102 Paderborn, Germany
{pjanacik, tales}@uni-paderborn.de

Abstract. Despite the advances in wireless, energy-constrained ad hoc networks, there are still many challenges given the limited capabilities of the current hardware. Therefore, our aim is to develop a lightweight, yet powerful operating system (OS) for these networks. We reject the brute force method of provisioning all necessary OS services at each node of the system. Instead, our approach aims to distribute the set of requested OS services over the network to reduce and balance load, improve quality of service, increase fairness and predictability. To limit the burden imposed on the network by the service distribution mechanism, only a subset of nodes, the coordinators, chosen by an underlying state-of-the-art topology control, are concerned with this task. Coordinators observe the state of nodes and OS services within their one-hop vicinity, i.e. their decision area, incorporating different aspects, such as energy, utilisation, or available resources in their decisions. Although each coordinator acquires information and triggers migrations of service states only locally within its decision area, a global-level result emerges, as decision areas naturally overlap. In this manner, an increased amount of work load e.g. in one decision area "floats" to the surrounding decision areas attracted by better conditions. In ns-2 simulations we demonstrate that the mechanism of emergence, which produces many fascinating results in natural systems, can successfully be applied in artificial systems to considerably increase the efficiency and quality of OS service distribution.

1 Introduction

Given current hardware limitations of wireless nodes, e.g. commercial off-the-shelf sensor nodes (see [1]), there are severe restrictions on the software executed on them. For the same reason, operating systems (OS) for this type of nodes, like *TinyOS* [2], do not provide the means to handle more complex applications. To cope with these challenges, we use the paradigm of OS service distribution within our lightweight, distributed operating system *NanoOS* [3]. The OS consists of different services such as scheduling, synchronisation, time, etc. Traditional OS offer the set of all needed services at every node of the system resulting in excessive resource waste. Moreover, this limits the possible number

Please use the following format when citing this chapter:

Janacik, P., Heimfarth, T., 2006, in IFIP International Federation for Information Processing, Volume 216, Biologically Inspired Cooperative Computing, eds. Pan, Y., Rammig, F., Schmeck, H., Solar, M., (Boston: Springer), pp. 199–208.

of OS services utilised at one node at the same time. In contrast, our approach distributes the set of needed OS services over different nodes leading to a lower per-node load, a greater amount of possible service types, and the option of load adjustment. In particular, a distribution service observes the network and initiates migrations of OS service states (associated with service requestors) to achieve the following aims: *load balancing*, i.e. the uniform distribution of load over available nodes and services, *fairness*, i.e. the equal treatment of service requestors, *quality of service*, i.e. short answering times, and *predictability* of service quality. Providing these properties is a *global*-level aim, which is achieved solely from numerous interactions among *lower*-level components, i.e. the nodes. Moreover, the rules specifying these interactions are executed using only *local*, i.e. one-hop, information without reference to the *global* pattern (or aim). The *emergent* property (as defined in [4]) of our system is of utter importance in the scenario of volatile, energy-constrained networks: it translates to a highly increased amount of robustness, resilience, and a considerably lower communication overhead.

To lower the burden imposed on the network, our approach makes a subset of nodes, the *coordinators*, responsible for service distribution. This set is chosen dynamically by an underlying state-of-the-art topology control (such as [5, 6, 7]), so that each node has at least one coordinator in one-hop distance. Coordinators run a *distribution service* that is responsible for observing the state of the system within their one-hop neighbourhood, i.e. their *decision area*, and for deciding on the migration of OS service states. As already discussed above, at first glance, the mechanism for service distribution is local. But given the natural overlap of decision areas, there is also an inter-decision area migration. This way, load can "float" to neighbouring areas, so that a global-level result emerges. Using ns-2 [8] simulations, we demonstrate the considerable improvements in terms of the above-defined aims provided by our approach. We are aware that reducing the distance between OS service requestors and providers, efficient service discovery, or failure handling are also crucial in wireless, energy-constrained ad hoc networks. These topics are however beyond the scope of this document and will therefore be addressed in other publications.

This paper is organised as follows: Section 2 presents the state-of-the-art, while Section 3 subsequently describes the proposed emergent distribution of OS services. Section 4 then presents the results of our simulations. Finally, Section 5 ends this paper with brief concluding remarks.

2 State-of-the-Art

Current ad hoc or sensor network node hardware imposes severe restrictions on the software executed on top of it. Therefore, *TinyOS* [2] e.g. tries to solve this problem with its extremely small footprint. But since all components of a TinyOS instance have to fit into one node, its functionality is severely limited, so that it cannot cope with more complex applications. The *MagnetOS* approach

[9], as another example, is very different from most OS: its aim is to offer a single-system image of a unified Java virtual machine (JVM) across nodes. Migration of objects in MagnetOS is carried out over one or multiple hops in the direction of the greatest communication, reducing the distance between call-initiators and -receivers. Our work, however, has different aims: improving load balancing, fairness, quality of service, and predictability. In the related field of dynamic distributed scheduling algorithms, there has also been research on the reduction of communication cost and load balancing. However, such approaches like [10, 11] were developed for static networks of UNIX workstations and are not suited for mobile, volatile, resource- and energy-constrained networks. Further, they impose the burden of service distribution on all workstations in a network.

3 Emergent Distribution of OS Services

After providing an outline of our approach in the introduction and reviewing the state-of-the-art, this section describes the system components and how division of labour between nodes is employed. Subsequently, the main part of this section concentrates on migration source and target determination.

3.1 System Components

We assume a wireless network consisting of resource- and energy-constrained, mobile hardware nodes. Our OS, composed of services, and applications, composed of tasks, run on top of it. In addition to the functionality of traditional OS, our OS provides an *uniform system call environment* across the mobile nodes and further services like a *distribution service*, observing the system state and initiating migrations, or distributed event, memory, and synchronisation services. As depicted in Figure 2 (a), *OS services* and *application tasks* are subtypes of the abstract *processing entity*. An OS service maintains states associated with each of its requestors, which are sharing it and may reside on different, remote nodes. Services may act as both, service requestors and providers, while tasks only act as requestors.

3.2 Division of Labour between Nodes

In order to reduce the burden imposed on the network by the mechanism of service distribution and to enable the fusion of relevant system data, we assign the task of service distribution only to a subset of nodes, called *coordinators*. This subset, created by a state-of-the-art topology control (such as [5, 7] or our work from [6]), should consist of a low number of nodes, while ensuring that each node has at least one coordinator in one-hop communication distance (as depicted in Figure 1 (a)). Further, this implies that the number of coordinators scales with the density and number of nodes. The idea of our work is that each coordinator runs a distribution service that monitors the coordinator's *decision*

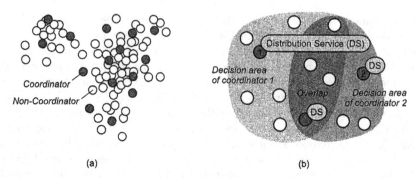

(a)   (b)

Fig. 1. Division of labour between nodes. (a) Different node types. (b) Decision areas of coordinators and distribution service placement.

area, which contains all non-coordinators in one-hop distance. Figure 1 (b) shows the overlapping decision areas of coordinators 1 and 2. We assume the amount of overlap to be a tuneable parameter of topology control. Coordinator status changes take place as *reaction to changes* of the environment (e.g. node density), but also *over time*, so that nodes "take turns" being coordinators balancing the burden of service distribution.

3.3 State Migration Source and Target Determination

Migration, initiated by the distribution service, consists of the migration of states, which are associated with the requestors of services, between existing OS services, but also the migration of states to newly-started OS services. Figure 2 (b) illustrates a typical scenario, where migration is applied. The OS service running at node 4 is overburdened, as indicated by the service request queue length. At the same time, the OS services at nodes 3 and 5 are almost idle increasing the overall execution overhead. To improve the configuration, some OS service states from the service at node 4 would be migrated to the service at node 6. The services at nodes 3 and 5 would be fused, on the other hand, by migrating all states from one to the other service. To be more concrete, the migration decision policy (intuitively speaking) has the following main operational goals: First, prevent too long service request queues; second, disburden services at nodes, whose remaining energy level is considerably below the average energy level of nodes in the decision area of the coordinator; moreover, avoid the execution of services with very short queues, since these do not justify the associated overhead and hold resources which may prevent the start of new services. To enable migration decisions, every distribution service is provided with the information utilised in the descriptions below from all nodes and services in its coordinator's decision area (by underlying protocols).

In our model, we assume the utilisation of a service to be indicated by the *average length of its queue for pending service requests* in terms of processing time needed. For the sake of simplicity, we will only refer to it as (service

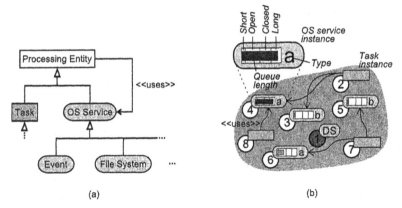

Fig. 2. Processing entities. (a) Relationship between processing entity and its sub-classes. (b) Distribution of processing entities over the network, illustrating a problem scenario. Key: DS—distribution service

request) queue length below. In order to enable decisions based on the degree of utilisation, our approach distinguishes the following categories of service request queue lengths (see also Figure 2 (b)):

Short: Low utilisation
Open: Fair utilisation
Closed: Fair or slightly higher utilisation, rejecting new requestors
Long: Critically high utilisation, rejecting new requestors

There are different *priority classes* to characterise the *severity* of the problem at the migration source (according to the policy described above): (1) Long queue; (2) queue open or closed and energy low at hosting node; (3) queue short. For an additional, more fine granular ranking within priority classes, we use the following *OS service fitness metric* that rates the service incorporating the hosting node, e.g. whether the service load is appropriate and the host's resources are not exhausted: $M_{service\_fitness} = \omega_{CPU} \cdot M_{CPU} + \omega_{mem} \cdot M_{mem} + \omega_{ql} \cdot M_{ql} + \omega_E \cdot M_E$. It uses metrics taking into account CPU and memory utilisation[1] $M_{\{CPU,mem\}} = \frac{avail\_\{CPU,mem\}}{max\_\{CPU,mem\}}$ describing the proportion of available to maximum resources, the queue length metric $M_{ql} = 1 - \min(\frac{ql}{ql_{long\_min}}, 1)$ reflecting the relation of the actual queue length to the minimum long queue length, and the energy metric

$$
M_E =
\begin{cases}
1 & \text{if} \quad E_{host} \geq E_{avrg\_decision\_area} \\
1 - \frac{E_{avrg\_decision\_area} - E_{host}}{E_{avrg\_decision\_area}} & \text{else}
\end{cases}
$$

describing the proportion of remaining energy at the host to the average amount of remaining energy at nodes in the decision area. ω_{CPU}, ω_{mem}, ω_{ql}, and ω_E are

---

[1] Different members of sets exclude each other in the following formula.

weights for the corresponding metrics, such that $\omega_{CPU} + \omega_{mem} + \omega_{ql} + \omega_E = 1$. They can be adjusted in order to reflect characteristics of a certain hardware type, e.g. ω_{mem} can be increased if memory is the more valuable resource. Moreover, the above functions use $avail\_\{CPU, mem\}$, reflecting the amount of available CPU and memory resources, $max\_\{CPU, mem\}$, describing the maximum available corresponding resources at a node. ql_{long_min} represents the minimum queue length for the "long" category and ql the actual service request queue length. $E_{avrg\_decision\_area}$ contains the average of remaining energy levels in the decision area, whereas E_{host} describes the remaining energy level of the service host.

The service in the *highest* priority class with the *lowest* $M_{service\_fitness}$ ranking is chosen first as *migration* source. In order to reduce interference of overlapping decision areas, only a distribution service at a coordinator, which is connected to a non-coordinator with the best link from all links connecting it to surrounding coordinators, may choose a service from such a non-coordinator as migration source.

Finding a *migration target* works similar to the migration source finding process, but using the following *priority classes*: (1) Open queue and sufficient energy at hosting node; (2) short queue; (3) no service running at hosting node. Priority class 3 is only an option, if the queue length of the migration source is above the minimum long queue length, so that near-idle services are not migrated unnecessarily. The decision process proceeds similar to finding a source, except that the whole decision area is taken into account. The service in the *highest* priority class with the *highest* $M_{service\_fitness}$ ranking is chosen first as migration target. After migration initiation, migration source and target are locked, excluding them from the migration process for a specified period of time in order increase the stability of the system.

4 Results

We implemented our emergent distribution of OS services and a reference approach using C++ and the ns-2 network simulator [8]. For lower layers, we used our topology control [6] and ant colony-based routing [12]. The reference approach employs a greedy, demand-based OS service placement without service migration and topology control, in conjunction with ad hoc on-demand distance vector (AODV) [8] routing from ns-2. To simulate running processing entities (PE), we specified a set of PE types. For each PE type, a recurring sequence of behaviour items is defined. Each *behaviour item* includes information on its execution duration, CPU, memory, and OS service requirement (a service type or none), as well as, the processing time needed by the required OS service. The assignment of application task instances to PE types and nodes was randomised.

The simulations further employed a 914 MHz Lucent WaveLAN DSSS radio, the two-ray ground reflection model, 80 joules initial energy per node and an

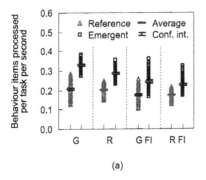 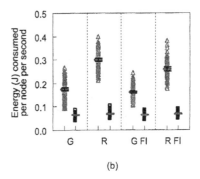

(a)   (b)

Fig. 3. Performance (a) and energy results (b). Key: G—grid, R—RPGM, FI—failure injection

802.11b MAC protocol, provided by ns-2. To cover static and dynamic scenarios we used two settings: (1) A *grid*, 44 nodes, 3 x 15 arrangement, horizontal and vertical distance of $d = 25$ m between nodes, 1000 s simulation time; (2) a *reference point group mobility* (RPGM) model [13], 64 nodes, 4 x 16 groups, logical group centres movement 2–8 m/s based on random walk model [8], 850 x 850 m area, 900 s simulation time. In order to simulate volatile and failure-prone networks, we injected failures during simulation. Our *failure injection* (FI) model employs k failure points (FP) $f_{1,...,k}$. At the start of a run, FP probabilities $p_{f1,...,k}$ are set randomly between p_{min} and p_{max}. Next, each node makes a probabilistic decision based on $p_{f_{1,...,k}}$, whether to fail at FP $f_{1,...,k}$. Each FP f_i is associated with a failure time t_{f_i} in ascending temporal order, so that for some $i \in 1,...,k$, $t_{f_i} < t_{f_{i+1}}$ applies. Failing at an FP f_i means for a node that its network interface is out of order between t_{f_i} and $t_{f_{i+1}}$. A failure at the last FP ($i = k$) persists until the end of the simulation. We used two FP ($k = 2$) and failure times ($t_{f_{1,2}}$) at 333 and 667 seconds of simulation time. The minimum FP probability (p_{min}) was set to 0, the maximum (p_{max}), to 0.5.

The presented figures were obtained using the following settings: 100 runs, reference and emergent approach, grid and RPGM topology, with and without FI; lower and upper bounds of confidence intervals, with probability of error $\alpha = 0.05$, to indicate the significance of the presented results (marks for not applicable or too narrow intervals for a reasonable visualisation are omitted).

4.1 Performance and Energy Consumption

Figure 3 (a) depicts the processing speed of both approaches. The emergent approach outperforms the reference approach by a clear margin, which is also an indication for a higher quality of service. The energy consumed by both approaches is depicted in Figure 3 (b). Again, the emergent approach clearly outperforms its reference counterpart. FI does not influence energy consumption considerably, possibly, since the failed nodes do not actively participate

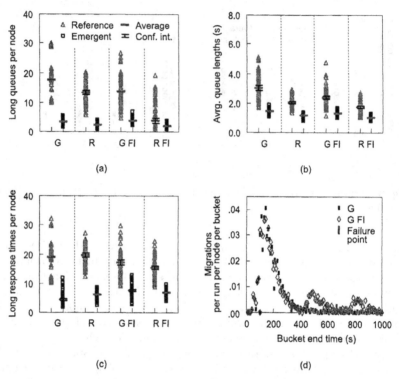

Fig. 4. Load balancing, fairness, quality of service, predictability (a–c) and migration behaviour (d) results. Key: G—grid, R—RPGM, FI—failure injection

in communication, thus saving the corresponding amount of energy. Further, the figure clearly demonstrates that the variance of energy consumption of the emergent approach is intelligibly lower, which is also an indicator for a higher predictability.

4.2 Load Balancing, Fairness, Quality of Service, Predictability

Quality of service depends on service request queue lengths in general, whereas load balancing, fairness, and predictability depend on the uniform distribution of queue lengths throughout the system. Therefore, our next studies are focused on these indicators. Figure 4 (a) depicts the number of long service request queues (i.e. "which are in the long category") per node in each of the runs. Measurements were taken at service reply issuing. Evidently, the number of long queues in the reference approach is several times higher. Nevertheless, some RPGM FI runs for the reference approach exhibit a very low number of long queue lengths. This is supposedly owed to the reference approach, starting a high number of services that are utilised only to a minimum extent, which increases overhead and prevents new services from being started. In contrast to the reference approach, the figures for the emergent approach appear to stay constantly low with only little variance, indicating good quality of service and a high predictability. Further, the high amount of long queues in the reference approach hints at the lack of fairness: some service requestors are served significantly slower than others, which greatly affects, and leads to high variances of service requestors' own processing speeds.

Looking at average queue lengths in Figure 4 (b), the conclusions are similar, but the averages of both approaches are more close-by. This could be explained as above by reference service distribution starting a high number of little-utilised services. Emergent service distribution, in contrast, attempts to avoid running near-idle services in order to minimise overhead and provide enough room for the start of new services. This is, however, to its disadvantage in this particular metric. The results for service response times in Figure 4 (c) additionally take into account communication delays and are very similar to the figures in (a).

4.3 Reaction Behaviour and Stability of Migration

Figure 4 (d) depicts the migration activity in a grid topology. Migration times encountered are sorted into buckets of 10 seconds. All runs exhibit an initial peak, reflecting initial optimisations. Without FI, migration settles down thereafter, yielding a highly stable solution for the rest of the simulation. If however the need for optimisations is brought about by FI at 333 and 667 seconds, migration reacts swiftly shortly after the occurrences, settling down subsequently leading to a stable solution.

5 Conclusion

Within the scope of our efforts to create a lightweight, yet powerful operating system (OS) for wireless, energy-constrained nodes, this paper introduces an efficient method for the distribution of OS services. Our approach only imposes load on a selected subset of nodes, the coordinators. They observe the state of the system locally within their decision areas. Given the natural overlap of these areas, when one decision area suffers e.g. under high load, this load "floats" to the surrounding areas attracted by better conditions. Therefore, although each coordinator acquires information and triggers migrations of service states only locally, there is an emergent global result.

Given the restrictions of current hardware, an efficient distribution method is crucial for our OS. Even more, we strive to provide an OS behaviour that is rather associated with OS which exhibit a much larger footprint: load balancing, fairness, and predictability, combined with a high quality of service. Using ns-2 simulations we show that our approach reduces energy consumption by a significant amount compared to a reference system. Further, quality of service is increased by more than 80 % in most cases, while load balancing is improved by 200 to 400 % exhibiting a low deviation from the average values.

This in particular results in considerably improved fairness and predictability. The state obtained by the proposed mechanism is characterised by stability and swift adjustment to changes in the environment at the global level, emerging from execution of solely local actions based on local information. Concludingly, the observations give yet another piece of evidence that emergence as a mechanism often encountered in nature can be transferred to computer systems while preserving its inherent character.

References

1. The Scientist and Engineer's Guide to TinyOS Programming. http://ttdp.org /tpg/html/book/book1.htm, accessed January 7, 2006.
2. J. Hill, R. Szewczyk, A. Woo, S. Hollar, D. E. Culler, and K. S. J. Pister. System architecture directions for networked sensors. In *Proc. of ACM ASPLOS*, pages 93–104, Cambridge, MA, November 2000.
3. F. J. Rammig, M. Goetz, T. Heimfarth, P. Janacik, and S. Oberthuer. Real-time operating systems for self-coordinating embedded systems. In *Proc. of IEEE ISORC*, Gyeongju, Korea, April 2006. Accepted for publication.
4. S. Camazine, J.-L. Deneubourg, N. R. Franks, J. Sneyd, G. Theraulaz, and E. Bonabeau. *Self-Organization in Biological Systems*. Princeton Studies in Complexity. Princeton University Press, first edition, 2003.
5. A. Cerpa and D. Estrin. ASCENT: Adaptive self-configuring sensor networks topologies. *IEEE TMC*, 3(3):272–285, 2004.
6. P. Janacik, T. Heimfarth, and F. Rammig. Emergent topology control based on division of labour in ants. In *Proc. of IEEE AINA*, Vienna, Austria, April 2006.
7. F. Ye, G. Zhong, J. Cheng, S. Lu, and L. Zhang. PEAS: A robust energy conserving protocol for long-lived sensor networks. In *Proc. of IEEE ICDCS*, pages 28–37, Providence, RI, May 2003.
8. The network simulator. http://www.isi.edu/nsnam/ns/, accessed July 8, 2005.
9. R. Barr, J. C. Bicket, D. S. Dantas, B. Du, T. W. D. Kim, B. Zhou, and E. Gün Sirer. On the need for system-level support for ad hoc and sensor networks. *ACM SIGOPS OS Review*, 36(2):1–5, April 2002.
10. H.-U. Heiss and M. Schmitz. Decentralized dynamic load balancing: The particles approach. *Information Sciences*, May 1995.
11. C. Lang, M. Trehel, and P. Baptiste. A distributed placement algorithm based on process initiative and on a limited travel. In *Proc. of PDPTA*, 1999.
12. P. Janacik, O. Kao, and U. Rerrer. An approach combining routing and resource sharing in wireless ad hoc networks using swarm-intelligence. In *Proc. of the ACM/IEEE MSWiM*, pages 31–40. CTi Press, 2004.
13. X. Hong, M. Gerla, G. Pei, and C.-C. Chiang. A group mobility model for ad hoc wireless networks. In *Proc. of ACM/IEEE MSWiM*, August 1999.

Author index